Dental Mission Manual

FOR PORTABLE, SHORT-TERM DENTAL TRIPS

By the Members of the Christian Dental Society

Praying you'll serve God always!
Dr. Bob & Diane Meyer

Blessings! Dr. Gody

ISBN: 1514291304
ISBN 13: 9781514291306
Library of Congress Control Number: 2015909337
CreateSpace Independent Publishing Platform
North Charleston, South Carolina

Acknowledgements

———•———

Dr. Bob, current president of the Christian Society (CDS), and Mrs. Diane Meyer (BSN, MST), veterans of over fifty dental mission trips, compiled and wrote this manual using current literature and the expertise gleaned from hundreds of trips by many CDS members.

Ms. Sharyn Markus (MLS, MA), our knowledgeable and conscientious editor, has served on varied dental missions. Mr. Mark and Mrs. Susan Curtis from The Curtis Group Dental Practice Marketing Group designed our CDS logo and Mission Manual cover, are CDS Advisory Council Members, and have served on missions.

Those who have specifically contributed ideas and experiences are recognized in alphabetical order: Dr. Mark Albers, Mrs. Debbie Bailey (BSDH), Dr. Kathleen Barlow, Dr. Victor Bradford, Mrs. Shari Buttenwieser (BSDH), Dr. Jim Carney, Dr. Gayle Cheatwood, Dr. Frank Cho, Dr. T. Bob Davis, Ms. Lynelle DeRoo (BSDH), Dr. Bill Dodson, Dr. Steve Eikenberg, Dr. Gregory Ellis, Dr. Brian Fitzpatrick, Dr. Pete Fotos, Dr. Dale Giebink, Dr. Russ Gilliam, Dr. Larry Goedeck, Dr. William Griffin, Dr. Monica Oliveira-Hewitt, Dr. Scott Hewitt, Dr. Gary Horn, Dr. Daniel Hudson, Dr. James Jesperson, Dr. Ron Lamb, Dr. Bill Lefler, Dr. John Ley, Dr. Robert Liebler, Dr. Chun In Jerry Lin, Dr. Tom Love, Dr. Dick Martin, Dr. Blake McKinley, Dr. Kevin Mitchell, Dr. Dave Moretz, Dr. Al Nessmith, Dr. Michael O'Callaghan, Dr. Jim Orban, Dr. John Pfefferle, Dr. Brad Perrett, Dr. Ed Poremba, Dr. Randy Sanders, Dr. Bill Sasser, Dr. Denis Scharine, Mr. Paul Shada, Dr. Jennina Townsend, Dr. Michael Vaughan, Dr. Sean Vostatek, Mrs. Tina Wendel, Dr. Blake Westra, Mrs. Sueellen Williams (BSDH), Dr. Dave Wisse, Dr. James Wolf, Dr. Roy Wrather, and Dr. Jody Yarbro.

We deeply appreciate all CDS members, past and present, as well as the dental practitioners and the personnel who serve on mission trips. Gratitude is extended to families, prayer partners, outreach organizations, office staffs, pastors, teachers, mentors, dental supply and maintenance workers, and so many others who have contributed to God's work.

Dedication

This manual is dedicated to the supportive spouses, family members, friends, and auxiliaries who accompany and fill vital roles for dental personnel on mission trips. Other people are at home encouraging, praying, sacrificing, and sustaining our communities while loved ones are serving.

Dental Mission Manual
For Portable, Short-term, Dental Trips
Table of Contents

Manual Clarifications

———

* When a sentence occurs in *italics and quotes* with the speaker not identified, it is the words or the experience of a Christian Dental Society member.

* The term "Christian" is generally understood in the United States of America. However, in some countries, varied terms such as "follower of Christ" or "believer in the Lord of the Universe" are preferred. The national hosts may be consulted on appropriate religious terminology.

* In this manual, a "developing country" denotes a place where people have lower life expectancies, education, and income. A "developed country" has a highly structured economy and advanced technological infrastructure relative to other less industrialized nations. These terms are not meant to be judgmental. (See Chapter 17: Labeling Countries.)

* The term "national or local host" refers to the international residents of a developing country—distinguishing them from the dental team members who usually reside in a developed country.

* All Bible verses, written in a separate font, are from the *New International Version.*[1]

* Although this manual was current at publication, please update information by sending to the CDS home office at cdssent@netins.net. Even though the Word of God is eternal, few policies are more changeable than airline requirements, governmental decrees, and travel advisories.

* All proceeds from the sale of this book and any donations will go directly to the CHRISTIAN DENTAL SOCIETY for the purpose of encouraging, assisting, and equipping dental personnel to use their gifts to further God's kingdom.

Introduction

The Christian Dental Society (CDS) exists to encourage and to equip dental personnel for short-term, portable, dental missions, and to provide help and suggestions for people contemplating such missions. This manual is intended to improve dental care and faith-based mission trips to areas of need at home and around the globe. Tips are included to save non-productive effort and stress in organizing dental missions, with the hope of making each trip more positive and rewarding. Proven techniques from CDS members are presented, as they have learned from their experiences and want to share their wisdom.

A six-chair dental clinic is set up in the Kenyan bush.

Mission dentistry can be an act of generosity and compassion. No matter where the team travels, someone will be standing near who has a toothache and whose life could be rapidly improved by dental skills. Even more importantly, treating dental disease can show people that someone cares for them, no matter how desperate their lives may be. Dentistry provides a uniquely valuable resource for an outreach program. Jesus often did the same—the Gospels are full of stories where Jesus healed the sick, and His example illustrates that dentistry is a unique, dignified, and blessed calling.

Simultaneously, mission dentistry can refresh memories of why dentists entered the profession—the idealism, the compassion, the desire to help others—which may have been lost in the fog of insurance paperwork or bureaucratic indifference. The team can brighten lives and can teach non-dental staff about a rewarding healing profession. Even though mission dentistry involves hard work, it can be the kind of "good stress" which lets everyone sleep well at night; and it can be among the most positively memorable parts of a career.

A dental mission includes dental professionals and non-dental volunteers and can last any length of time—from a few days to the long-term staffing of a permanent facility. Dental personnel participate in over a thousand medical or dental missions each year to areas of the world where oral healthcare is substandard or nonexistent. Each mission is different and may range from a one-chair clinic manned by two people to a multiple-chair clinic with a large, mixed team of host nationals and dental practitioners from various nations.

Reasons for a shortage of dental care can include insufficient numbers of trained clinicians, societal practices, poverty, natural disasters (hurricanes, tsunamis, floods, earthquakes, and droughts), war, or famine. The CDS has successfully and quickly established portable dental clinics in areas ranging from rooms in local homes, orphanages, street youth centers, transition houses, summer camps, schools, seminaries, hospitals, churches, outreach centers, medical clinics, military posts, refugee camps, prisons, yurts, tents, boats or ships, and under trees. Furthermore, these portable clinics can reflect state-of-the-art standards of care for infection control, safety, and convenience.

Christian Dental Society's Statement of Faith

Trusting in the Lord Jesus Christ as our Savior:

* We believe in one God, existent in three persons: Father, Son, and Holy Spirit.
* We believe God is the Creator and Ruler of the universe.
* We believe the Son of God, Jesus Christ, was conceived by the Holy Spirit, lived a sinless life, died for our sins, was resurrected from the dead, ascended into heaven, and will return to earth in glory.
* We believe the Holy Spirit indwells every believer in Christ and is our helper, teacher, and guide.
* We believe the Bible is the Divinely inspired Word of God and has authority in all matters of faith and conduct.

Christian Dental Society's Mission and History

The Christian Dental Society's mission statement declares: "As Christian dental practitioners, we aspire to share the Good News of Jesus Christ, while encouraging and serving others at home and abroad." The CDS cooperates with all Christ-centered churches in their dental mission programs and is independent of any organizational or denominational affiliation.

During the 1962 American Dental Association convention, twelve dentists met to discuss the dental needs of church-related hospitals and clinics all over the world. They organized the "Christian Dental Society" in 1963 as a mechanism for like-minded Christian dentists and dental personnel, from anywhere in the United States, to unite in fellowship and support for dental missions. In 1965, the CDS was granted non-profit, tax-exempt status under Section 501(c)(3) of the IRS Code. The CDS office is located in Sumner, Iowa, where the organization's administrative assistant resides as the only paid staff member. The CDS is a volunteer-run society funded primarily by membership dues and gifts. The CDS encourages members to plan trips themselves, networking with their own churches, groups, or other organizations with pre-existing mission goals.

For fifty years, the Christian Dental Society has been a leader in dental missions worldwide. The need for short-term and long-term dental volunteers is overwhelming. With the advances in transportation and portable equipment, dental personnel have the ability to relieve pain and suffering globally in God's name. The Church has long recognized that meeting a person's physical needs is one of the most effective ways to show Christian love and to share the Good News of Jesus Christ. Dental care is an invaluable tool in reaching out to others.

As Dr. L. Greene (short-term missionary) says, "God does not want our ability—He wants our availability! God does not call us because we're equipped; He equips us for the call."[2]

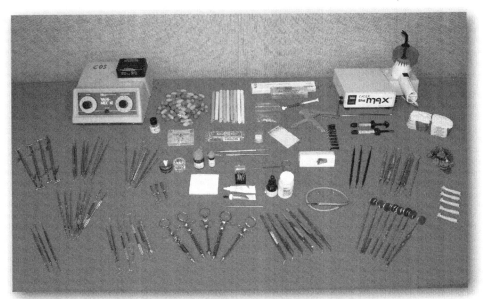

The CDS' restorative kits are loaned to dental teams.

Christian Dental Society's Membership Benefits

—————

❋ **Spiritual blessings** are received by members as they provide dentistry and minister to disadvantaged people at home and abroad.

❋ **Annual meetings of** the CDS' board of directors and the CDS membership occur at the American Dental Association convention. The CDS promotes fellowship and networking among Christian dental professionals who desire to reach out to others with mission dentistry.

❋ **Seasoned volunteers** lead the CDS and share missionary travel pointers and dental tips with those desiring to provide dentistry in austere settings in a multitude of countries.

❋ **CDS lends** dental instruments and equipment (restorative and surgical instruments; light-weight, portable, operative units, compressors, chairs; and sterilization set-ups) for a nominal fee for short-term mission projects.

❋ **Designated Funds** account provides for CDS mission dentists or team members to receive tax benefits for donations and costs of volunteer trips.

❋ **The website** for CDS (www.christiandental.org) is extensive and includes resources, lists of Christian ministry organizations requesting dental volunteers, networking opportunities, and valuable recommendations to facilitate dental mission trips.

❋ **Informative newsletters** (three annually) and CDS news-briefs are distributed.

❋ **Facebook CDS site** (located under "Christian Dental Society") informs and connects.

❋ **Members advertise** their dental offices, since CDS lists members' names, the locations, and the office websites on the CDS website. *"I receive several patients each year who have looked up "Christian dentists" on the Internet and have found my location."*

* **Mission trips** are organized and run by CDS members for the participation of students and others. New team members learn about missions while serving.

The CDS' surgical kits are loaned to dental teams.

CHAPTER 1

Overwhelming Need

STATISTICAL DATA

"Dental caries is the most common, chronic disease in the world, but few people, even in public health acknowledge this fact." (Dr. B. Conrod, President FDI World Dental Federation)[3] *"We thought dental need statistics might be inflated when we first started doing overseas dental missions. The more we travel, the more we believe these statistics are accurate. After dental mission trips to 35 developing countries, we realize most people have no access to dental care."*

* "Over 90% of people in the world do not have access to routine dental care." (Dr. D. Shanley, former Dean, Trinity College Dental School, Ireland)[4]

* "Worldwide, the prevalence of dental caries among adults is high, as the disease affects nearly 100% of the population in the majority of countries." (Dr. P. Peterson, World Global Oral Health Programme, Switzerland)[5]

* "Dental decay remains largely untreated and there are widespread inequalities both between and within countries. Many village health care centers in Africa report that oral pain is among the five most frequent health complaints." (Dr. R. Beaglehole, public health consultant and clinical dentist)[6]

* "To the person with a toothache, even if the world is tottering, there is nothing more important than a visit to the dentist." (George Bernard Shaw)[7]

* "Every tooth in a man's head is more valuable than a diamond." (Miguel de Cervantes)[8]

Dentist/patient ratios are deplorable worldwide. According to World Health Organization statistics, over 30 countries around the world have less than one dentist for 100,000 people.[9] For most developed countries the ratio is about 1 dentist/2000 people. In Africa at large, the dentist/ patient ratio is 1/150,000; Ethiopia 1/1,300,000; Haiti 1/160,000; India (rural) 1/300,000; Papua New Guinea 1/372,000. Many other countries have only one dentist for tens of thousands of people. These "dentists" often don't deliver the standard of care that dentists from developed countries provide, and many of the dental personnel have little formal education. "The vast bulk of oral treatment must be carried out by personnel without formal training in dentistry." (Dr. D. Shanley)[10] "Every day I see tooth problems, but I have no dental training. People live in much pain." (Dr. Zaka, Madagascar medical doctor)[11] *We were delighted when an American medical doctor and a physician assistant working in Africa asked us to show them some dental basics, since the dental need is so great. After several hours, however, they admitted it was just too complicated and challenging for them personally to add dental to all their other medical duties; and they decided they would try to recruit dentists to come whenever possible.*

Nonexistent hygiene is a tragedy in most of the developing world. Oral preventive educational measures, hygienists, and hygiene cleanings are usually not available. Most people live with gingivitis (infected gums) which often progresses to periodontitis (loss of bone support around the teeth). Most adults have significant mineralized calcium deposits. *We have treated dental patients in numerous developing countries and have not encountered a single hygienist or treated any national patients who have had hygiene cleanings.*

Dental unavailability is the norm outside major cities in many countries and to those people who remain perpetually poor. "Eighty per cent of all oral health care is concentrated in 20% of the population." (International Federation of Dental Education Associations)[12] "Even though some countries seem to have availability to quality dental care (such as in Cairo, Egypt), 90% of the people live a subsistence existence, while wealth and privileges go only to the top 10% of the population who can access large population centers." (Dr. M. Hanna, Egyptian physician)[13] "Two-thirds of dental graduates from the

Philippines migrate to the U.S, where most of them do not work as dentists but as other health professionals. The overall shortage and unequal distribution of dentists is complicated by a growing trend of 'brain drain,' as oral health professionals migrate from their country of origin to work in a different country, often attracted by higher salaries and better work environments." (Dr. R. Beaglehole)[14]

    *   "No matter how we may attempt to rationalize it, profound disparities in oral health and disparate effects of oral diseases have been documented on our watch and during our time of leadership and stewardship for oral health! The range and the magnitude of these disparities should trouble us all." (Dr. C. Evans, College of Dentistry, University of Illinois at Chicago)[15]

    *   "The gaps in health outcomes, seen within and between countries, are greater now than at any time in recent history." (Dr. M. Chan, World Health Organization Director)[16]

Dental issues are not thought to be life-threatening so many developing country health planners and politicians spend what little resources they have on medical facilities, and they provide meager dental assets. These leaders are often unaware of the magnitude and the impact of dental need and believe dental treatment and preventive services are an optional luxury. (See Disease Connections in the following section.) Often there are no safety nets for people who are hurting dentally. "Caries is a disease of social deprivation, just as it is a disease of bad diets." (Dr. O. Fejerskov and Dr. E. Kidd)[17]

    *   "Lack of surgical provision (of cleft palates) commits otherwise healthy individuals to lifelong disfigurement and functional impairment, as well as educational and social exclusion." (Dr. S. Hodges, pediatric anesthesiologist)[18]

Dental care receives insufficient attention. "Of the more than 8,000 World Health Organization employees globally, only three professional-level staff work exclusively on oral health." (Dr. R. Beaglehole)[19] *"We met an Egyptian family practice physician, trained in America and running a residency teaching program for physicians in a missionary hospital in Aswan,*

Egypt. He came to visit us in America and complained of a toothache. When asked why he did not get it fixed in Egypt, his reply was shocking: 'I would rather have a toothache and lose a tooth than catch hepatitis or HIV.' As a top physician in a teaching institution in a fairly developed country, he could not obtain reasonable dental care. In Egypt, there were dentists, but many did not sterilize and people only go to a dentist when the pain became unbearable or the infection life-threatening."

Dental pain and dysfunction are often burdens which people are simply expected to endure. Poor aesthetics can provide barriers to employment and acceptance. Relieving these problems can greatly improve lives while generating hope and good will. *"In Swaziland, we worked at one of the largest hospitals in the country where there was little dental care available. Swaziland has no dental school and only eight dentists in the entire country, who primarily work on the privileged few. We extracted infected, non-restorable teeth on almost every doctor, nurse, and administrator in that hospital. We have experienced first-hand the almost total lack of reasonable dentistry in every developing country we have visited. Because oral care, dental education, and hygiene are so neglected throughout most of the world, dentistry is a wide open door for us to go almost anywhere at any time and to have a positive impact."*

School absenteeism is often due to toothaches. "Tooth decay is reported as the most common chronic childhood illness, with 51 million school hours lost to dental-related illness each year." (Report of the Surgeon General)[20]

   * "Eighty-five per cent of six-year-old Philippine children had signs of dental infection—such as abscesses, ulcerations, fistulas, and open pulps." (Dr. R. Beaglehole)[21]

   * "In Thailand, 90% of pre-adolescents reported need related to oral health." (A. Sheiham, Dental Public Health Professor, University College London Medical School)[22]

   * "Children live for months with pain that grown-ups would find unendurable; the gradual attrition of accepted pain erodes their energy and aspiration." (Jonathan Kozol, U.S. writer and educator)[23]

Ineffective dentures are common in many countries, and poorly made appliances can exacerbate pain or dysfunction. This indicates both the value of prevention and the need for improved skill in denture fabrication. "No one should suffer from oral diseases or conditions that can be effectively treated or prevented." (Dr. R. Carmona, past U.S. Surgeon General)[24]

Oral cancer is a significant problem in many developing countries. Preventive education and, possibly, early detection and referral could be life extending.

Oral infections are often "treated" by antibiotics and pain medications, rather than definitive treatment of infected teeth. Giving antibiotics indiscriminately can lead to bacterial resistance and lowered effectiveness when antibiotics are needed for other reasons. Antibiotic use does not address the primary cause of the infection (the need to fix or to remove the tooth), contributes to misdiagnosis, and often is simply ineffective. *"There are such unbelievable needs in developing countries. People will come for miles by foot or canoe to get to a competent dentist and will camp for days in line to be seen. You cannot imagine the need for dental care in these countries until you actually go, work, see, and feel the desperation for help. It will give you a greater appreciation of the dental skills you have to help others."*

Widespread poverty is shown by the fact that "80% of the world's population lives on less than US $2 a day. These low-income people rarely have resources for dental care. A simple tooth extraction can cost up to US $100." (Dr. R. Beaglehole)[25] "Healthcare needs around the world are staggering. Thirty thousand people each day die from preventable disease. A child dies of hunger every sixteen seconds. Forty per cent of the world lacks basic sanitation facilities. Over one billion people have unsafe drinking water. Nearly 50% of the people in the world are children, and 40% of the population of the world is under age fifteen (less than 20% of North Americans are under age fifteen.) Many of the global children have a dismal future, as they are poor, marginalized and forgotten. Health services are few and far between for most children in the world." (D. Livermore, PhD)[26]

Disease Connections

Oral diseases demonstrate that the body and the mouth are inseparable—the mouth can significantly affect the body just as the body affects the mouth. The oral cavity acts as the site of origin for dissemination of pathogenic organisms and microbial toxins to distant body sites. A number of epidemiological studies suggest that oral infections may be a risk factor for systemic diseases. Human endodontic and periodontal infections are associated with complex micro-floras in which approximately 500 species have been encountered. Oral health is important not only to prevent oral disease but also to maintain general health. "The compartmentalization involved in viewing the mouth separately from the rest of the body must cease. Oral health affects general health by causing considerable pain and suffering, changes what people eat, and affects their speech, quality of life, and well-being." (Dr. A. Sheiham)[27]

Ineffective health orally, with resultant systemic bacteremia, has been implicated in the following medical maladies, as documented by Drs. L. Xiaojing, K. Kolltveit, L. Tronstad, and I. Olsen of the Faculty of Dentistry, University of Oslo, Norway.[28]

 ❖ Diabetic issues and the relationship with periodontitis may be the strongest of all connections between the mouth and the body. Inflammation that starts in the mouth seems to weaken the body's ability to control blood sugar as it impairs the body's ability to utilize insulin. In turn high blood sugar levels provide ideal conditions for infection to grow.

 ❖ Cardiovascular problems such as atherosclerosis, infective endocarditis, and myocardial infarction are linked to inflamed blood vessels and bacterial infections from chronic inflammation.

 ❖ Pregnancy issues—to include miscarriages—are being related to infection and inflammation in general which seem to interfere with a fetus' development in the womb. Babies born too early or at a low birth weight often have significant health problems, including lung conditions, heart conditions, and learning disorders.

 ❖ Bacterial pneumonia is most commonly caused by aspiration of oral-pharyngeal flora into the lower respiratory tract.

- Cerebral infarctions are caused when bacteria attaches to fatty plaques which clogs arteries and breaks off.
- Rheumatoid arthritis and related pain decreases when periodontal disease is treated.
- Obesity issues have been linked to gum disease, and periodontitis progresses more quickly in the presence of higher body fat.
- Oral cancer concerns increase as the body's immune system becomes compromised. Poor oral hygiene and the resultant bacteremia often occur with cancer.
- Nutritional dysfunction often occurs in people not able to masticate healthy foods due to lack of teeth from dental disease.
- Scientific research continues to reinforce and to find more connections between poor oral health and systemic medical problems.

CHAPTER 2

Mission Benefits

Outreach Goals`

Dental ministry is a remarkably effective tool for using physical healing to open the door for the spiritual healing of people. Dental pain and disease can be a barrier to physical, mental, and spiritual well-being. Because of the universality of dental disease, nearly everyone is a candidate for dental services; therefore, the influence of outreach dentistry is widespread. Compassionate care prepares patients for a sympathetic hearing of the Gospel. Many who will not listen to other missionaries will accept those providing health care, since dental disease and pain are pressing issues. Dentistry provides a practical display of God's love and the concern of Christians serving in His name. *"I remember sharing Christ with a patient who had oral candidiasis and a generally weak appearance. She indicated a decision to receive Christ. I also talked to a hospital patient who was so weak he couldn't speak. But he could listen as I shared John 3:16 from the Bible with him and asked him if he wanted to accept Christ. He nodded his head. Later that night he died."*

    "In the dental chair I had a woman with severe pain from a broken down lower molar which needed to be extracted. Using every available method of dental anesthesia, the tooth could not be touched without the patient moaning loudly in excruciating pain. As the interpreter calmly reassured the patient and ministered to the spiritual needs of the patient, I had to step back and 'resort' to prayer as I was on the verge of letting the patient leave. The tooth, despite every effort possible could not be even touched. After prayer, I decided to give it one last chance and, without any additional anesthesia, was able to extract the tooth without a hint of pain. As soon as the tooth was removed, it was like an evil had been released from the woman. With great enthusiasm she embraced the hope of Christianity and became a changed person."

The Great Commission is addressed by ministering to others with dental missions in the name of Jesus. The Great Commission is God's command to reach out to the world: "Therefore go and make disciples of all nations, baptizing them in the name of the Father and of the Son and of the Holy Spirit, and teaching them to obey everything I have commanded you. And surely I am with you always, to the very end of the age" (Matthew 28:19-20). "You will be my witnesses . . . to the ends of the earth" (Acts 1:8).

Spiritual growth in people participating in short-term missions often brings life-changing experiences. A trip can enhance personal spiritual growth. An altered prayer life, a commitment to resist materialism, and a newfound orientation toward servanthood often result from a mission experience. Serving gives new and expanded vistas of the Christian experience. Pastor Don Richter says, "A mission trip is a contemporary form of pilgrimage."[29] *"I suppose it's a little selfish on my part because there is nothing greater than the huge smiles I get from helping the poorest of the poor.* It is more blessed to give than receive (Acts 20:35). *The amazing thing about missions is that often in giving of our wealth, time, and talents to show Christ's love to others, we receive in return the immensely more valuable treasures of heaven and are filled spiritually and emotionally to overflowing. This is the power of the gospel, which we seek to spread to others, returning like a boomerang and making our joy fuller."*

    ✦   *A trip helps me cultivate a servant's heart."*

FOLLOWING CHRIST

Christ's example of caring is followed when we heal others. "Jesus went through all the towns and villages, teaching in their synagogues, preaching the Good News of the kingdom and healing every disease and every sickness" (Matthew 9: 35-38). Therefore, as Christian dentists, we are obligated not only to make disciples but also to use our special skills of healing. In many Bible passages, Christ ministered to people by healing their physical needs. The Gospels tell of 26 specific persons Jesus healed, with references to many others. The apostles continued to heal physically and spiritually: "When Jesus had called the Twelve together, he gave them power and authority to drive out all demons and to cure diseases, and he sent them out to preach the kingdom of God and to heal the sick" (Luke 9:1-2).

Miraculous healing is not the way in which most sickness will not be healed today. God usually heals through the skill, care, and compassion of a medical or a dental practitioner, along with the support of others. Nevertheless, healing is a prominent part of the Gospels; and it is an important part of many Christian worship services, especially in developing countries. When health care professionals can help heal physical ailments, the kindness often prepares the patient for an evangelistic message and spiritual healing. "Heal the sick, raise the dead, cleanse those who have leprosy, drive out demons. Freely you have received, freely give" (Matthew 10:8).

Healing touch brings trust. Touch is a universal language of love, and it can instantly convey warmth. Jesus said, "A new command I give you: Love one another. As I have loved you, so you must love one another. By this all men will know that you are my disciples, if you love one another" (John 13:34-35). *"Because of the healing touch of dental practitioners, a patient allows them into their personal space. We cannot emphasize how important the touch is to expressing our loving compassion, bridging gaps, and establishing rapport. People who come to us with a physical need have had to put their fear aside, step forward in faith, and show willingness to let us help them. With the healing touch often comes an almost instantaneous trust and openness to hear a message about God."*

Scriptures instruct us to care for others. "He who is kind to the poor lends to the Lord, and he will reward him for what he has done" (Proverbs 19:17). "He who oppresses the poor shows contempt for their Maker, but whoever is kind to the needy honors God" (Proverbs 14:31). "Religion that God our Father accepts as pure and faultless is this: to look after orphans and widows in their distress and to keep oneself from being polluted by the world" (James 1:27). "If anyone has material possessions and sees his brother in need but has no pity on him, how can the love of God be in him? Dear children, let us not love with words or tongue, but with actions and in truth" (1 John 3:17).

Inspiring trips short-term my encourage participants (especially the young) to consider long-term service. *"Youth mission trips can produce far more enduring outcomes than merely entertaining teenagers with lock-ins, wild stunts, pricy multimedia, or luxurious camps or retreats. Missions crack open the hearts of youth to biblical content and commands in a way that fun-and-games can't. It ignites their minds far faster than lectures. It captures the attention of youth who want to do rather than to sit. It can draw jaded students into a lifetime of making a difference in the world. A service event can be an entry point to meeting God."*

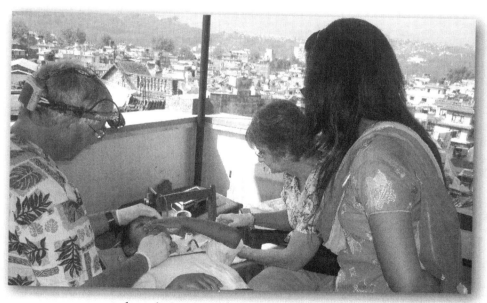

A dental clinic is held on a Nepal roof top.

Relational Outcomes

Christ's ambassadors are the term many volunteers desire to be called as they reach out as Christ's disciples. *"Children from Dakar, Senegal showed us how* *religious and political misinformation fosters hate and distrust in the world. Using dentistry to fix a painful tooth opened the door for us to visit a Muslim compound where many children were terrified of us. The children grew up under the threat of being boiled in oil and eaten by white, American Christians as the ultimate punishment for misbehavior. By the end of our visit, however, the children were laughing, sitting in our laps, and the whole compound's perception of Christians had changed."*

Unity occurs among the Church of Jesus Christ and international mission groups when teams travel to spread God's love. The team learns about missionaries supported by their local church and how to pray for the needs, the struggles, and the victories in the national church and community. They become emotionally and spiritually tied to another congregation or organization. Team members learn how to share their faith—it can actually be easier to share it for the first time in an international setting. Joanne Shetler (missionary to the Balangao People in the Philippines) said, "The tribes in the Philippines still say that the best thing the airplane ever brought was the visitors. They told us their faith wouldn't be so strong if it weren't for all those who came to share their testimonies. To hear the same truths about Jesus Christ from people from all over the world validated those truths and greatly enlarged their faith…and meeting with the nationals greatly increased the faith of the visitors!"[30] *"Jesus prayed for unity among believers so that the unbelieving world would be able to recognize that Jesus really was from God, that He really was the Messiah."*

  * *"The fellowship that believers enjoy is especially sweet when it crosses ethnic and cultural boundaries. Differences in skin color or language cannot inhibit the unity brought about by the presence of the Holy Spirit in the lives of believers. It still amazes me that I can meet a Christian for the first time in an international country, and in less than two minutes we have more in common than I do with an unbelieving neighbor I have known for nearly two decades."*

  * *"In Egypt we worked with Habitat for Humanity, which helps build homes for the less fortunate in the world. We had traveled to a new Muslim village of 5,000 people to construct the first Habitat house there. The villagers were very distrustful of our team, and the first day they would not allow us to perform dentistry. After working a day helping them build, we gained their trust and they asked us to assist them dentally. By the time we left that village, in only*

a few short days, we had become honored guests; and they were willing to defend us with their lives if harm should befall us. Hearts and minds were changed."

♦ *"One area of impact often not considered is in providing dental care for the more affluent in the country—diplomats, business people, government officials, and other leaders . I saw ambassadors and high government officials; and, in some cases, I had the chance to share spiritual ideas with them. In many countries, people like these are not well reached with the Gospel, yet they wield great influence in the society. They are often open to spiritual ideas; yet, there are few who seek to minister to them."*

Family/friend relationships are built within most teams. *"A family mission trip helped a sixth-generation dentist open the eyes of one of his four daughters to become the seventh-generation dentist within the family."*

♦ *"It is great to take spouses and family members whenever possible, as the mission experience often is life-changing, and it is important to share that with significant others."*

♦ *"A lawyer wife, who worked all day sterilizing instruments, beamed often as she watched her dentist husband and teenagers providing dental care and experienced the family bond and growth they had together while serving others."*

♦ *"I met one of my dearest friends on a mission trip to Jamaica about ten years ago. Since then we have gone on a dozen trips together, and we have inspired each other. It should be no surprise that our deepest, most meaningful friendships will be with those with whom we serve the Lord."*

♦ *"My wife and I have never been more 'in-sync' than when we have a common goal of helping others. Our marriage has been blessed and continues to be exciting through missions. Some moments can be stressful, and everything does not always work perfectly; but with any adversity comes growth, and we have always come out more loving and understanding towards each other."*

♦ *"After a spring break dental mission to Belize, all family members agreed we'd had the best trip ever—even though we'd gone to many tourist places for vacations before. The mission often surfaces in our conversations of our most memorable family moments."*

♦ *"Team members build lasting bonds of friendship with nationals and return often to work with the same people. Some have had the chance to host their international friends on visits to America."*

Supportive encouragement is provided to those who serve as career missionaries on the field. Traveling gives insight into God's kingdom worldwide. Teams learn how to pray for missionaries—their needs, struggles, and victories. It enriches and encourages career missionaries on the field. *"My first mission trip, to Belize, started out as a real bummer. My expectations were that I would change the world or at least this particular corner of it. To my chagrin, the area in which I served was predominantly Christian already, with well-established churches that were dentally needy but spiritually well-endowed. The Holy Spirit convicted me of the inappropriateness of my attitude through several passages that speak clearly to our calling to minister to fellow believers.* '...to prepare God's people for works of service, so that the body of Christ may be built up' (Ephesians 4:12). *For us to ignore the needs of other Christians so that we can add a few evangelistic notches to our belts is in direct contrast with the Christ-centered gospel that we seek to proclaim. Not surprisingly, as Acts 2 shows, love between Christians can also be a very effective testimony to the unbelieving world of the truth of the gospel."*

    ❖   *"Mission trips have broadened my worldview as I've learned to worship God with other cultures and to exercise the faith I've seen in others around the world."*

Service examples are set by team members who travel. Family, friends, church, and community are all watching the members give globally. A mission trip brings opportunities to witness and to share Christian beliefs in dental practices and our community. Service raises the importance of missions for the home church. Max Lucado, "the best preacher in America" (according to *Reader's Digest*) and author of 50 books, writes in *Outlive Your Life*: "You want to do good. You want your life to matter. You want the world to be glad you lived."[31] *"We took our teenagers when we went on a mission trip. Our teenagers were impacted positively by serving others."*

    ❖   *"We knew a 73-year-old woman who had never liked the gap between her crooked front two teeth. She had saved money to fix them; but after hearing what the CDS did to help children, decided she would rather give that money to help the less fortunate. Now whenever she looks in the mirror and sees her front teeth, she thinks of all the good she was able to do and relishes the uniqueness of her smile."*

Self-sacrificial giving and good outcomes in the world encourage everyone. Mission trips give insight into God's work worldwide. Helen Keller said, "Although the world is full of suffering, it is also full of the overcoming of it."[32] *"It always encourages us to dwell on the positive aspects of the world. We have seen orphanages helping the abandoned; street centers equipping the homeless; drug addicts coming clean and finding hope; prostitutes turning their lives around; hospitals and schools helping those who can't pay; seminaries and conference centers that spread Christian love and hope; the excitement of refugee children devastated by war being given shoe boxes of love; transition houses teaching young adults a trade skill; radio and television ministries that encourage and educate; and so much more. The world is full of people using their gifts and talents to make a difference, and we are inspired both at home and abroad."*

* *"We have witnessed evil, suffering, and persecution in the world and have also been greatly encouraged as we have seen much good come despite it. The mission field is filled with marvelous stories of overcoming and of unexplained happenings (miracles)."*

* *"I had two young brothers killed by a drunk driver in a seemingly meaningless vehicle accident. Nearly thirty years later our mission pilot, using his own small plane, was giving his time and resources to serve by taking us to Mexico for a dental mission. As we conversed, we found we both came from the same small town and that he had been in our house after my brothers' deaths in the accident. The pilot had been influenced by my family's Christian example of forgiveness, and now he was serving others (including us)!"*

* *"When wondering how people can even survive due to the lack of essentials like food, water, shelter, and parents, these experiences teach us of the indomitable human spirit. The outpouring of love, the hugs, the smiles, and the verbal, singing, and dancing expressions of many patients' appreciation goes far beyond monetary rewards."*

Dental teamwork can add enrichment to the life of a person who had thought of dental care as disgusting or repulsive. *"A dentist's husband—who at first stated he would never assist or get close to blood—changed his mind after working as his wife's dental assistant. He said, 'For the first time I have a true appreciation for how hard my wife works, how much good she does for others, and what a joy it is to help her.'"*

They celebrate success in a Jamaican dental clinic.

Purposeful Dentistry

Purposeful serving fulfills a person's quest to use his/her God-given gifts to be significant and to make a difference. "Each one should use whatever gift they have received to serve others, faithfully administering God's grace in its various forms" (1 Peter 4:10). "... put off the new self . . . work, doing something useful with his own hands ('dentistry is our interpretation!'), that he may have something to share with those in need . . . Be kind and compassionate to one another" (Ephesians 4:24-32). Others write extensively about this:

    ❖   Os Guinness, author, respected theologian, and social critic wrote *The Call*, a book about finding and fulfilling the central purpose of our lives. Guinness says, "Become an entrepreneur of life and see all of life as an enterprise transformed by God's call. Count the cost, consider the risks, and set out each day on a venture to multiply your gifts and opportunities and bring glory to God and add value to our world."[33]

♦   Pastor Rick Warren, the founder and senior pastor of an evangelical mega-church, wrote *The Purpose Driven Life*. Selling 30 million copies, this book is a guide to a 40-day spiritual journey that helps discover the answer to life's most important question: "What on earth am I here for?"[34] "Whoever trusts in his riches will fall, but the righteous will thrive like a green leaf" (Proverbs 11:28).

♦   Bob Buford, a successful businessman and founder of Leadership Network wrote *Half Time*, where he coins the phrase—"changing your game plan from success to significance." He asks, "What do you want to be remembered for?"[35] Buford also wrote, *Finishing Well*, encouraging us to make the second half of our life better than the first. "As long as you're able to do something meaningful, why would you go into some kind of holding pattern before and/or after retirement?"[36] Why retire to the "golf course," self-entertainment, or "Leisureville" exclusively? One newly-graduated dentist said, "I dreamed that my life would make a difference in the world at large. Why not go where the need is great and your influence is unmatched? I decided that one more dentist in Mississippi would not make much difference, but one more in the Ivory Coast would."[37] *"One of the most evangelically rewarding dental missions was when my son and I traveled on a small airplane to Mexico for a weekend dental mission. Not only was my son influenced to a life of service, but also we had the opportunity to work with a Gideon, bi-lingual pastor who acted as our interpreter. After we got the patients out of physical pain and had established a trust relationship, the pastor had the opportunity to address the individual's spiritual and emotional suffering. Several patients, right in the dental chair, came to place their hope in Christ."*

♦   *"There are many patients for whom relatively simple dental care can make a big difference. Composite restorations transformed a young girl with teeth that were unattractive due to caries or congenital malformation. A patient with a carious tooth may come expecting extraction but be happily surprised to find that the tooth can be saved."*

* *"Two hours down a rough dirt road, we set up a six- chair clinic in the middle of Massai country in Kenya. The tribal leader was a pastor whose smile revealed four missing maxillary incisors from a childhood fall, sustained when running from a wild animal. We provided a partial, igniting the whole tribe into singing and dancing to the Lord!"*

EDUCATIONAL SHARING

Teaching/sharing the knowledge of dentistry, sterilization, and oral hygiene with international medical or dental professionals and students is a blessing. *"The mission field is a perfect teaching environment in many respects. First, there are plenty of patients, and not nearly as much record-keeping required as in the developed world. Secondly, inexperienced health practitioners or students often will have the opportunity to provide more hands-on treatment, with the short-term, seasoned missionary professionals nearby for back-up. Thirdly, because of the desperate need for care in most parts of the world, patients will be as grateful for the opportunity to see a student or a developing professional as they would a licensed dentist. While on a mission trip, Christian dentists who share their expertise in humility and love can be a powerful force for the gospel in the lives of professional health personnel or students."*

* *"In Madagascar, I spent two weeks training a physician who took care of 400 street children with a Christian center. The national doctor's most common problem was pain and infection from toothaches. Children could not eat well and lay awake at night in pain from diseased teeth. The Madagascar doctor quickly learned how to diagnose dental problems, deliver dental anesthesia, and remove painful infected teeth. We left him with basic extraction instrumentation and supplies. All the teachers were trained in oral hygiene and each child was given a toothbrush. The next day, the teachers showed the children how to brush their teeth around the communal fountain. The toothbrushes were kept at the school because if they had been sent out with the children, the families might have sold the toothbrushes or traded them for other essentials."*

* *"In Ecuador we learned that the children were trading their new toothbrushes for candy!"*

The teachers show the children how to brush in Madagascar.

* *"A professional exchange of information occurs within the team and with international national dentists, physicians, and health practitioners. We, in America, do not have all the answers and always welcome the chance to share and learn from national professionals."*

* *"A host national dentist in Uruguay, after seeing the CDS portable equipment, said, 'I can do that!' He is now helping orphans in isolated settings. A Guatemalan dentist, who worked with us, said, 'I will now help a few patients in my practice, even if they can't pay.'"*

AMAZING ADVENTURES

Adventurous travel brings interest, excitement, and wonderment to life. Participating in safaris in Africa, riding camels around the pyramids in Egypt, having a lemur climb on a shoulder in Madagascar, riding an ostrich in Kenya, being given a Siberian wolf pelt from the commander guarding the Russian-Mongolian-Chinese border, embracing the risks of caring for refugees in a volatile part of the world, or learning to brush teeth with local twigs in Senegal are a few of the highlights reported by CDS members. "The world is a book, and those who do not travel read only a page" (St. Augustine).[38] "Travel, in the younger sort, is a part of education: in the elder, a part of experience" (Francis Bacon.)[39] *"We are enriched by the beauty and grandeur of our world, the diversity of its people, and the wonderful cultures, interesting politics, and religious faith of others. On a mission trip we live with, work with, and enjoy the people in their environment— free from the fetters of tourism."*

Purposeful vacations or mission trips are educational and give perspective to life. They increase appreciation for what we have and decrease dependence on material things. *"Mission trips are also a stark reminder that we don't really need as much as we think we need. My time in Jamaica's mountains allowed me to meet those people who work eight hours a day at a coffee factory, sorting through coffee beans by hand, barely making enough to keep food on the table. When it came time to worship the Lord, however, there was a joy and sincerity of heart that most Americans could envy. Perhaps a lot of the 'stuff' we accumulate actually serves as an obstacle to recognizing the Lord as our provider."*

* *"In Madagascar, we saw women squatting all day long in the hot sun with a hammer making gravel by hand. Now, I don't complain about my back at the end of the day."*

* *"The local children asked our teenagers how many shoes they had, and our kids were ashamed to tell them about their full closest. Suddenly the latest fashion did not hold the same appeal, as our teenagers realized these children had no shoes, lived on a dirt floor, had to carry water, and had no electricity in their homes."*

* *"Many of us live like royalty compared to the majority of the world. When poverty is experienced close-up, we cannot help but reevaluate our priorities."*

OTHER BENEFITS

"Altruistic behavior decreases stress, increases immunity, relieves pain, improves emotional health, decreases anxiety, relieves depression, increases longevity, and improves social interaction. These outcomes have been shown in studies. Interestingly, these health benefits are tied to giving of oneself. You don't get them by giving your money alone." (Dr. David Stevens, executive director of the Christian Medical and Dental Associations)[40]

Charitable trips are eligible for a tax deduction either from the dentist's business or on an Individual Schedule A Tax Form, for those who itemize. The Christian Dental Society "Designated Funds Account" provides a place for mission dentists or team members to receive tax benefits for donations and costs of volunteer trips. *"Tithing one's time through annual, short-term, one-to-two-week projects can fit well with the obligations of an active practice. In addition to service at home, personal involvement in missions abroad, where the need is overwhelming and the impact is great, is one of the most fulfilling and spiritually enriching experiences one can have."*

CHAPTER 3

Mission Planning

—◆—

VARYING LOCATIONS

Many opportunities for mission locations present themselves, and the world can be a large and daunting—yet an exciting and adventurous—place. God can use anyone with a desire to serve on short-term, overseas mission trips. *"Leaders of large, multinational, Christian organizations often tell us that there is desperation for dentistry everywhere and that they will welcome it at any time. We do not even have to ask, it is a given."*

◆ *"All countries have many people with painfully abscessed teeth, and dental hygiene is almost non-existent. Dentists can take great artistic satisfaction when someone's smile is no longer a liability for seeking employment. (A nice smile can be a major advantage in areas where tourism is a major source of jobs.) It can thrill dental practitioners to know a person may be able to use his/her teeth for many years after a restoration or a sealant is placed or when s/he has let people know—for the first time—how dental diseases can be prevented."*

Experienced leaders and established organizations offer the best mission trip experiences initially. Many faith-based and humanitarian agencies work overseas.

◆ Numerous, well-established, Christian organizations beg for dental help, which can be found on the Internet under such topics as "dental missions," "international missions," "medical dental missions," or "international and global organizations."

◆ The Christian Dental Society (www.christiandental.org) is a great resource for dental mission assignments and for help in planning and equipping missions. Dates and locations of trips are also listed under www.dentalmissiontrips.org.

- The American Dental Association has an informative website of Christian/humanitarian missions at www.internationalvolunteer. ada.org.

- The Christian Medical and Dental Associations (CMDA) (www.cmda.org) is an outstanding medical and dental organization offering mission opportunities and spiritually uplifting conferences and training opportunities each year.

- The Global Missions Health Conference (www.medicalmissions. com/conferences/guide) held in Louisville, Kentucky each November is a large meeting and an excellent place to be encouraged and to network for mission locations.

- Home mission trips, denominational preferences, or contacts with church or family members, relatives, friends, missionaries, and Christian organizations have all provided CDS members with opportunities to serve on dental missions.

Mission location choices involve a number of considerations such as:
- Where do we have a connection, a desire, or a calling?
- Do we understand the language or are translators available?
- How much time do we have?
- What are the financial considerations?
- What are the logistics needed for the site (housing, safe food, transportation)?
- What are the health considerations for the team (immunizations)?
- What are the needs of the site—is it a new project?
- What are the political, social, and religious stability concerns of the site?
- Are there legal requirements to be addressed (licenses, registrations, permits)?

Health/safety sources help determine the choice of a given destination when deciding where to serve. *"We are prudent where we take teams."*
- Centers for Disease Control (www.cdc.gov/travel) have information on health risks and precautions associated with most international countries. Travelers' hotline: 1-800-232-4636 or 1-404-332-4559.

* World Health Organization (www.who.int) is the health arm of the United Nations and has information by topic and by country.

* Central Intelligence Agency (www.cia.gov) has a "World Fact Book" with maps, facts on the people, the government, and the economy for all countries. It is well-researched and updated often.

* U.S. State Department (www.state.gov/travel/) provides consular information sheets, as well as information on travel advisories, embassies, and consulates.

* Check other state departments for information: Australia (www.smartraveller.gov.au); Canada (www.voyage.gc.ca); and United Kingdom International and Commonwealth Office (www.gov.uk/).

* If visiting a country with recent political instability, civil strife, or proneness to natural disasters, it is helpful to register online with the State Department (www.step.state.gov/step/). With trip information on record, the State Department can readily locate and help travelers in a crisis.

* Emergency phone numbers for the nearest American consulate or embassy are found at www.usembassy.state.gov/. When traveling abroad, program emergency numbers into a cell phone or jot them down in a small notebook. Be sure to include numbers for local police and/or ambulances, since the local officials are the best for immediate assistance. Consular or embassy officials can help with problems involving passport replacement or in locating an English-speaking lawyer or doctor. (Note that the State Department's emergency assistance numbers—888/407-4747 or 202/647-5225—only work at home and are more useful to friends or family who may be gathering information on your behalf.)

Timing Suggestions

A year ahead is a good time to start planning for a trip for all parties involved. Missionaries' schedules are an important aspect of the timing of a mission trip. If the missionaries host many teams, their calendar may be busy. Asking permission of the sponsors is important, as the team's goal is to serve the nationals. Sponsoring organizations often find that dental mission teams are a challenge even for experienced leaders. Dental volunteers must cooperate with leadership staff and be as flexible and as enthusiastic as possible. *"Our idea of a project is often very different from the hosts' ideas for the same task."*

Favorable weather or environmental conditions in the international country should be considered when scheduling the mission trip, as this maximizes effectiveness and enjoyment. Since the need for dentistry is so great throughout most of the world, team leaders can plan trips when the conditions are most favorable and safe for the team and the patients. Bad weather can impede the team's capabilities and the patients' ability to transport to clinics. Disaster relief, of course, does not allow a team to pick the best time. But, if possible, teams should skip rainy or hurricane seasons. The Caribbean hurricane season ranges from June through November, with the greatest risk for storms from August through October. In SE Asia, monsoon season is from December through early March. An independent weather forecasting service (www.accuweather. com) covers hurricanes. The web site for the Weather Channel (www. weather.com) and the World Weather Information Service (www. worldweather.wmo.int) is the forecasting arm of the U.N.'s World Meteorological Organization (WMO) and has weather updates for more than 1,200 cities. The WMO tracks severe weather events at www. severe.worldweather.wmo.int/. *"On our first trip we went to Nicaragua in the middle of summer, and it was oppressively hot, humid, and buggy. We learned!"*

* *"I have seen it so humid that clothes would not dry for several days. You will learn to be quite adaptable in these 100% humidity environments. Read any information available. People who live there are the best source of information."*

* *"July in Mongolia was the warmest month in the year, but it was still cool. We dressed accordingly."*

* *"We went to Peru in July, since the seasons were opposite on the other side of the equator, and it was winter during our summer."*

* *"In Central America, the dry, peak season runs from mid-December through April. Don't go in the extreme weather because the trip may turn into an episode of 'Survivor.'"*

- *"In central India, dust, heat, and smog can be intolerable, and you will be better off knowing those times."*

Sight-seeing goals may be taken into consideration. The best time to see local holidays (or avoid them, if they could interfere with the team's effectiveness) may add weight to the scheduling decision. *"It was thrilling to see Mongolia's colorful Nadam on July 11th following our mission work. It was an Olympic-like event held in the capital city of Ulaanbaatar."*

- *"We like to go to Africa in May or June, as winter nears and the foliage is not as thick. The animals are easier to see on a safari when the vegetation is lower and less dense."*

- *"Elaborate, colorful celebrations make the Day of the Dead in Oaxaca, Mexico, or the week before Easter in Antigua, Guatemala a great time to travel. A guidebook is a good source on local festivals."*

- *"Avoid visiting Muslim countries during Ramadan. During the month-long fast, many cafes and restaurants are closed during the day, and the pace of work is reduced. Note that the Muslim calendar is lunar, and dates for Ramadan and other religious holidays shift back eleven days each year."*

Dental personnel were called to serve in Kenya.

Mission Callings

God's calling on a life is important to discern. Many would-be volunteers ask how to clarify a "calling from God" to missions. An individual does not have to be considering full-time mission work to serve on a short-term mission trip. The following are steps to help discover and to discern if an individual is receiving a call from God to any type of mission work. (Dr. Chapman D.S.S and Dr. Topazian, D.D.S)[41]

* Individuals must realize that not all are called to an international field. Some people are called to witness at home. All are called to pray, and all are called to tithe. If individuals feel compelled or "pressed" to travel internationally, they are possibly sensing God saying that He wants them to join a team, and they may be quite unhappy at the thought of staying behind. Not all risks are removed, but those called have peace concerning the trip. They become willing to endure

hardships and to sacrifice. *"God may be telling us to do something, even when it seems to be accompanied by a little discomfort or apprehension. It is normal to have concerns when stepping out of a comfort zone, but God may still be prompting action."*

• *"There is the point where staying home is not an option. Life is safer and more rewarding in the uttermost parts of the earth than at home because that is where God has called us to be."*

• A potential volunteer can take active, aggressive steps to investigate needs and opportunities for service. S/he could participate in mission work at home or overseas and train in evangelism, discipleship, and Bible study. S/he could read mission publications.

• A prayerful commitment to God is helpful, asking Him to confirm opportunities, and to block avenues which do not conform to His will for the individual's life. A daily, personal, devotional time and a vital spiritual life are essential to knowing how and where God needs servants. Worship regularly at a church and fellowship with Christian groups. The advice of trustworthy mentors, counselors, and colleagues is useful when chosen wisely.

• Working submissively with mission groups involves some loss of personal autonomy, which an individual must be willing to do "for the sake of Christ," as Paul wrote in Philippians 3:7.

• The choice of friends who are open to God's leading, and especially the selection of a spouse, is vitally important in encouraging one to mission service.

• Money must be handled wisely, especially the avoidance of nonessential debt and other encumbrances which may deter an individual from a goal of serving in missions. The trappings of a consumer-oriented lifestyle will diminish an appetite for service and can load one with debt which prevents service in a needy location. *"Generosity can be a wonderful antidote to selfishness and financial anxiety."*

• Expecting a supernatural sign to declare one's destiny regarding missions is not necessarily going to happen. Many people with no religious motivations will leave home and risk danger and disease for financial gain or adventure. Those volunteers who believe people are lost without the Gospel should be at least as motivated.

Team size can vary depending on the mission focus, host capabilities, and the resources available. A group of five to fifteen people can be a manageable size for many places. A larger group can be difficult to house, to feed, and to transport (a large van usually fits 10-12 people). A smaller group may lack the critical mass to have the manpower and the collective skills to accomplish a task.

Participant qualifications can be flexible, but it is recommended that all team members have willing hearts and an attitude of service and ambassadorship. Dedicated helpers must be healthy in body and mature both in faith and demeanor. Desirable team members are well-prepared, responsible, and have the goals of winning souls, discipling lives, relieving distress, and working for God's kingdom. *"We try to balance the team so each member has a "buddy" to relate to—someone his/her age or interest level. It is important that team members are inclusive and not cliquish."*

❀ *"We encourage family members to serve together since trips often change people, and it can be important to share this with significant others."*

❀ *"We have taken non-Christians, but they must be aware of the spiritual goals of the team. It is important that they agree to support the witness of the group. Sometimes the impact of the trip will help them grow spiritually which is our prayer always."*

Choosing participants involves the team leader's discretion and mature judgment. Although decisions should have a liberal dose of grace, leaders are called to discern between the spirit of truth and the spirit of error. The question is if potential team members are teachable. *"There are people who shouldn't go on mission trips overseas, just like there are people in my church who shouldn't be put in positions of leadership."*

❀ *"I had a man who was committed to evangelism. For several months before the trip, he prepared, polished, and refined his testimony. It was ten, typewritten pages and took thirty minutes to present. The third time the missionary said he needed to cut it down to five minutes he got in a snit and sulked in a corner of the clinic for the rest of the trip. I never let him go on a dental mission trips again. We should be full of grace, but we should also have discernment."*

Members' convictions can make a difference on a trip. All team members must consent and conform to the requirements of the trip—whether it is standards of dress, religious sensitivities, or other issues unique to the field. The team represents sponsoring organizations that have often taken stands on issues. In most cases, it is better to take team members who agree with the beliefs of the churches and the sponsoring organizations. *"On one trip we had several people with little religious leanings. It caused problems and that at least should have been discussed ahead."*

* *"The comments at our meetings about simple, modest dress never registered with one teen we took on our trip. She made arrived at the airport in a backless, tight, halter top that caused me (the team leader) to spend most of the airline trip wondering what to do. Finally, as the airplane descended, I leaned across and suggested she wear her jacket to avoid unwanted attention. She must have been uncomfortable in the 100-degree temperature, but she did comply. She brought other wardrobe controversies upon herself throughout the trip."*

* *"The most common conflict within youth mission teams is the issue of a dress code. The issue seems to defy preparation. Clothing in the U.S. represents a personal expression of freedom. But, it is not necessarily what other cultures would call modest or even appropriate. We get howls of 'not fair!' when the line is drawn. In the Latin culture, for example, even dresses that bare the shoulders are considered to be offensive. Remember that you can preach and sing all you want; but if the people to whom you are ministering have already identified you to be unwholesome or offensive, your witness is ruined. Sensitivity goes further than avoiding evil.* I Thessalonians 5:23 says to 'avoid the appearance of evil.'"

* *"Several team members drank alcohol in public, which we had to discuss. We hadn't addressed the issue before the trip, but thought there was an understanding against drinking. Alcohol consumption can give the wrong impression about Christians and Americans, especially in some cultures where it is forbidden. The lack of consensus on that issue caused several problems on the trip."*

Judgmental attitudes are not advisable when allowing team members to join the team who have the desire to serve, unless there are extremely good reasons to refuse their presence on the trip. God inspires and calls others to come. *"One woman put off others on the team with her boisterous personality before the trip. But on-site, she spread joy and energy, soon capturing a place as a most beloved team member due to her encouraging and buoyant nature. The locals adored her as she easily learned their names and spoke broken Spanish with them. Our job is to stay open to letting people find fulfillment by following their own instincts and callings."*

* *"One church lady overheard my wife talking about the trip and insisted she should come. We worried about her ability to walk and her high blood pressure. It turned out that she was a perfect roommate and helper for the hygienist who showed up at our first meeting unexpectedly. She also was the only one who spoke sign language for a little patient who needed it, thus securing our admiration as a God-send on the trip after all!"*

Varied team members serve on a Mongolian military base.

Lifestyle Hints

Fine health—physical, mental, and spiritual health—before a mission trip helps overcome the stresses of long-distance travel. Limiting factors for volunteers include mobility issues since most countries don't cater to disabled people. Chronic illnesses such as COPD or heart disease may be limiting. *"We often comment that one has to be in good shape to haul bags over long distances in airports. Jet lag, lack of sleep, and stressors of mission clinic work, unfamiliar foods, changing schedules, new relationships, and more variables take people out of their comfort zones and stress individual physical and mental resources. Being in good shape physically, mentally, and spiritually helps one overcome and even thrive with all the unique challenges and opportunities."*

Immunity building and dietary health are enhanced for team members by following wholesome living habits. Sound advice includes avoiding processed foods and polyunsaturated vegetable oils, adding digestive-enhancing yogurts, and including fresh, whole, immune-enhancing foods, such as vegetables, whole grains, and ocean fish. A doctor or a nutritionist could suggest supplements. *"Some volunteers recommend taking oral probiotics which contributes to the health and the balance of the intestinal tract and helps fight illness and disease. Consult a doctor or ask for information at a local health food store."*

Conduct Agreements

Team agreements should be presented at an early stage when taking team member applications. The agreements will outline expectations and will clarify the standards for the trip. Using a Code of Conduct will avoid surprises and problems from individuals with preconceived ideas or personal opinions. The code is not meant to discourage participants but to encourage understanding and unity. Below are three general Code of Conduct outlines that can be adapted for specific teams.

Conduct Agreement Example # 1: (Since this one is fairly general in nature, applicants may not be required to sign it.)

* Stay flexible and roll with the punches. Regardless of what happens say, "No worries." Members will think of the best interest of the team and the mission goal, not their own agenda. No matter what the team has prepared to do well, God may have other plans which He will reveal upon arrival. It would be a sin to stick with our plans when He reveals a different road.

* Imitate a servant. Pitch in and help anywhere possible. No job is more important than another. Be a ready helper.

* Keep positive. Don't complain about anything—don't even think about it, if possible. Make the best of every situation.

* Remain supportive. Keep a good attitude, especially about other team members. Remember, "Everyone is a little strange, but never me! (Ha, ha)"

* Be punctual. Be at appointed places on time so the group doesn't have to wait.

* Show responsibility, especially with belongings, and be as aware as possible when traveling.

* Act wisely. Keep safety in mind at all times.

* Portray light-heartedness. Smile often and have fun with the group and the nationals. Keep the work environment friendly and know that every aspect of life is a witness.

* Model spirituality. Join in prayer times, devotionals, Bible reading, journals, church attending, and group time.

Conduct Agreement Example #2: (This one is longer and more specific.) The following elements are crucial to the effectiveness, the quality, and the safety of mission trips. As a member of the team, I agree to these ideas:

* Remember that I am a guest working at the invitation of a local ministry.

* Recall that I have come to learn as well as to teach. I may run across procedures that I feel are inefficient or attitudes that I find closed-minded. I will resist the temptation to inform our hosts about "how I do things." I will be open to learning other people's methods and ideas. (*However, we will be teaching our hygiene and dental care concepts to North American students using developed country standards.*)

* Respect the host's view of Christianity. I recognize that Christianity has many faces throughout the world and that the purpose of this trip is to witness and to experience faith lived out in a new setting.

* Develop and maintain a servant's attitude towards all nationals and my teammates.

* Bless my team through cooperative participation. I will attend all group meetings.

* Follow my team leader(s) and his or her decisions. I will be on-time to all meetings.

* Refrain from gossip. I may be surprised at how each person will blossom when freed from the concern that others may be passing judgment.

* Refuse to complain. I know that a mission trip can present numerous unexpected and undesirable circumstances, but the rewards of conquering such circumstances are innumerable. I will be positive and supportive.

* Support the labor that is going on in the country with the particular church/churches or person(s) with whom we are working. I realize that our team is here for a short while, but that the local church is here for the long term. I will respect their knowledge, insights, and instructions.

* Communicate positive political comments and discuss assets of our host country.

* Be inclusive in my relationships. Even if my spouse or boyfriend/girlfriend is on the trip, we will make every effort to interact with all members of the team, not just one another.

* Avoid any activity that could be construed as a romantic interest towards a national person. I realize that certain activities that seem innocent in my own culture may be inappropriate in others.

* Wear modest clothing and accessories throughout the trip. I understand that some clothes acceptable in the U.S. may not be acceptable culturally in other countries.

* Have responsible eating habits. I understand that the food may be different from what I am accustomed to. I understand that I should eat every meal in ample amounts as my body will respond more healthily when cared for nutritionally under mission conditions.

* Drink/sip plenty of safe water throughout the day and evening to stay hydrated.

* Abstain from the consumption of alcoholic beverages, the use of tobacco, or the use of drugs.

* Avoid any un-Christ-like behavior while on the trip. I will represent God and His people well.

* Accept authority. Should significant conflict arise or appear imminent between team members or others on the field, the team leader has the authority to send an offender home at the offender's additional expense under the team leader's timing and conditions. Safety of all participants and the group as a whole is foremost in such decisions, while effectiveness and cooperation are significant considerations.

I agree to abide by the Code of Conduct stated previously.
Applicant's Signature: _____
Printed Name: _____
Date:_____

Conduct Agreement Example #3:

It is my desire to participate in a dental mission trip being sponsored by the Christian Dental Society. I realize that, regardless of whether or not I am a Christian, I will be representing the Christian Dental Society during this trip. For this reason, I commit to refrain from any behavior that could reflect poorly on the Christian faith. My pledge includes, but is not limited to, the following:

* I will attend devotional sessions and will give them my full attention.

* I will seek to treat my patients as I would want to be treated under similar circumstances, and I will make their wellbeing a higher priority than my own clinical experience. Matthew 7:12, Philippians 2:3-4

* I will refrain from an over-indulgence of alcohol, and I will not use any illegal substances. 1 Corinthians 6:19-20

* I will refrain from sexual activity with anyone who is not my spouse and not share my accommodations with anyone of the opposite sex who is not my spouse or family member. 1 Thessalonians 4:3-5

* I am aware that if I choose to participate in behavior that reflects poorly on the Christian Dental Society, the leaders of the trip have the right to send me home immediately at my own expense.

Agreed to by: (print name)_____

(sign name)_____

Date: _____

CHAPTER 4

Electrical Considerations

Electrical power is a major consideration when running equipment in developing countries. It is important to know the difference between 110-120 voltage (used in the United States) and 220-240 voltage (used in many countries). When touching a bare wire of 110 volts, it will definitely bite. 220 volts is very powerful, causing an immediate muscle spasm that keeps a hand from releasing the bare wire—having the power to kill. When faced with 220-volt power, an adequate step-down transformer (converter) must be used for 110-volt equipment. Many dental operating units accept either 110 or 220 volts, as do many of the newer curing lights, amalgamators, head lights, cameras, phones, and computer battery chargers. Any electrical unit which has a motor (for example, an amalgamator) requires a larger converter to cover the amperage needed to run the unit.

Plug adaptors can vary for international counties. Information on international current and power plugs can be found on the Internet: www.kropla.com/electric2.htm or www.dbicorporation.com/internat/intpower. ntm. Converters or plug adaptors can be purchased at most electronic stores or from the Internet. The sponsoring organization may have converters and adaptors already, so it is appropriate to ask. Many nationals who sponsor teams do have some adaptors, but they may not have enough.

Power strips with circuit breakers help protect equipment against power surges, especially when using a portable generator. Their use is highly recommended.

Extension cord sizes are another important consideration. The small 16-18 gauge extension cords—which most lights and fans use—do not carry enough current through the smaller wires to run the dental operating units. The cords will heat up and/or damage the dental operating unit.

When using a 5 KW generator, a 12-14 gauge extension cord is needed to carry power.

Wattage power needed to run a one- to a six-chair clinic is calculated by this formula: needed power in watts = voltage (110 or 220) times the current in amps. Someone on the team must know this information, as the power considerations are essential. *"Our Aseptico dental operating unit requires 110 volts X 6 amps or about 800 watts to run, which is not excessive considering its accomplishments. Because the unit needs more power to overcome the inertia when turning the motor over, it requires about 1400 watts of start-up power. Most developing countries—when they have electricity—generally have enough electrical power to turn the lights on and to run a fan, but not enough electricity to meet the electrical demands of even a simple dental clinic. We generally need a 3 KW generator to run a one-chair dental clinic, if the normal electrical current is not dependable. For larger clinics of up to five chairs, we can function with a 5 KW generator, as all the units are not on simultaneously. To decrease the load on the generator, I can often use the local power source to run one unit or the sterilization heating element. The host national obtains a generator, and our team pays the cost. We make sure it has enough watts to meet our needs, with enough gasoline purchased to keep it running."*

Electricity availability for restorative dentistry may not be a priority if extractions and hygiene are the goals of the mission. *"I would still recommend taking a battery-operated handpiece to help with the sectioning and removal of more difficult teeth. Whenever possible, we take the equipment to perform restorative dentistry."*

CHAPTER 5

Portable Equipment

Without equipment, the diagnosis and the extraction of most teeth as well as oral hygiene instruction and cleanings can be accomplished, but everything is easier with a few portable items. The Christian Dental Society produces and sells or rents the light-weight portable dental chair listed on the website www.christiandental.org. The CDS also rents portable dental operating units, sterilizers, surgical and restorative kits. (See pictures before and after the CDS Membership Benefits on page xvi.)

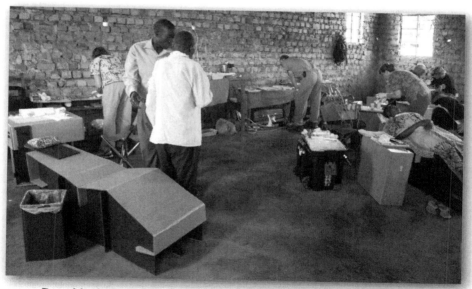

Portable, light-weight dental chairs are used in a church in Uganda.

Dental chairs enable the operator to position the patient favorably. The proper chair efficiently allows the dental professional to work longer without back strains or injury. When a dental chair is not available, and sit-down dentistry is desired, a wooden bench propped up on one end, with a blanket to soften the wood, works reasonably well. Small, plastic-covered pillows can be made to support the patients' heads. For stand-up dentistry, an elevated chair can be used. Head rests can be attached to the chair back, which assists in the positioning and support of the patient's head. A wall can be used behind the patients to brace their heads. *"We use a plasticized, durable, light-weight chair available through the Christian Dental Society for $400. Two chairs fit in one airline carry-on box, totaling only 42 pounds."*

    * *"Keep the stress off your back! If you have to lean over, brace yourself with your other arm, extend your legs beneath the level of your neck, operate at the 12:00 or 3:00 position, frequently tighten your abdominal muscles, and consider using a stretch-band during breaks to relieve shoulder spasms."*

Dental stools support the lower back and allow the dental practitioner to work more comfortably and longer without muscle strain. *"A trifold, portable stool (the brand-name is Camptime) with back support works well and can be purchased from the Christian Dental Society, at some sporting goods stores, or on the Internet."*

Operating units for dentists come with a high-speed and a low-speed handpiece, suction capability, and an air/water syringe. A dental operating unit is needed for restorative dentistry, surgical extractions, hygiene cleanings, endodontics, or prosthetics. There are a variety of portable dental operating units available. Some require a separate compressor or source of compressed air to run and others are self-contained. The CDS has both types available for dental mission trip rental. Look for a sturdy, dependable unit that is light enough to carry on the plane and has the ability to run on either 110 or 220 volts. Beware of some unreliable, mail-order units that have no ongoing service to maintain the equipment. *"We currently use Aseptico's 33-pound, self-contained Task Force Deluxe dental unit which is easily transportable as checked baggage on the plane and costs about $2400 with the 20% missionary discount. We further protect the unit by* *placing it into a rolling Sears' tool box or a medium hard-sided, rolling luggage bag for ease of transporting. Many airlines currently allow the transport of this unit on the plane as a carry-on bag, which saves baggage space for other dental items."*

Portable equipment can be purchased from dental supply organizations including: Adec (www.a-dec.com), Aseptico (www.aseptico.org), ASI Medical (www.asimedical.net), Bell International (www.bellinternational.org), Avtec Dental (www.avtecdental.org), DNTL (www.dntlworks.com), and M-DEC (www.portabledentistry.com).

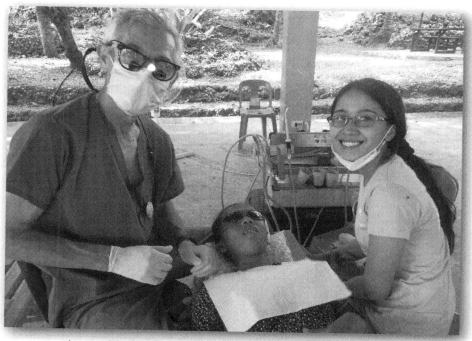

A portable dental operating unit is used in the Philippines.

Battery-operated handpieces with a straight and contra-angle head are extremely handy when there is no electricity or dental operating unit. A high-speed 1:5 or 1:3 multiplier contra-angle head attachment, although expensive, significantly increases the cutting capability of the unit. Overuse will overheat this attachment. There are also portable solar panels available to recharge the battery. When doing extractions, a handpiece to section a tooth or to remove bone can be invaluable with a difficult extraction. On the mission field, this can happen several times a day. A battery-operated handpiece can also allow the dentist to smooth or to adjust a tooth, to remove caries, or to polish teeth. Most have enough torque to open a tooth needing a root canal. Some choices of battery-operated handpieces include the Bell dental handpiece (www.bell-dental.com), the micro-portable handpiece from Avtec dental (www.avgtec.com), and Aseptico's Porta-a-Tip (www.aseptico.com).

A dental light is essential for the dental professional to see adequately in the dark corners of the patient's mouth. *"Mini-LED lights with rechargeable batteries, mounted on magnifying or protective eye-wear, are the best source of light, and are what I use in my private practice. LED spelunker head lights mounted on head bands also function adequately and can be found at most sporting goods stores. It is important to remember the charger."*

Curing lights are needed for restorative dentistry to set the bonding agents, resin restorations, and basing agents. *"Rechargeable, battery-operated LED curing lights are the lightest and easiest to use."*

An amalgamator mixes dental amalgam, as well as certain cements and other Glass-ionomer restorative materials. A 110-V amalgamator, which has a motor, needs a larger step-down converter when used with 220-V.

A rubber dam set-up is recommended when doing restorative procedures, especially on the mission field where effective high-speed suction is often lacking, when working with untrained assistants, and when communication is difficult due to language differences. A rubber dam helps control the operating field, with better isolation and moisture control, making it easier on the dentist, the patient, and the assistant. *"In many cases, especially in the lower posterior, the rubber dam makes restorative restorations easier, faster, and safer. It is definitely worth the effort when doing restorative procedures on the mission field."*

Appropriate sterilization is a must! (This is discussed in Chapter 10.)

Air-abrasion units and hydro-abrasion units propel extremely small particles of aluminum oxide with or without water onto tooth or prosthetic surfaces and are a great adjunct to quality restorative dental care. Abrasion units can be attached to an air source through a quick disconnect on a dental operating unit while others can be attached to the high-speed handpiece hose. Abrasion techniques help remove decay and assist in preparing the tooth for bonding or sealing by cleaning and roughening the tooth or prosthetic surfaces.

An ultrasonic scaler is critical for efficient treatment and to save fatigue of the hygienist's hands and wrists. In a developing country setting, where few, if any, have ever had their teeth cleaned, the calculus is abundant and tenuous to remove. The air-driven, sonic scalers (for example, the Titan) attaches like a handpiece and operates with the tip moving in an orbital pattern at a low frequency of about 3,000-8,000 cycles/second (which is how many times the tip comes in contact with the tooth). The ultrasonic scalers involve a power unit connected to a water source that plugs in. Ultrasonics vibrate at much higher frequencies than sonic scalers (25,000 cycles/sec and higher) with a more linear pattern. The ultrasonic handpiece utilizes either magnetostrictive devices (for example, Cavitron, Parkell, Coltene) created by a resonating stack of metal strips or piezo devices (for example, EMS, Satelic, Amdent) with vibrations produced by oscillations of a quartz crystal in the handpiece. The primary difference between sonic and ultrasonic scalers is power. The sonic scaler is a low-power device that removes plaque and fresh calculus. For the heavy-duty cleanings on the mission field, the power of an ultrasonic scaler is necessary. *"Sonic scalers do not work on heavy calculus. I am much better off just using hand scaling rather than a sonic scaler, but this quickly fatigues my wrists. Ultrasonic scalers are the best when faced with heavy calculus."*

Dental x-rays with portable, hand-held units are becoming more compact and less expensive. X-ray sensors connected to a small computer or tablet deliver instantaneous images. The disadvantage is that computers, software, and sensors—especially—are expensive. The option to purchase self-contained packets with fixer, developer, and film is an inexpensive alternative to sensors and computers and to the traditional dark chamber with fixer and developer. Dentafilm Ergonom-X self-contained film packets are available at www .Amerdental.com or www. practicon.com. and can be purchased on the Internet. *"We have found x-rays to be cumbersome, time consuming, and expensive in many settings. In more established settings, x-rays are definitely recommended and are becoming easier and cheaper."*

Check all equipment before going on the trip and service it as necessary.

Inexpensive equipment from less than reliable sources is best to avoid. Be skeptical of poorly made items or used equipment purchased on the Internet or through "supply houses" that have not withstood the test of time. These units easily break, are difficult to repair, and can compromise the capability to treat patients. *"Problems often present with new dental equipment not fully field-tested, and old equipment not well-maintained. Frequently, I have found that they don't hold up during transport or when used in a field environment."*

Maintenance and repair of equipment should not be ignored, as there are usually no medical repair specialists on the mission field. The ability to provide care is compromised if equipment cannot be fixed, jerry-rigged, or adjusted. The host nationals, although they may be helpful, cannot be depended upon to have the know-how or parts to fix the equipment. It is smart to take reliable, pre-tested equipment that the team members know how to use and to not assume that because it worked last time, it has survived shipping dangers and time in storage. *"I find that it is wise to maintain my equipment and instruments by cleaning, disinfecting, or sterilizing them after each trip. If something needs repairing, I don't wait. I always evaluate what worked and did not so I can prepare better for the next trip."*

Extra parts should be taken for essential items that can break or get lost easily.

• An extra rubber seal for the pressure pot sterilizer lid, as it can be burned and damaged if someone forgets to put water in the pot, is a must.

• The air/water syringe tip, the suction tip adaptor, and the end of the anesthetic syringes can be easily lost, so take extras.

• O-rings, screws, nuts, bolts, and other small repair parts can be accumulated over time, which are specific to the equipment used.

Maintenance articles include, but are not limited to, such items as a Leatherman (multi-purpose) tool, heavy-duty scissors, spare fuses, handpiece lubricant, super glue, assorted zip ties, batteries, and electrical tape. Little hex wrenches to open or to tighten items on equipment come in handy. Duct tape has many uses but must be transported in checked baggage.

Local nationals can often help if equipment breaks and team personnel can't repair the items. The nationals are often adept at fixing mechanical objects and know how to work around problems. If items aren't repairable, the locals may know where to get a replacement. If nothing can be done, the professionals that are affected must stay flexible and make adjustments. *"Our amalgamator broke in Ecuador, and we contacted the local Rotary Club. They bought us a new one there!"*

Repair items, emergency drugs, and electrical plug adaptors generally fit into a plastic, see-through, fishing tackle box for easy accessibility and transport.

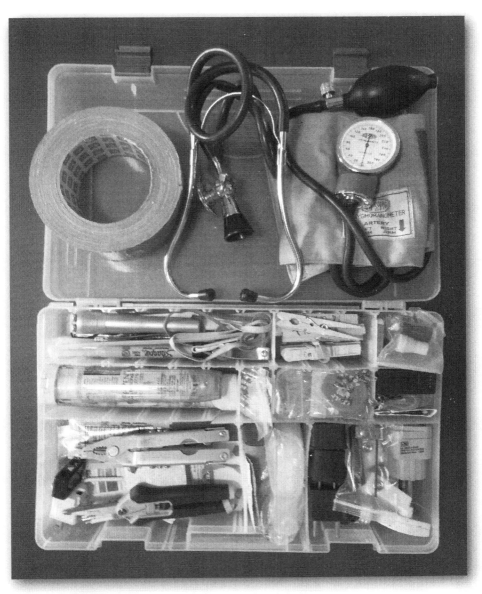

A maintenance and emergency medicine kit is organized in a plastic container.

CHAPTER 6

Restorative Information

RESTORATIVE MATERIALS

Composite fillings are considered the material of choice for most restorations, especially in the anterior mouth and for small posterior restorations. The variety of bonding agents and composites are often operator-specific, as there are numerous systems. *"We generally give dentists a plastic fishing tackle box with dividers so they can bring their own composite restorative materials. It is easier for dental professionals to work with familiar materials."*

Amalgam fillings are considered for restoring large posterior fillings. Amalgam is still the least expensive, strongest, longest-lasting, and most easily used restorative material available for posterior restoration. Both the Food and Drug Administration and the American Dental Association consider amalgam safe. *"I still consider amalgam the restoration of choice for posterior large fillings, especially on the mission field, where patients have no routine dental care."*

Glass-ionomer, as a restorative material or base material, can be a valuable adjunct to composite or amalgam in selective cases and is used for Atraumatic Restorative Treatment. Base material under large fillings is often composed of glass-ionomers or a combination of resin and glass-ionomers. Glass-ionomers come in a powder liquid form for hand mixing or in capsules that can be mixed in an amalgamator, if available.

Dental sealants are a valuable, preventive, dental treatment. This resin material is placed in the pits and fissures on the chewing surfaces of permanent molars and premolars that are susceptible to dental caries, due to the anatomy of the chewing surfaces of these teeth.

Dental cement is useful to place a stainless steel crown on a tooth or to re-cement a crown.

Atraumatic Treatment (ART)

Atraumatic Restorative Treatment (ART) is a viable restorative technique, primarily for application in developing countries. ART is an acceptable treatment alternative on selective cases in more austere settings. In 1994, the World Health Organization endorsed ART. Dr. Roger Smales, D.D.S. documented this technique. [42]

The ART approach intercepts small and medium-sized decay using only hand instruments or a slow-speed handpiece to remove the majority of the carious tooth substance, generally without dental anesthesia. The cavity is then restored with a conventional glass-ionomer such as Fuji IX. Glass-ionomers have a chemical adhesion to tooth structure, are bio-compatible, and demonstrate sustained fluoride release.

ART effectiveness is especially useful for these cases: early childhood caries, the extremely fearful patient, the mentally/physically handicapped, or as a sedative restoration to arrest or to slow down caries. It requires minimal cavity preparation, decreases trauma to the tooth, and is generally painless. ART does not generally remove all decayed tooth structure and is not considered to be a permanent restoration. It lasts from months to a few years but can be a valuable tool for caries treatment options in unconventional settings.

ART is performed when skilled human and and/or other resources are not readily available or affordable to treat dental caries by more conventional means. ART allows caries treatment in remote areas and in the field environment, as it is performed with unsophisticated dental equipment and/or minimal instrumentation and supplies. This cost-effective technique is simple enough to train non-dental personnel or primary healthcare workers in its use.

ART is contraindicated if there is the presence of a swelling or a fistula near the carious tooth or if the pulp is exposed. ART should not be attempted if there is a history of the tooth hurting for no reason, if the tooth responds to biting pressure, or if a chronic inflammation with an irreversible pulpitis or a necrotic nerve is suspected. Other major limitations to ART include an inability to use hand instruments to access and to remove caries, large carious lesions below the gum line, or an inability to control moisture or bleeding.

CHAPTER 7

Dental Care

—◆—

OVERALL TIPS

Overwhelming needs are found everywhere for surgical, restorative, and hygiene services. The team's priority is to point the way to God by demonstrating His love. Any personal contact makes a significant impression on every patient who is positively impacted. In doing the greatest good for the greatest number of people, each patient can be touched even if all the treatment needed cannot be accomplished. Expectations must be reasonable, and dental personnel should be content in whatever good can be done—not only through dental outcomes, but also through spiritual results. *"Many dentists or hygienists are hesitant to go on missions because they feel they might have to compromise the high standards of care they maintain in the developed world. If they could only see that the love they give others—even with a little touch of dental treatment—has a huge impact on people who are often so marginalized that they feel no one cares for them. Just the presence of a dental professional speaks volumes to the needy. The locals do not expect or even realize the high standard of care that is perpetuated in the developed world. Those in a developing country are often so blessed by any gesture that is given, and the credit for the treatment often goes to God."*

Portable dentistry usually consists of extractions, fillings, or an occasional endodontic or prosthetic procedure. With hygiene support, cleanings are always needed and greatly appreciated. Poor oral hygiene, toothaches, and dental infection are rampant almost everywhere. Hygiene and extractions are the easiest services to support and to equip when doing a dental mission and often provide the greatest good for the most patients. When treating with extractions only, without hygiene support, requests for cleanings and restorations are generally declined, as so many people are in pain and need the dentists' time. Electrical requirements are minimized or eliminated when using a battery-operated handpiece and sterilizing with a gas, propane, or fire-heating source.

Providing surgical care exclusively is an attractive way for new mission dentists to acquire dental mission competence, as it eliminates costly restorative materials, curing light, amalgamator, restorative instruments, a rubber dam set-up, and endodontic and prosthetic supplies. However, most dentists want to save teeth and prefer a mixture of surgery and restorative opportunities. It soon becomes apparent that there will be no end to extraction possibilities, and it can be more satisfying to restore smiles, to save critical teeth with endodontics, or to make an interim partial on selected cases. *"We want to open doors to Christian ministries and to encourage and to assist the long-term missionary efforts through our witness and use of dentistry and not just focus on extracting another tooth."*

Providing hygiene instruction should be basic to any dental mission and can best be done by a hygienist, although ancillary personnel can be trained to teach basic brushing and flossing techniques. (See Chapter 12.) The presence of a hygienist on a dental or a medical team is truly a blessing and, even if treatment is not accomplished, much can be done in the preventive category of care. Hygienists do not need to join a dental-specific mission or have a dentist accompanying them. In any mission endeavor, much can be accomplished while teaching prevention and while performing gross debridement of plaque and calculus with hand instruments. Any hygiene service given is truly a use of God-given gifts and is greatly appreciated. Teaching proper brushing, flossing techniques (flossing is rare in developing countries), nutritional counseling, and caries control can do more long-term good than cleaning, restoring, or pulling teeth. More hygienists need to understand how valuable they are to any mission team and that their presence on a mission—with or without a dentist—will bring enrichment, gratitude, and great blessings for themselves and others. *"I always tell hygienists that they are the most loved and appreciated members of all dental personnel. Their gifts of preventative education and hygiene are the most desired service in developing countries. They often get more hugs and gratitude than dentists receive!"*

Standard instrumentation is used to accomplish basic surgical, restorative, and hygiene procedures. Dental professionals have their own methods of treatment, and the array of instrumentation can be broad. Surgical and restorative kits can be rented from the CDS (www.christiandental.org). *"As a team leader, I provide the standard instruments, but always encourage dentists/hygienists to bring along any special instruments they prefer which are not in our basic kits."*

Plastic trays are the most convenient, safest, most frequently used accessory to hold surgical or restorative instruments and to transport them to and from sterilization. A tray is a flat, lipped, easily cleaned surface to work from. The tray, covered with half of a patient bib or paper towel, works well. The trays are also used to store restorative supplies and materials for easy access by each restorative dentist. Burs, bonding supplies, wedges, matrix bands, basing material, and more can be transferred to the contaminated tray off the restorative tray as needed. Sterilization personnel place the hot instruments on a tray to cool them. Each operator should have four trays.

These instruments are organized for a six-chair portable clinic.

Pack, store, and transport instruments and supplies for accessibility, efficiency, and convenience in fishing tackle, plastic containers which have dividers to separate items. Containers come in a variety of sizes and configurations and are available wherever fishing supplies are sold. When transporting, packing 2" x 2" gauze around the instruments protects them during the rough handling of bags by the airlines. Forceps can be stored in one container, elevators in another, and surgical elevators, retractors, suture holders, and mouth props in another. Most restorative instruments, matrix bands, and holders fit into one container, and the rubber dam set up fits in another. A smaller container holds all the burs for easy organization. With this system, only the instruments or items required for a procedure are pulled out, making it possible to return to obtain a few more items if the surgery becomes more complex. This decreases the number of instruments used and reduces how many must be taken on the mission.

For set-up, the containers are placed on a flat surface where they are immediately available and organized. Sterilization personnel are taught to replace the sterilized instruments, and all is ready to transport to the next location by just closing the container without any extra handling. When sterilization personnel are learning (so many of the instruments look similar to the untrained eye), they can just place the instruments on a side tray for a more experienced worker to replace.

Practitioners' provisions are often operator specific, and there are a number of items that can make dental treatment easier in unfamiliar clinics. Good communication with the nationals decreases surprises. Often promised items are missing even with the best pre-planning and the good intentions of sponsoring organizations. *"When packing for a dental mission to Eastern Europe, we were promised a fully operational, two-chair clinic. We found a filthy room with holes in the floor. Piled in the hallway were junky dental units which would never function. Fortunately, we had brought everything needed for a portable dental clinic, and we set-up in an adjacent room."*

   * Professionals should ensure the items that they want to use listed in Appendices B, C, and D will be in the clinic or will be taken by the team. If not, the practitioners should bring those items themselves.

   * Personal items are important to include: loupes, a headlight, preferred masks, properly-sized gloves, smocks/scrubs, anesthesia, needles, burs, and desirable instruments that may not be included in the basic set-up. Personal instruments should be marked for easy return.

* For restorative treatment, practitioners should consider bringing basing and bonding agents, composite, articulating tape, sealants, and interproximal wedging materials in an organized container. Bring rubber dam set-ups as they are usually not included in the basic inventory.

* Hygienists should definitely bring an ultrasonic as it will save their hands when removing abundant and tenacious calculus deposits. Sonic scalers which fit on dental operating unit air hoses do not have adequate power. Appropriate electrical power and a water source are needed for ultrasonic use.

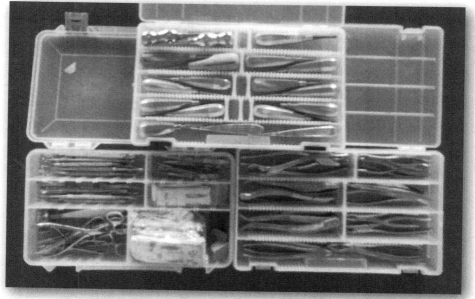

Surgical instruments are organized in plastic containers.

SURGICAL ITEMS

Surgical needs depend on how many dentists are working, their surgical skill level, how many teeth are being taken out on each patient, whether the dentists mix restorative or other procedures, and the sterilization time. With the pressure pot sterilizer system, the turn-around time for instruments is about thirty minutes. This includes washing, rinsing, bringing the pot to pressure, sterilizing for ten minutes, and cooling for five minutes. For surgery only, four sets of surgical instruments per practitioner are recommended. For fillings only, three sets of restorative instruments are recommended, since restorative procedures take longer. For a mixture of surgery/restorative treatment, there should be two sets each of surgery and restorative instruments. A checklist found in Appendix B includes the following items for surgery.

* Dental equipment includes a dental chair, an operator stool with a backrest, and a dental operating unit with a handpiece and suction capability for surgical extractions if available. Handpieces must attach to the unit and must function appropriately. They should be checked before departing. It is important to remember suction tips, air/water syringe tips, handpiece lubricant, surgical burs, an acrylic bur, smoothing burs, and tooth cutting burs. It is wise to bring a surge protector for the unit, extra fuses, and an extension cord.

* With sporadic, very limited, or no electricity expected, or if a dental unit is not available, it is helpful to bring a battery-operated handpiece with surgical burs for the occasional difficult extraction. An aspirating syringe can be a helpful adjunct to irrigate and to keep the bone cool. A cup is used for spit, and gauze may provide moisture control.

* If the dentist is more comfortable standing for surgical procedures, a head rest attached to the back of a chair is a valuable adjunct.

* Dental x-rays are becoming more portable and less expensive. They are a valuable adjunct to diagnosis and treatment but are not considered essential for basic surgery procedures.

* Dental loupes or eye protection for the dentist may include a LED battery-operated headlight. Spelunker LED headlights on a head band also function well. A battery charger or extra batteries should be packed. Including eye protection for assistants and patients are necessary.

* Gloves must be the correct size and type for each operator and assistant. Face masks are also operator specific and should be selected to fit each practitioner.

* Anesthetic syringes and mouth mirrors are used for each patient. An explorer and/or periodontal probe is often helpful. Placing instruments on

a tray covered with half of a patient bib greatly assists surgical set-up access and transportability. Operators should focus on the chief complaint and not try to remove all the bad teeth. Local anesthesia (usually two carpules per patient on the average) is best brought from the developed country as the efficacy of local supplies may be questionable. Some carpules of anesthesia without epinephrine is appropriate for selected patients. Many dentists use topical anesthesia that is placed with a cotton tip applicator. The anesthetic needles should match those the practitioner normally uses (short or long, 25-guage to 30-gauge). Some dentists bring an intraligamental syringe and extra-short 30-gauge needles. It is best if only the professionals place and remove needles, sharps, and anesthetic carpules. Used sharps are deposited in a plastic water bottle (sharps container) which is burned with the paper products. A needle recapping guard is useful.

* 2" x 2" gauze pieces soak up tissue fluids and blood, help maintain the surgical site, and act as pressure bandages when the patients bites on them after extractions. Some personnel use larger (3" x 3" gauze) as the patient is less likely to aspirate or swallow them, but most prefer the 2" x 2" size. A disposable cup or small baggie is helpful for placement of extra gauze and medications for the patient to take home. Patients can also spit into the disposable cups.

* Patient bibs, which can be cut in half, make excellent patient drapes to protect patients' clothes and are held on with bib clips. The other half of the bib is used as a barrier for the instrument tray.

* Forceps vary greatly, but most teeth can be removed with upper and lower universals. Serrated beaks grip better and help with rotation. Pedo-sized and regular-sized forceps are recommended. The # 23 cow horn is the only special forcep many dentists prefer for lower molars, and some prefer using the 53R and 53L for upper molars. Dentists are encouraged to bring the forceps they are most comfortable with.

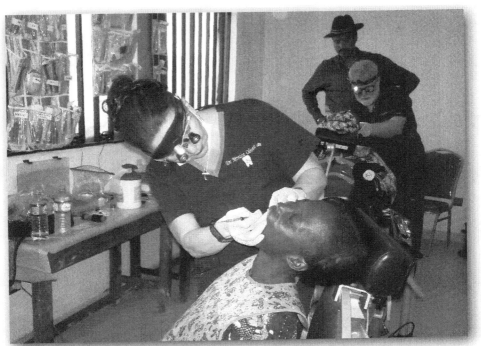

Surgery is done in the standing position with a head rest attached to the chair.

* Elevators and luxators are often practitioner specific and having the "right one" helps immensely. Often teeth can be removed using only these instruments.

* Periosteal tissue elevators are needed on almost every tooth to free tissue attachments. Since there are several types, the dentists can bring what they prefer. *"If you have never used the Woodson #1, I recommend it. A ½ Hollenback makes an excellent periosteal elevator for pedo teeth and for many adult teeth which do not require extensive tissue reflection. It can also incise the PDL nicely. Sometimes the luxator can also be used to release tissue."*

* Curettes and scalers help remove infected tissue and clean adjacent teeth.

* Curved hemostats facilitate removal of tissue tags, bone fragments, pieces of teeth, and loosened teeth.

* Root tip picks vary, can be boxed with the elevators, and are occasionally needed.

- Cheek retractors are operator specific and are not always used.
- Mouth props come in small-child, child, and adult sizes and are useful in protecting the temporal mandibular joint, especially for lower extractions and for holding the mouth open.
- Bard Parker holders and scalpels are useful (most use a #15 or a #15c blade).
- Sutures, suture holders, regular and tissue scissors, and tissue tweezers are used sporadically to manage the soft tissue. Suture material varies. 4-0 Vicryl, violet color, on an FS-2 needle is suggested, as it handles like silk and resorbs by hydrolysis in a few weeks without inflammation. For fine suturing, 5-0 Vicryl on a P-3 needle does well. Vicryl is a superb subcutaneous suture when closing in layers. If removal of a silk suture cannot be ensured, its use is not recommended, as it takes a year to resorb and starts to draw infection into the wound within a week. Cat Gut and Chromic Gut are not ideal if the dentist will not be present to monitor and to ensure its removal. Gut sutures are difficult to handle and resorb by inflammation. Fortunately, gut usually unties itself in a short time and, if not, resorbs rather quickly.
- A bone file and a rongeur remove and smooth bone but are used infrequently.
- A mono-bevel chisel and hammer to chip bone away and a bi-bevel chisel to split teeth may be helpful if the dentist is trained to use it. Most dentists prefer a bur.
- Tissue hemostatic agents, gel foam, and dry socket paste can be useful at times.
- Fugi IX is a glass-ionomer which comes in a powder and a liquid that can be mixed and is a great restorative option to have even if planning on doing surgery only. It sticks to the tooth, releases fluoride, arrests decay, and fills holes in teeth. (See Atraumatic Restorative Technique in Chapter 5.)
- Analgesics (for example, Motrin 200 mg tablets and Tylenol 325-500 mg tablets) provide the patient with pain relief. Stronger narcotic analgesics are not usually recommended. It is also advisable to have written tooth extraction instructions which can be handed out to the patient or to

someone in charge who speaks English and can interpret for the patient. (See Appendix H.)

* Antibiotics (for example, Pen VK 500 mg tabs, Amoxicillin 500 mg tabs, and Clindamycin 150 mg tabs) help with major infections, when the patients exhibits systemic signs, when the immune system is compromised, or for endocarditis or prosthetic joint replacement prophylaxis.

* A patient mirror for instruction is often useful.

* Containers to hold all the instruments and supplies help in the organization, storage, and transport of instruments and supplies.

* Sterilization is a must! (See Infection Control in Chapter 10 and Sterilization Checklist in Appendix E.)

* Oral hygiene instructions given by a hygienist or trained auxiliary personnel are important and are usually conducted before surgical procedures. Toothbrushes, toothpaste, and floss are useful to give out to all patients. (See Chapter 11.)

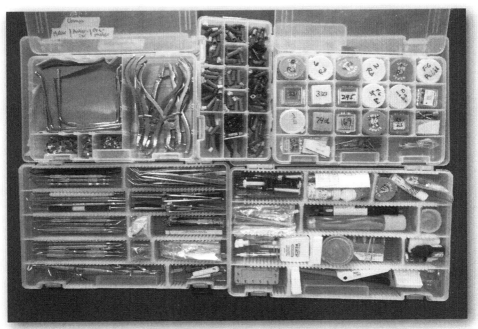

Restorative instruments are organized in various plastic containers.

RESTORATIVE ITEMS

Restorative needs depend upon how many dentists are working, the skill and the speed of the operators, how many fillings are being completed for each patient, if the dentists are also doing surgical procedures, and the sterilization turnaround time. Including restorative procedures on the mission field are more complex than providing only extractions but are often more fulfilling and are always greatly appreciated. Three sets of restorative instruments per dentist are suggested. If the tooth requires a large restoration with a possibility of a nerve exposure, it is good to warn the patient that if the decay goes into the nerve, the tooth will have to be extracted. Root canals are rarely an option. A checklist found in Appendix C consolidates the following items for restorative.

* Dental equipment includes a dental chair, an operator stool with a backrest, and a dental operating unit with high- and low-speed handpieces, suction capability, and an air/water syringe. Handpieces must attach to the unit and must function appropriately. They should be checked before departing. It is important to remember the appropriate suction tips, the correct air/water syringe tips, and the handpiece lubricant. It is wise to bring a surge protector, an extension cord, and extra fuses for the dental unit. The unit must work with the voltage available in country or procure a proper 220-240-volt to 110-120-volt converter. If electricity is sporadic, insufficient for the power demands of the clinic, or if there is no electricity, the host nationals should obtain a generator large enough to run the clinic. (See Chapter 4.) The gasoline to run the generator must also be purchased.

* Dental x-rays are becoming more portable and less expensive for dentists. They are a valuable adjunct to diagnosis and treatment but are not considered essential for basic restorative procedures.

* Air-abrasion and hydro-abrasion are commonly used in dentistry to help in decay and stain removal. This technique also cleans and prepares the tooth surfaces for better bonding.

* Loupes or eye protection for the dentist may include a LED battery-operated headlight. Spelunker LED headlights on a head band also function well. A battery charger or extra batteries should be packed. Including eye protection for the assistant and the patient is necessary.

♦ Gloves must be the correct size and type for each operator and assistant. Face masks are also operator specific and should be selected to fit each practitioner.

♦ Placing instruments on a tray—covered with half of a patient bib—greatly assists in restorative set-up access and transportability. *"I often have one tray for restorative materials, burs, etc. and one for instruments. When needed, I transfer the restorative items to the working instrument tray. For example, I just transfer the needed burs to the instrument tray to avoid contaminating the whole block."*

♦ Anesthetic syringes and mouth mirrors are used for each patient. An explorer and/or periodontal probe are often helpful. When focusing on the chief complaint and when not restoring all of the bad teeth, two carpules of local anesthesia per patient is sufficient. The efficacy of anesthesia purchased in the developing world may be questionable, so it is generally recommended that practitioners bring their own anesthesia. Some carpules of anesthesia without epinephrine is appropriate in selected patients. Many dentists use topical anesthesia that is placed with a cotton tip applicator. The anesthetic needles should match those that the dental personnel normally uses (short or long, 25-guage to 30-gauge). Some dentists bring an intraligamental syringe and extra-short 30-gauge needles. It is best if only the professionals place and remove needles, sharps, and anesthetic carpules. Used sharps are deposited in a plastic water bottle (sharps container) which is burned with the paper products. A needle recapping guard is useful.

♦ Both high-speed and latch burs are useful on a bur block for easy access. Burs, although sterilized, do wear out and extras are needed. Dental burs are dental-operator specific, as some like carbide burs and others prefer diamonds. There is great variation in sizes. It is important to include surgical burs, an acrylic bur, finishing burs, and polishing burs. *"We recommend dentists bring several bur blocks containing their favorite burs, plus extras of the burs they most frequently use. We carry a divided, plastic box that organizes extra basic burs."*

♦ LED cordless curing lights are the easiest and the lightest to use. A single operator wanting to do a significant amount of restorative should consider bringing two curing lights in case one malfunctions. Two dentists each can bring a light and share if one goes bad. The charger must be included.

⁑ Composite is the material of choice for anterior teeth and often works well in posterior teeth also. Composites and bonding agents vary greatly, are operator specific, and may expire quickly in hot climates. Since these materials are often unavailable in developing countries, it is advisable to bring them from home. The composite gun, etching syringes and tips, flowable composite syringes and tips, and sealant syringes and tips are all important. Packing and interproximal (plastic) instruments are used for composite placement.

⁑ An amalgamator and amalgam are useful for large posterior restorations as the preferred restoration. A silver filling will generally last longer and be less technique-sensitive in patients who may never see a dentist again. The amalgamator may need a larger converter if used in a country with 220-240 volts. Amalgam carriers and an amalgam well facilitate carrying the amalgam to the mouth. Excavators, chisels, packing, and carving instruments are needed.

⁑ Interproximal materials include an assortment of matrix band holders and matrix bands (pedo, regular, and wide) for placing interproximal amalgam, and clear matrix bands are needed for composite fillings. There are numerous systems to bring to ensure tight contacts and natural anatomy. Bring wedges, tissue forceps (tweezers), sandpaper polishing strips, and floss. A #12 blade on a Bard Parker handle facilitates smoothing the margins on interproximal composite restorations.

⁑ A rubber dam set-up includes a punch, forceps, frames, anterior, premolar and molar clamps, and rubber dam material which fit nicely in a fishing-tackle, plastic, divided container. *"When you can use a rubber dam to isolate the tooth and control the patient, it makes restorative more enjoyable, efficient, predictable, and safe."*

⁑ Scalers and curettes are needed to clean teeth and to help prepare margins for fillings.

⁑ Articulating forceps and marking tape are used to check the patients' bites.

⁑ Base or liner material is often recommended for deeper cavities. Light-cured glass-ionomer/resins are effective and easy to use.

* Glass-ionomer material is used for Atraumatic Restorative Treatments (ART) on primary teeth and in some caries-prone individuals. Use the powder and the liquid that will be mixed or the capsules if there is an amalgamator for alloys.

* Astringent and retraction cord help with hemostasis and the retraction of tissue.

* A hand-held mirror for each operator aids in educating patients and in explaining procedures.

* A TMS pin and post kit are used by some dentists.

* A stainless steel crown (SSC) kit with cementing material, crimpling pliers, and scissors are sometimes useful. It is generally best—when faced with overwhelming needs—to avoid pulpotomies and SSCs on primary teeth and to focus on the permanent teeth. Primary teeth are best left alone to hold space, if they are not hurting the patient, not causing a major infection, or not interfering with the eruption of the permanent teeth. Taking out primary teeth early invites crowding and may do more harm than good.

* Pulpotomy supplies are necessary if there is a plan to do them (for example, on a primary second molar before the eruption of the permanent first molar to help maintain space).

* Analgesics (for example Motrin 200 mg tablets and Tylenol 325-500 mg tablets) provide pain relief if doing extensive fillings.

* Antibiotics (for example Pen VK 500 mg tabs, Amoxicillin 500 mg tabs, and Clindamycin 250 mg tabs) are indicated for major infections, when the patients exhibits systemic signs, when the immune system is compromised, or for endocarditis and prosthetic replacement prophylaxis.

* Containers to hold all the instruments and supplies help in the organization, storage, and transport of instruments and supplies.

* Sterilization is a must! (See Infection Control in Chapter 10 and Sterilization Checklist in Appendix E.)

* Oral hygiene instructions given by a hygienist or a trained auxiliary person are important and are usually done before restorative or surgical procedures. Toothbrushes, toothpaste, and floss are useful to give out to all patients. (See Chapter 11.)

Hygiene Items

Hygienists' needs depend on whether they are teaching only or are also treating patients. Hygienists may be using hand instruments or ultrasonic scalers with a dental operating unit. Hygienists may diagnose, place sealants, give anesthesia, and even perform some tooth extractions. Hygienists are often the most sought-after dental practitioners since most patients desire cleanings. There are few or no hygienists in most developing countries. Gingivitis and periodontal disease are rampant; and, even in those whose mouths are relatively clean, there is calculus build up and interproximal inflammation. Floss is seldom available or used. Hygienists are the most qualified to teach oral hygiene and prevention, which includes a discussion of how sugars and acids affect oral health. Hygiene is often the most productive use of the team's time and resources, with the greatest potential for a lasting impact. A checklist is found in Appendix D of the following hygiene items.

　♦　Dental equipment includes a dental chair, an operator stool with a backrest, and a dental operating unit discussed under restorative. Also look under restorative necessities for information on anesthesia, loupes, eye protection, headlights, gloves, and masks as they are similar to those for the restorative dentist.

　♦　An ultrasonic scaler (sonic scalers are not powerful enough) saves the hygienist's hands and wrists, as most patients have never had a cleaning, and the calculus is abundant and tenacious. Bring three or four tips. A dental operating unit, with a handpiece, air/water syringe and suction capability greatly facilitates what the hygienist can accomplish. *We try to ensure our hygienist has a chair, dental operating unit, headlight, ultrasonic, and an assigned, dedicated assistant and interpreter. What they are able to accomplish is as valuable as anything the dentists are doing.*

　♦　Suction capability with suction tips should come with the dental operating unit. However, patients can spit into a cup when there is no suction capability, but this is more difficult, less hygienic, and time-consuming.

　♦　Assorted hand scalers and curettes are operator-specific. If treating two patients per hour, hygienists should bring three to four sets and a sharpening stone.

* A handpiece for polishing with a prophy angle and paste is a nice service, but it is not usually time efficient, considering that so many people need basic debridement and oral care instruction.

* A hand-held patient mirror is necessary for individual instruction. More mirrors are needed for giving group instruction. Compact make-up mirrors often can be purchased inexpensively and are easy to carry.

* Toothbrushes are valuable to hand out to each patient when teaching oral hygiene.

* Disclosing tablets or solution are used to teach brushing. Paper cups to rinse and multiple patient mirrors will be needed.

* Flossing instruction is also valuable, but floss may not be easily available. Many patients who are conscientious may be using (or may be taught to use) twigs, fishing line, toothpicks, or string/thread to clean interproximally.

* A large tooth model with a brush and possibly a chart with pictures, helps teach oral hygiene to groups. This instruction potentially pays the greatest dividends. A hygienist can teach brushing, basic nutrition, flossing, the cause-and-effect of acid on tooth decay, the importance of fluoride, bottle mouth caries prevention, and periodontal disease facts. A sample chart is described in Chapter 12.

* Sealants are wonderful to perform on selective patients. A dentist can provide a curing light or bring one if planning many sealant procedures. Etching gel and sealant syringes with tips are needed along with dry angles, cotton rolls and (2 x 2) gauze for isolation. For adequate sealants, an air/water syringe and suction will work well, although some hygienists have accomplished sealing teeth using only syringes to wash and to dry teeth. An air-abrasion or hydro-abrasion unit helps to clean and to prepare the tooth surface for sealants.

* The restorative section has a list of medical items which may be needed.

* Containers to hold all the instruments and supplies help in the organization, storage, and transport of instruments and supplies.

* Sterilization is a must! (See Infection Control in Chapter 10 and Sterilization Checklist in Appendix E.)

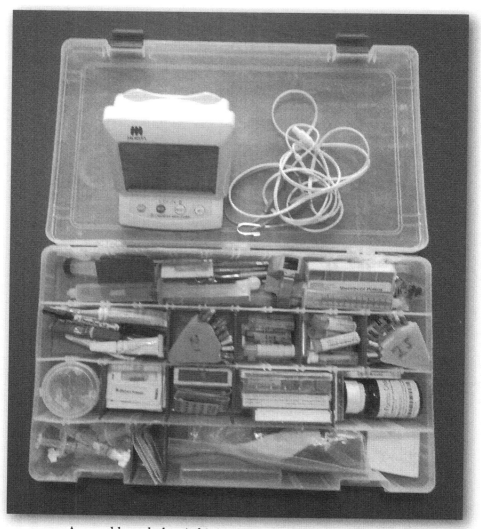

A portable endodontic kit is equipped with an apex locator.

ENDODONTICS AND PROSTHETICS

A root canal is occasionally desired to save a critical tooth. The team can carry a basic endodontic kit in one plastic, divided box, and an apex locator can reasonably determine working length. The dentist can perform a root canal using hand file sets (21mm and 25mm) and can irrigate with an endodontic syringe tip on a plastic syringe filled with diluted bleach. Also needed are assorted paper points to dry the canals, a root canal sealant paste, gutta-percha master and accessory points, an endodontic spreader for lateral condensation, and a match to heat off the gutta-percha ends using an endodontic plugger. Root canals—on easily restored, critical, anterior teeth—are a worthwhile capability to carry to the mission field. Restoring someone's smile, rather than removing a tooth, is especially rewarding.

A prosthetic kit allows the replacement of primarily anterior teeth, fits into a small tackle box, and includes the following items: an assorted set of three upper and three lower impression trays, alginate, stone, a mixing bowl and spatula, a small lab knife to trim the model and to remove the partial off the model, assorted denture teeth, some red rope wax to place the teeth in the model, separating medium, resin in a dispensing container, monomer with an eye drop carrier to "salt and pepper" the resin, monomer for the model, several acrylic and polishing burs, and a small rag wheel with a polishing abrasive. Bringing a small bottle of monomer in the kit does not alert customs. *"When I fabricate an interim partial, I recommend taking an impression, checking color, and pouring up the impression in stone before the patient leaves. The patient is instructed to return after the partial is completed. To minimize time away from patient treatment, the partial can be worked on between patients, during breaks, after lunch, or at the beginning or the end of the day. The patient and others often enjoy watching, providing a great opportunity for a Christian witness and to show care."*

Endodontic/prosthodontic procedures are usually reserved for notable individuals with specific needs, as these procedures take more time. However, they can pay great dividends for the credibility of the mission team and its outreach. *"I have made partials (which takes about an hour of my time) for church leaders who lost their teeth while tortured in prison for defending their faith, for pastors who would not smile, for a young female who could not attract a husband, for someone who built churches around the world, for a church choir director so she could sing more proficiently, and for a children's teacher who greatly feared the dentist and spread that fear to her students, and others."*

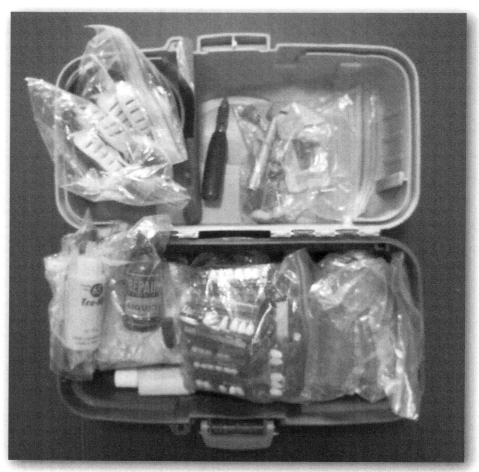

A portable prosthetic kit is stored in a fishing tackle box.

CHAPTER 8

Disposable Supplies

CALCULATING AMOUNTS

Disposable supplies and items needed can be calculated by counting the days of work, multiplying by the number of hours worked, multiplying by the number of dentists/hygienists, and then multiplying times two patients per hour. This calculation assumes a combination of restorative and surgery procedures. Adding 25% more of each of these items ensures adequate amounts. Calculating for five clinic days of eight hours of treatment, where two patients an hour are seen, totals sixteen patients each day and eighty patients in a week for one dental practitioner. Round that number up to 100 patients. If the treatments are primarily surgical procedures, increase the numbers to three or four patients per hour, as surgical treatments take less time than restorative or hygiene treatments. Match the size of the gloves to the professionals and the assistants. Patient bibs are cut in half—one half for the patient tray and one half for a bib. This table of disposable supplies for 100 patients is a reasonable representation of how to calculate quantities:

How to Calculate Disposable Supplies

Disposable Supplies for 100 Patients			
Supply Item	# Per Patient	Total #	Packaging
Anesthesia carpules	2 per patient	200 carpules	4 boxes of 50
Anesthesia needles	1 per patient	100 of size used	box of 100
Topical anesthesia & cotton tip applicators	1 bottle & 1 cotton tip applicator per/pt	1 bottle of topical and 100 applicators	1 bottle & package of 100
Gloves for dentist	2 pair per patient	400 of size and type for dentist	4 boxes of 100
Gloves for assistant	1.5 pair per/pt	300 of size for assistant	3 boxes of 100
Patient bibs	1.5 per patient	150	carry in bags
Gauze 2 x 2	12 per patient	1200	6 packs of 200
Cotton rolls	2 per patient	200	4 packs of 50
Disposable cups	1 per patient	1 per surgery pt	package of 100
Dentist & assistant masks	1 per 5 patients	20 for dentist & 20 for assistant	1 box of 50
Toothbrushes: adult and child as needed	1.2 per patient	120 as always need extra	child/adult
Trash bags	1 per 15 patients	7 plastic bags	7 grocery bags
Disinfection wipes	1 per patient	100	1 container
Pain medications: Motrin 200 mg or Tylenol 325 mg	15 per surgery patient	1000 tabs: assume 70 need medications	2 bottles of 500 pain meds
Sutures	1 per 20 patients	5 each	5 each

Supply tips include these hints:

* Acquire as much information as possible ahead of time. Common sense and simplicity are the key.

* Check in advance about supplies available in the international country. Sometimes it is better to bring everything, and sometimes items can be purchased in-country.

* Check expiration dates on all supplies, as customs may confiscate or impound medications which have expired.

* Purchase dental anesthetic in developed countries, as teams have had difficulty finding adequate anesthetic in developing areas.

* Take note of the supply situation after each trip (too much or too little), so that planning is improved for future trips.

Obtaining Items

Donated equipment that is often used and dated is given frequently by well-meaning dentists or supply houses for use in developing countries. *"People seem to donate their 'Junk for Jesus' without thinking that in the developing country it will not only be very expensive and difficult to get into country, but also almost impossible to maintain without replacement parts and someone who knows how to repair it."*

* *"I become angry when I see the trash given to missionaries. Why not give them the best and keep some of the older items at home?"*

Returning dentists who serve frequently on dental missions add to their capabilities by purchasing more items at intervals. They often start out borrowing curing lights, handpieces, amalgamators, instruments, and supplies from their home dental office or renting from another source, and then they gradually procure much of their own portable dental equipment and instruments. Dentists who return to the same place often find ways to equip an overseas clinic over the years.

CDS rents portable chairs, portable dental operating units, sterilizers, surgical kits, and restorative kits (www.christiandental.org.) These items may be used on dentists' or hygienists' early trips, and later they may obtain their own.

World Dental Relief (www.worlddentalrelief.com) provides a wide selection of supplies, instruments, and equipment at a greatly reduced cost. They also rent surgical and restorative kits and sterilizers.

Supplying organizations who equip medical/dental missions include Project Cure (www.projectcure.org), Hands of Hope (www.handsofhopenw.org), MAP International (www.mapinternational.org) and numerous others.

Permanent clinics may already be set up overseas by some organizations that provide much of the equipment, instruments, and supplies. Dentists can easily join an existing, permanent mission clinic for various lengths of time.

Dentists collaborate with other home-town or local dentists involved in charitable dental work. They can share equipment and instruments when taking larger teams.

Dental equipment and supply organizations that have helped set up clinics and supported missions in varied countries include Aseptico, Colgate, GC America, Henry Schein, Kerr, Patterson, Septodont, Ultradent, and others.

Mission sponsors include local churches, religious sponsorship organizations, national and community organizations, and local dental clinics.

Self-funding by participants is done frequently. Some team members feel led to give through volunteer work, and some team members send out support letters requesting funding (See Chapter 19.)

Tax-deductible expenses throughout the mission process should be kept in a folder or on a tally sheet.

CHAPTER 9

Clinic Set-Up

GENERAL CONSIDERATIONS

Prayer begins each day. "Do not be anxious about anything, but in everything, by prayer and petition, with thanksgiving, present your request to God. And the peace of God, which transcends all understanding, will guard your hearts and your minds in Christ Jesus" (Philippians 4:6-7). This sets the tone for the day. Prayer can be given at meals, during transportation to and from the clinic, and/or at the clinic site.

A clinic day in India starts with team prayer.

Treatment capabilities are communicated by the visiting team leader as clearly as possible to the national leaders so they can maximize the team's abilities for patient treatment and ministry as discussed in Chapter

15. Dental capabilities are emphasized so that accurate expectations may be established concerning what the team can accomplish. *"We hope and pray that we'll have the appropriate number of patients selected for us to treat. Disappointing or upsetting anyone reflects poorly on the ministry."*

Name badges or name stickers are helpful for everyone on both the visiting dental team and the national team. Names are often difficult to pronounce and unfamiliar cross-culturally. Name tags also identify clinic participants and give authority, inclusion, and ownership to the national volunteers. Some team members have their names embroidered on their scrubs. *"We put name cards in plastic name protectors that can be pinned on or that can be attached on a neck string. (See the Jamaican student team picture in Chapter 14.)*

   ❖   *"We found name identification to be so important that we bought a button-making machine for about $100. We use our organization's logo as a background and inscribe the team members' and missionaries' names on the logo. This can be done on a computer and the badges run off six at a time using the 2.5 inch size. We make many nameless buttons (which have the same underlying logo) and take a permanent marker so that the locals who come to help can also wear a button. Putting the buttons together is a simple and quick procedure once the tag is designed."*

Local/national staff is responsible for organizing the clinic area. They provide the clinic with a reasonable space to work, interpreters for each practitioner, a suitable generator and fuel when needed, several tables, and chairs for the staff and the patients. These basic, logistical items should be available upon the team's arrival. Toilet facilities and a water source for washing and sterilization on site are helpful.

Clinic set up is ideally accomplished prior to the first clinic morning. There are many details to ensure a fully functioning clinic, including adequate electrical power and properly functioning equipment. In a new setting, especially with inexperienced mission teams, everyone feels better when there is time to set up and to get organized. Once patient treatment begins, there is still a significant learning curve. The clinic will flow more efficiently from the beginning if questions and problems can be addressed earlier. Many times this is not possible when the team arrives at a location where patients are waiting. Preparation, organization, communication, patience, and flexibility all come into play, as every situation has different challenges.

Clinic arrangement can be visualized first in relation to the power source so that the dental operating units and the sterilization center can obtain electricity. (See Chapter 4.) Existing lighting and ventilation should be noted. (In hot climates, it is advisable to procure a fan.) Patient flow is analyzed to maximize the workspace and the convenience of movement. For each operatory, there must be adequate space, protection from the elements, and tables, benches, or chairs for the placement of supplies and instruments. Adding more operators and chairs brings complexity to the set-up. Since there may not be a large enough space in one area for all the operators, flexibility and adaptive ideas may call for the use of several nearby rooms. *"We have set up in houses of multiple rooms, shelters, in tents with uneven dirt or sand flooring, in numerous small school rooms with low ceilings, in medical exam rooms just large enough to hold a dental chair, in offices, in hallways, under trees, and more. It is ideal to have a larger church or building where the whole clinic fits into one room with a hard floor, good light, and air circulation."*

The sterilization station and the instrument table must be centrally located to minimize the distance between the dental operating areas. Under the guidance of the leaders, the team must quickly utilize the usually "less-than-ideal" situation. After they begin working, the caring team continues to make adjustments and to improve the operation as they learn what does/doesn't work well. *"In the military, we called this ongoing analysis of operations 'position improvement.'"*

Evangelistic sharing is important in the waiting area, as the dental clinic draws many people. The local ministry team, in conjunction with mission team members, should be encouraged to take advantage of talking with patients while they are waiting to be treated or afterwards. *"As we often say, physical healing and the power of touch rapidly develop a trust which allows the doors to be opened to spiritual healing."*

* *"At the clinic site we've used puppet shows, audio-visual presentations, or brief sermons and testimonials. In every situation, we had trained counselors ready to share their faith and to assist those ready to accept Christ as Lord of their lives."*

Treatment limitations sadden teams and it is difficult to turn people away without help given. However, teams must accept and rejoice that what they do accomplish makes a difference to "that one at that time." Especially for first-time volunteers, the difficult fact exists that not all who present themselves for help can be assisted—because of the complexity of the problem, the lack of resources, the time constraints, or the energy level of the volunteer team. It is folly to work at breakneck speed the first two days, only to hit the wall and to be ineffective from the third day onward. In a world so full of dental needs, the question is often asked about how we can truly make a difference. "We can do no great things, only small things with great love." (Mother Theresa)[43]

* "I am only one, but I am one. I cannot do everything, but I can do something. And I will not let what I cannot do interfere with what I can do." (Helen Keller)[44]

* "We often relate the starfish story, which talks about a child, who, after high tide, was throwing the starfish who had washed up on the shore back into the water. An older, cynical person asked the child why she was wasting her time and effort helping a few starfish, as there were so many dying ones. The child preceded to pick one up, and, throwing it back into the water proclaimed, 'It made a difference to that one.'" (Loren Eiseley, American author and educator)[45]

* "To the world you may be only one person. But to one person you may be the world because you have touched them with compassion… touched their heart with love, and relieved their pain." (Author Unknown)

* *"Lasting improvement in the health conditions of a populace is made through small increments of sustained effort, not by one supercharged flurry of activity. A relationship of mutual trust and understanding usually develops over a considerable span of time. Progress is often not noticeable until the volunteer takes the time to reflect on what has happened over the years. It is for this reason that return visits to the same location are helpful for sustainable improvement in the community."*

Crowd control within the clinic helps maintain harmony and peace. (See Gate Keepers later in this section.) *"We strongly dislike a line of patients who gather in gaggles. With that clamor of confusion, staff anxiety increases as they wonder if they'll ever catch up."*

* *"Focus on doing the greatest good for the greatest number of people. Every patient is important and a child of God. Try to keep the mood light, calm, and quiet, without hurry or deadlines. Encourage everyone to have patience and flexibility."*

Curious people are attracted to the clinic, and they draw close to watch or to attempt to get treatment. It is recommended that non-essential people stay out of the clinic, as additional noise and confusion stresses patients and practitioners alike. When the clinic is noisy, dentists cannot communicate with the patient and the interpreters. Patients often desire some privacy, which may be difficult. Patients should not have to face the crowds, especially if they are self-conscious, hurting, or bleeding. *"Many nationals have never seen a person with different colored skin, eyes, or hair, or all the strange equipment and instruments, so they try to get close. Do not be afraid to gently explain to people that their enthusiastic, loud conversations and laughter are disruptive to the dental clinic."*

* *"Some cultures do not accept that men and women are being treated in the same room at the same time."*

A controlled atmosphere that is relatively quiet is what most American dentists and hygienists are accustomed to. A group dental setting with many distractions may truly affect their ability to function comfortably. *"We generally assess the disruption tolerance level of the practitioners when taking a larger team and try to accommodate for individual preferences."*

Family-oriented cultures accept the presence of relatives into more situations than Westerners do, and many people have never seen a dental procedure before. This willingness to allow family members to participate in a significant event, and the acceptance of curiosity over something we may consider mundane should be considered by the treatment team even as safety considerations remain.

Proper security is essential through locks and/or guards overnight, as the dental equipment and the instruments are costly. If dental items cannot be adequately secured, the team may have to pack and take them "home" each day. *"At one point we could not even leave the dental equipment in the locked car for several hours when visiting, but took it into the home with us."*

Moving locations every day happens frequently, and the clinic must be set up and packed up each day. This takes energy and time to close up operations in one location and then work out the myriad of details of setting up a clinic in a different setting, thus decreasing patient treatment time. It is preferable to set up the clinic ahead of time, stay for a day or two, work out any challenges, maintain and service the equipment, and be fresh to start the day.

Dental Treatment

Team attitudes and demeanors matter more than what they may do or say.

Dental patients who will be treated are primarily determined by the host nationals who the dental team is supporting. It is not generally the short-term dental practitioners who control which patients will be seen. (The section on Gate Keepers covers this important point.)

Treatment priorities are decided by the dentist who must provide a combination of restorative and exodontia in a place that has little or no dental access or follow-up care.

* The focus is on each patient's chief complaint. "Jesus sent us to help you, how can we help you?" "Do you have any pain?" "What is your primary dental concern?"

* Limiting treatment to about thirty minutes per patient is usually best while generally treating the most pressing problem. If possible, patients can come back later for other concerns.

* Dentists focus on surgical and restorative procedures. Unless there is extra time, cleanings by the dentist are not encouraged, although

most patients need it. With hygiene support, the dentists help prioritize hygiene patients.

* When treating children, it is best to avoid pulling primary teeth—especially molars that are holding space. Most practitioners take out only the teeth that are infected, hurting, or interfering with the eruption of permanent teeth, since there is usually no follow-up care. Even if the tooth is decayed, but painless, it is holding space for the permanent tooth.

* With children, the restoration of permanent anterior teeth and fixing permanent molars is a priority. If possible, the use of amalgam will help large posterior fillings last longer and is less technique sensitive. Filling primary teeth is generally a second priority and is avoided when there are greater needs and limited time.

* On all patients, hurting teeth should be removed. Large fillings can compromise the nerve, as there is usually no follow up. Patients should be warned that the tooth will be extracted if the decay goes into the tooth's nerve. It is usually better to leave the tooth if it's not hurting, even if the decay is into the nerve. A root canal can be done on a critical, immediately restorable tooth—usually a front tooth—but this has to be the exception due to time constraints and the availability of an endodontic set-up.

* Permanent anterior teeth with cavities are a priority. Restoring a smile and saving anterior teeth is especially appreciated by patients. To satisfy the chief complaint, it is often necessary to ignore broken-down, posterior teeth, and to fix interproximal decay on the incisors.

* It is best not to attempt taking out third molars unless it represents a true emergency.

Two-patient treatment at a time, with one chair per dentist, works well. Many have tried to line up many patients and/or use multiple chairs, but the following method, using one dental chair, works quite efficiently. This procedure decreases potential confusion between patients, the dentist, the interpreter, and the assistant, as patient treatment flows smoothly:

1) The interpreter seats a patient, positioning the head to the top of the chair. The interpreter asks about the patient's chief dental concerns

and if s/he has pain. If there is a parent or a guardian for a child, it is often helpful to involve him/her in the exam.

2) The dentist will have a tray with a mirror, an explorer, and an anesthesia syringe to do a quick exam focused on the chief complaint. It is best not to use a patient bib yet.

3) If the patient does not need anesthesia or the area will become numb immediately, place the bib and do the work or consult with the patient right away. (For example, if the patient can be quickly anesthetized—like on the removal of a primary tooth or minor procedure, which just needs local infiltration—then the dentist can begin work immediately on that patient.)

4) If the patient needs work and anesthesia, explain the situation to the patient and numb the area. The dentist picks the needle and places it on the syringe to avoid any chance of needle sticks to untrained assistants. Topical is recommended prior to anesthesia. After anesthesia, the interpreter has the patient get up and wait for anesthesia to take. (That is why it is best not to have the bib around the patient's neck at this time.)

5) The interpreter explains that the patient will take a Motrin or Tylenol pre-op if doing an extraction. (The medication is usually given by the assistant.)

6) The interpreter seats the second patient and finds out his/her chief complaint.

7) While the patients are being exchanged, the dentist takes the treatment tray and gets the instruments needed for the first patient and sets the tray aside.

8) The dentist uses another tray with a mirror, an explorer, and a syringe to diagnose and to anesthetize the second patient. After the dentist gives anesthesia to the second patient (and the assistant gives a pain pill if it will be an extraction), the interpreter exchanges the first patient—who is now numb—into the dental chair.

9) Meanwhile, the dentist takes the second tray, acquires the instruments needed for the second patient, and sets it aside. The first tray is retrieved, which has the instruments ready to treat the first patient.

10) With the help of the interpreter, the assistant has placed a patient bib and protective eyewear (optional) on the first patient, provided the

patient with a stuffed animal to hold (which comforts many patients and gives the patients' hands something to do) and has made sure that the unit is ready with a proper suction tip. Treatment is provided, followed by post-operative instructions if necessary. The dentist removes the needle before the tray goes to sterilization. As the patient is dismissed, the assistant dispenses a few extra pain pills and gauze in a paper cup if needed.

11) After the first patient is treated, the interpreter exchanges the first patient with the second patient who is now numb.

12) The assistant cleans the unit, removes the burs, and wipes down or replaces contaminated handpieces, air/water syringes, and suction tips. (The handpieces and plastic suction tips can be safely sterilized in the pressure pot.) The second patient is seated, and the assistant places a bib and protective eyewear on him/her and offers a stuffed animal, if appropriate.

13) The dentist obtains the tray s/he had previously prepared for the second patient and can now treat the second patient.

14) After the second patient is treated and the unit is cleaned, the process begins again with the next two patients.

15) It is best (almost mandatory) to have the needle placed and removed by the dental professionals to avoid needle sticks and for everyone's safety. If a suture needle or surgical blade is used, the dentist also removes it and places it in the "sharps" container before taking the dirty instrument tray to sterilization. An empty water bottle with a cap can be used as the "sharps" container.

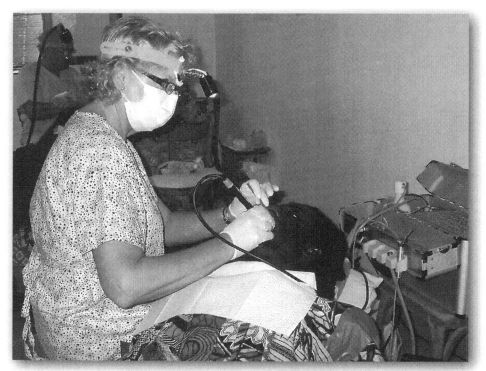

A hygienist is using an ultrasonic scaler in Uganda.

Hygienist guidelines vary. Teaching groups oral hygiene and nutrition yields the most lasting impact in many cases. Surgical needs may override cleanings, and the hygienist may help with diagnosis, administering anesthesia, and extractions.

    *   The dentists, hygienists, and national host must decide the scope of hygiene treatment and carefully select the patients, since the need will usually be overwhelming. Generally, gross debridement with an ultrasonic yields the most good for the greatest number of patients. With many needs, try to limit treatment time to about 30 minutes per patient. Select groups of youth may be treated with sealants, fluoride, and polishing.

    *   Hygienists need to have a dedicated interpreter, as they never stop instructing patients and must be able to communicate. The effectiveness of the hygienist is increased when provided an assistant to help suction, clean, and manage patients. *"I always value dental hygienists on the mission field, and they are so needed and appreciated."*

Dental assistants are invaluable volunteers in the portable dental clinic setting. Most dentists and hygienists require an assistant to help even if four-handed dentistry is not always possible. An assistant is kept busy with seating and dismissing patients, obtaining supplies for the dentist, suctioning, assisting, cleaning the unit, taking dirty items to sterilization, helping with sterilization, giving pre- and post-operative instructions and medications, teaching hygiene, and many other tasks that may be asked of an assistant. Assistants help in setting up and taking down the clinic and are valued team members. A trained assistant is a plus, but family or other team members can quickly learn the basics of assisting as most procedures are not complex on the mission field. Pre-trip meetings and some advanced training and communication between the dentists and their assistants is always helpful. (Tips are included under "Establishing harmony" in Chapter 15.) *"We always try to take a trained or a teachable person to assist each dentist or hygienist. Warm, calm, and flexible people who can adjust to the sights and the needs of the dental procedures are an asset."*

Interpreters assist and learn while watching and can fill in with the suctioning and other procedures as they become adept at understanding the procedures. Often medical personnel from the host country make competent assistants. (They often speak some English since medical courses often are taught in English.) They understand pain management and can be relied upon to give post-operative instructions when someone else is not designated to provide this service.

Gate Keepers

Gate Keepers have a critically important and challenging job, as they control who the dental team will treat and monitor patient access into the dental clinic. Dental personnel desire to serve and will generally treat whomever the sponsors want treated—within the team's time and energy constraints. Access to the dental practitioners should fall to host nationals who are discerning, reliable, and friendly while they enforce limits. Gate keepers must be aware of how much care the dental team can deliver in harmony with the host mission organization's goals. *"We consider ourselves* *a short-term tool to be used by the host ministry but are not certain about whom we should treat or the local politics concerning favoritism, bribes, family connections, promises made, and the many patients wanting care."*

Respected nationals are often effective gate keepers as they must gauge the social, political, and cultural norms of the area. If not knowledgeable of the dynamics of the community, the gate keeper may be influenced or coerced by nationals desiring preferential treatment beyond the parameters of the sponsoring organization and dental team. Unrealistic hopes and upset feelings can result in damage to the host ministry. Gate keepers are best able to resolve conflicts on who is to be treated, rather than the guest dental personnel who are there only briefly. If there are exceptions—an emergency or special circumstance—the host's permission should be obtained before treatment. *"In one case the prospective patient was an enemy of the host. After consulting and negotiating they resolved their problem and we provided care."*

❖   *"We nearly had a riot in one clinic, where people invited their friends to cut in front of people who had been waiting in line for many hours. Host nationals should ensure that waiting lines remain friendly places or use an alternative to waiting lines."*

Influential nationals or the national helpers may expect preferential treatment. Cooperate and use judgment with the needs of host nationals. Westerners might request special treatment in a similar situation.

Treatment limits fall around 15-20 patients per dentist/hygienist per day when providing restorative and surgery procedures (dentists) and cleanings (hygienists). When only doing surgery (taking out just problem teeth), more patients can be treated. There are always other people around who can be seen as time permits. *"We try to do a little dentistry on as many people as we can. We do not attempt to do all the dentistry needed on each person. A dentist could spend many hours working on just one patient!"*

❖   *"Normally we do one or two extractions—or one or two fillings—on each individual so that we can see more people. We try to do a little bit on everyone so that each patient feels that s/he has received an equitable amount of dental care."*

* *"There is always 'one more to treat' (to include the national people who are helping us). It is better to under-promise what the team can do, as there are often extra people who will need to be treated."*

Crowd control is managed with numbered cards, sign-up lists, the choice of select groups, and prescreening. The host must be responsible for controlling patient access to the benefit of the ministry and not allow it to detract from the good will and positive impact a dental team provides. *"Open-ended lines attract curiosity everywhere, and the promise of something new is compelling and draws crowds."*

* *"We like to allow only a few people to wait at a time."*
* *"Work diligently with the host to avoid a riotous situation where expectations are greater than what the dental team can deliver. If hurting patients travel for miles and wait for several days for dental care that is not delivered, it can result in an undesirable outcome."*

Follow-up treatment can be designated to the gate keeper or a national host. Often there are dental or medical questions or concerns that need to be addressed outside the dental clinic. Post-surgical, restorative, prosthetics, endodontics, orthodontic or medical issues may have surfaced and follow-up care, especially with children, needs to be coordinated. Someone who knows the local culture and the options for follow-up medical or dental care needs to be available to discuss issues and options (if there are any) with the patients, family members, or care givers. Post-surgical, written instructions and some pain medications can be left with a responsible person upon the team's departure. (See Appendix H.)

Effective Interpreters

Dental interpreters are vital to the success of the patient's dental experience and the efficiency of the operation. Each dental practitioner needs a dedicated, conscientious, congenial, and compassionate person to reassure each patient and to communicate each patient's needs and expectations to the dental team. One interpreter for each dentist and hygienist will be busy full time in seating and settling the patients, interpreting the dental diagnosis, communicating patient questions, assuring that the patient understands what the dental professional can and will do, alleviating patients' distrust and fears, and giving oral hygiene and post-operative instructions. Without good communication between the dental personnel and the patients, it is extremely difficult to work. A dedicated interpreter who returns each day to the same dental practitioner is especially helpful, as the learning curve is steep. Praying for good interpreters is significant. *"We also hope that the interpreters may be Christians who will be sensitive to opportunities to share the Gospel with the patients."*

Prioritizing communication is important, especially if team members do not speak the host language fluently. Dentistry requires the ability to interact with the patient, even if it means resorting to hand signals, primitive vocal sounds, diagrams, props, and facial expressions. That is at least a form of interchange. One of the greatest frustrations is simply not being able to converse. The dental professional often helps the interpreter handle the special dental language terms or the ideas that are repeated. (See Appendix F for examples.) The interpreter must interpret almost word for word, without putting his/her own knowledge or bent on the patient's or the dentist's words. *"One interpreter was telling everyone that they had worms in their teeth, which we corrected as soon as we found out!"*

Fearless interpreters are needed to observe slightly painful and bloody procedures without difficulty. Some interpreters prefer to wear gloves and a mask, as they want to protect themselves when they see the dental professionals wearing those items. It helps them feel that the dental team cares about their safety.

Paying wages daily to interpreters might be necessary to get excellent personnel. The wage and payment—using a setting-appropriate wage for the given country—is arranged for by the team host. Usually the cost is minimal, and it can be worth it to get reliable, consistent help. The wage may be a bonus and encouragement for the local national. However, it is preferable if interpreters are willing to volunteer and to show personal interest and enthusiasm.

Two interpreters per patient may be necessary at times. (Example: Spanish to a local or tribal dialect.) It is important to keep the language simple and direct. Avoid idioms or phrases which do not translate directly into other languages. (Example: "Give me the first shot at it.") Also, concepts which locals know nothing about are confusing. (Example: "Put the pedal to the metal.")

Time-consuming interpretation often occurs when each spoken phrase must be repeated. The delivery is a series of talking and pausing, while the interpreter is encouraged to relate exactly what the dental professional said.

Speak normally and distinctly. It is common to raise the volume of one's voice when trying to communicate in another language, but that is not necessary and might be offensive and unappreciated. Calm, normally toned voices also keep the clinic setting relatively quiet.

Excellent interpreters are those who remain engaged with the patients. The interpreters need to help reassure anxious patients, as many are fearful for good reason. Many patients have heard of or had horrifyingly, painful experiences. Many others have never seen a dentist and are uncertain and distrustful. It is best to soothe patients with a healing touch and calm, kind words; and the interpreters must communicate effectively the sincere desire to help. *"We request that the interpreters avoid cell phone or friend distractions and describe how important their job is to the success of the mission. Some interpreters will not hold the patient's hand (as it is not appropriate for cross-gender hand-holding in some cultures), or they will sit far back, showing they are not engaged in the process. An effective interpreter is a good communicator with nurturing skills and a genuine concern for the patient. It occasionally happens that an interpreter is not empathetic or caring, is easily distracted, and doesn't desire to be part of the dental team. Then, we explore other options."*

Flash Cards can be used (or taped to nearby walls to be pointed at) for frequently stated phrases: open wide, pain where?, remove tooth, numb tooth, swallow, bite, clean mouth, you are brave!

Phrase lists of common dental terminology may be sent ahead or given to the interpreters upon the team arrival so they can think about how these sentences could be interpreted in their language. (See Appendix F.)

International language phrases can be learned by team members, including these:
   * Hello, good-bye, thank you, you're welcome, pardon me
   * Titles (pastor, sir, madam, teacher, friend)
   * Beautiful, delicious, wonderful, great
   * Yes, no, please, beautiful, and delicious
   * My name is…what is your name?
   * Tell me your age (children only)
   * I am a Christian, I love Jesus, praise the Lord, may God bless you, shall we pray together?
   * What is the cost?

A cheat sheet of language phrases is helpful—perhaps an index card to be carried in a pocket. *"I take a small, pocket notebook and have people write their name or special words in it—so I can refer to those words or names I will use often. Then, I write the words phonetically after each word or name, so I can pronounce it correctly."*

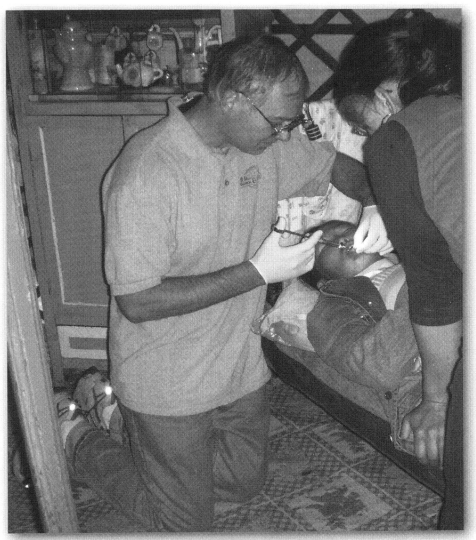

A valued interpreter helps with an extraction in a Mongolian ger.

Patients' Emotions

International patients—even children—are often very stoic in the dental chair. They are generally thankful for anesthesia and sit well for extractions and restorative treatment. Occasionally, patients are so terrified of dental treatment that they cannot be consoled and treatment must be deferred. *"One Dominican Republic pastor told us, 'I researched the topic of fear for my sermon. A poll of people's worst three fears put dentistry first, public speaking second, and death as third.' We couldn't believe that people would rather die than go to the dentist!"*

   *   *"We noticed that the children in Nicaragua feared us, which made sense when someone told us, 'Parents threaten their children with trips to the dentist for misbehavior here!' We were beyond shocked at the time, but have seen that in other places since."*

Treating children can be a challenge. It is best to start with the older ones who are hurting and very willing to get a painful tooth pulled. When they are treated without pain, the word quickly spreads that the dental team is acceptable. When a child is too apprehensive for dental treatment, let him/her watch with the help of a trusted caregiver to develop a rapport and to show the child what treatment is like. Parents and empathetic adults are often a great help for a child. *"If we start with a small, anxious child, who appears upset, we begin with a bad impression which is difficult to reverse."*

   *   *"We try to maintain a caring demeanor. When an occasional child refuses to be treated—sometimes when a parent is trying to force a child into the chair—the dental personnel refrains from getting upset or taking it personally. Move on to the next patient, as there are always so many needs."*

Dental shots are often the most traumatic part of the dental treatment. Difficulty communicating well in another language, cultural phobias, sensitization from past experience, and immaturity all contribute to a fear of the needle. The dental practitioners, the assistants, and the interpreters must exude confidence and calmness to anxious patients. Actions that help alleviate fear include: using topical anesthesia, distraction techniques like moving, rubbing, or tapping other parts of the body, and hiding the needle. *"Explaining to the patients that the shot is necessary so that the dental work can be done painlessly is important. Ideas they can understand help. (For example, "The shot is like a mosquito bite.")*

CHAPTER 10

Infection Control

Defining Sterilization

Sterilization is imperative. There is a significant difference between sterilization and disinfection; and it must be understood due to the prevalence of AIDS, hepatitis, herpes, tuberculosis, and infectious diseases from bacteria, viruses, protozoa, worms, and other maladies. It is an essential and a necessary practice to protect not only the dental team but also to prevent any transmission of disease from one patient to another. *"On numerous occasions we have seen or heard that dentists from developing countries do not adequately protect themselves or their patients from the transmission of disease. (Some dental teams from developed countries also do not sterilize appropriately.) Standards of care for treatment and for infection control are almost non-existent in many parts of the world."*

True sterilization is the total destruction of all living organisms—whether or not harmful—on a surface or an object. Appropriate sterilization includes the total destruction of all spores, which are the reproductive cells that are difficult to kill and that can cause multiple medical problems. Sterilization is accomplished by heat (340 degrees Fahrenheit for 60 minutes), by steam (24 psi for ten minutes), by chemical (ethylene oxide) autoclaves, by irradiation, by filtration, and by chemicals (glutaraldehyde—which takes 8-10 hours, or hydrogen peroxide—which takes 6-8 hours). All instruments inserted into the mouth should be sterilized.

High-level disinfection eliminates most harmful microorganisms (not including spores) from surfaces or objects. Disinfection is accomplished by using boiling water, glutaraldehyde (10-45 minutes, depending on the temperature of the solution), orthophthaldehyde (from 5-12 minutes, depending on the temperature of the solution), and hydrogen peroxide (30 minutes). The phenols, bleach, and alcohols are not considered high-level disinfectants and are primarily used to decontaminate surfaces and air. Disinfecting compounds can be highly toxic if spilled or inhaled, and transporting them can be dangerous. Sterilization is cheaper, easier, and faster if done with a pressure pot (field steam autoclave).

Adequate antisepsis is the application of liquid or cream antimicrobial chemicals to living tissue, either human or animal. The objective is to prevent sepsis—by either destroying potentially infectious organisms or by inhibiting their growth and multiplication. Some antiseptics are true *germicides*, capable of destroying microbes (bactericidal), while others are bacteriostatic and only prevent or inhibit their growth. Microbicides—which destroy virus particles—are called viricides or antivirals. Antisepsis is accomplished by using alcohols, iodine, quaternary ammonium compounds, chlorhexidine gluconate, hydrogen peroxide, or boric acid. A popular topical medication combines three antiseptics: neomycin (an aminoglyoside antibiotic), polymyxin B (an antibiotic primarily used for resistant gram-negative infections), and bacitracin (a mixture of related cyclic polypeptides).

Surface cleaning is simply wiping, dusting, washing, or otherwise removing the visibly obvious debris from a surface. This technique is a remarkably overlooked step in infection control. *"Patient chairs and headrests (plastic-covered, small pillows work well) are wiped after each patient. In addition to being a preventive measure, it shows respect for the next patient."*

UNIVERSAL PRECAUTIONS

"Universal precautions" using personal protective measures are employed to prevent the spread of disease. All blood and body fluids from patients—including blood, saliva, and infected tissue—should be considered infectious. Since most international patients come from remote areas with few infection-control measures, patients can be asymptomatic or unaware that they are carrying infectious disease, such as the human immunodeficiency virus (HIV), hepatitis B, hepatitis C, tuberculosis, influenza, and other infectious diseases. The best protection for volunteers is to use these proper, universal, standard precautions:

- Wash hands thoroughly or use antiseptic hand cleaners.
- Use gloves when in contact with bodily fluids.
- Wear masks, protective eyewear, uniforms or scrubs (and possibly gowns) when working in an environment where there is likely to be splatter of fluids.
- Handle sharp instruments cautiously.
- Use a rubber dam to minimize blood splattering.

Clinical accidents usually occur when an operator is in a hurry, is using an improper technique, or is tired. The field environment and the conditions might be completely different from those in a dentist's own office, making the possibility of such accidents even greater in a developing country. Dental health personnel need to take breaks from the clinic to avoid fatigue and to stay focused and detail-oriented.

Needle Protocol

At-risk practitioners can receive injury from dental needles, and other sharp instruments that can be infected by blood-borne pathogens (infectious microorganisms in human blood that can cause disease in humans). The pathogens to be concerned with include hepatitis B (HBV), hepatitis C (HCV), and human immunodeficiency virus (HIV).

Preventive measures to protect against injury may include, but are not limited to, these actions:

- Vaccination for hepatitis B must be required for all health-care workers who may possibly be exposed to blood, as it will protect them from hepatitis B exposure.
- Instruction must be given to all those handling contaminated items detailing injury avoidance, the potential infectious nature of blood-borne

pathogens, and the dangers involved in handling sharp instruments and needles.

* Education for all clinic workers concerning universal precautions and personal protective measures.

* Instruction on how to handle contaminated needles by use of a recapping guard or by sliding the needle into the cap. Needles must not be capped by holding the cap in a hand and placing the contaminated needle back into its protective cap. Only dental personnel place the needle, give the injection, and carefully recap the needle before disposal in a sharps container. Inexperienced personnel—who are not used to placing needles or to removing them from a dental syringe—should not handle sharps. *We have had no problems with needle-stick injuries since instituting the safety measure that only the dental practitioners touch needles.*

* Wearing heavy-duty rubber gloves to clean and to sterilize contaminated instruments helps to prevent sharps injuries and keeps infection control measures in place.

Infection risk for the recipient after a needle-stick or sharps injury must be minimized. The affected area should be rinsed and washed thoroughly with soap and clean water. An antibacterial cleanser is recommended. The practice of "milking out" more blood by squeezing the area is controversial and is not recommended by the Center for Disease Control (CDC). Antibiotic ointment and a clean bandage is placed over the wound. If the needle-stick or sharps injury is contaminated with blood or mucous, the blood-borne pathogens to be concerned about include hepatitis B, hepatitis C, and HIV.

* Hepatitis B Virus: According to current CDC guidelines, an exposure without the vaccination calls for the administration of hepatitis B immune globulin (HBIG) and the hepatitis B vaccine.

* Hepatitis C Virus (HCV): No vaccination or post-exposure prophylaxis (PEP) exists for hepatitis C. Recommendations intended to achieve early identification with direct viral testing and early treatment can occur at about six weeks post-exposure. HCV antibody sero-conversion occurs at four to six months, at which time HCV infection can be ruled

out. If symptoms develop, the volunteer must seek medical advice and testing from a medical treatment facility.

   * Human immunodeficiency virus (HIV): PEP guidelines from the CDC continue to be updated. If the infectious status of the source is unknown, his/her HIV status can be determined in about twenty minutes with a Food and Drug Administration-approved "Ora Quick home test." This test uses a simple saliva swab purchased from most drug stores or on the Internet for approximately $40. Unless it can be determined that the source is not HIV positive, the CDC recommends PEP be initiated within one hour of the injury. The current, four-week, preferred HIV drug PEP regime is documented in the updated U.S. Public Health Service Guidelines for the Management of Occupational Exposures to Human Immunodeficiency Virus and Recommendations for PEP, 2013. The protocol includes the combined use of two drugs. Truvad, used once daily, combines 300 mg of Tenovovir DF (Viread: TDF) and 200 mg of Emtricitabine (Emgtiriva; FTCD). The second drug, used twice daily, is 400 mg of Raltegravir (Isentress; RAL).

Side effects from these drugs (Truvad and Raltegravir) can be a limiting factor in PEP adherence. Side effects are generally self-limited but sometimes can last the duration of the 28-day PEP course and include the gastrointestinal side effects of nausea, vomiting, and diarrhea. Headache, fatigue, insomnia, and gastrointestinal upset are also possible. Antiemetic and antidiarrheal medications can be prescribed to help with PEP adherence. Changing to a different regimen can be considered if side effects become severe. Toxicities are rare with this currently preferred PEP treatment, are generally not life-threatening, and are reversible. Since renal toxicity from Tenofovir is the most troubling side effect of the preferred regimen, caution is advised in patients with impaired renal function. Wholesale costs for a 28-day PEP regime is currently about $2700 in the U.S.

HIV cases involving a dental professional exposure from an infected patient have not been documented to date. The chances of being infected from a minor needle-stick or sharps injury are extremely small. The HIV

PEP regimen may be difficult and costly to procure, may bring numerous side effects, and may not be necessary. Therefore, each mission team must assess the cost/benefit/risk tolerance to determine whether to procure a HIV test kit and PEP regime to take to the mission field. In the event of an exposure, those involved can also consider using anti-retroviral drugs in the country they are serving in for a modified PEP regimen. This method has been recommended as an alternative method by physicians working in developing countries.

STERILIZATION TECHNIQUES

Sterilize everything which comes into contact with a patient's mouth. Sterilization is defined as removing or destroying all forms of microbial life.

Chemical wipes disinfect inanimate objects (for example, hoses, trays, knobs, and protective eye glasses) which destroy most pathogens to a level that is not generally harmful to health.

Chemical antiseptics kill micro-organisms on skin or living tissue.

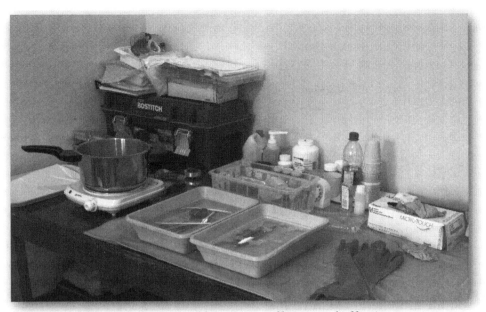

This sterilization table set-up is efficient and effective.

Sterilization recommendations in a short-term field setting can be done with a simple, yet effective, method (similar to a steam autoclave) using a 4-quart, stainless steel, Presto pressure pot, and a heating source. Heat and pressure efficiently kill all micro-organisms. The pressure pot comes with a pressure regulator which fits on the lid, and the steam vents at 16 pounds per square inch (psi). Twenty minutes at 16 psi ensures sterilization. By adding an additional weight to the pressure regulator (which can be purchased through the Christian Dental Society), the pressure is raised to 24 psi pressure, enabling sterilization to occur in 10 minutes. There is a "Pressure Pot Validation Letter" and directions for this method on the CDS website (www.christiandental.org) under "Resources." The validation letter is useful to take on trips, as pressure pots are not assumed to provide safe sterilization in some countries. Also, pressure pots have been used to make bombs, which can arouse custom officials' suspicions. If a pressure pot is confiscated, lost, or broken, the host national can usually procure a pressure cooker. *"The pressure pot can be bought in a hardware store for about $60. We use a 1000-1500 watt, small, single-burner, heating element which can be purchased in either 110 volts or 220 volts for around $50."*

* *"I am careful to pack the pressure pot without the lid attached to prevent concerns at official checkpoints."*

The pressure pot sterilization method is effective when these steps are followed. (Directions can also be found on the CDS website under "Resources.")

1) The dental professional removes the anesthetic needle, glass cartridge, and surgical blades at the dental chair to avoid needle-stick injury and places them in an empty, plastic, water bottle, which works well as a sharps container. When using a plastic water bottle, be aware that the plastic is thinner than an industrial sharps container and sharps can penetrate it. Dentists must handle carefully by the top or wrap it in cardboard secured with duct tape. From the dental chair, the dirty instruments are carried on a tray to the unclean side of the sterilization table.

2) Heavy-duty gloves are worn to decrease the chance of injury from the sharp instruments used in dental treatment. Blood and debris are removed using a tub of soapy water and brushes. The tubs are plastic food storage containers just large enough to hold and to clean the instruments. A drop of dish soap usually suffices for a small container.

3) The instruments are then rinsed in a tub of clean water before being placed in the pressure pot. Small items like dental burs and rubber dam clamps can be placed in a tea strainer for containment.

4) One cup of water is poured into the pressure pot (more or less depending on the efficiency of the heat source.) A little water should be left at the end of the cycle, as the seal on the lid can be damaged if the pot goes dry before the cycle is completed.

5) The lid is secured, making sure the handles click to seal. The pressure regulator is placed on the top and the pot is set on a heat source. *"We use an electric, single-element heat source, but a gas or propane stove works well, too. In a pinch, the pot can be placed over a fire or on whatever the nationals use to cook their food."*

6) Once the steam begins to vent around the pressure regulator, the timer is started for 10 minutes at 24 psi. (Twenty minutes is required at 16 psi.) Since there is often much noise in the clinic, a loud timer works best.

7)   After the 10-minute cycle, the pot is removed from the heat source, and the pressure regulator is taken off the pot, which allows the steam to vent quickly. The piercing sound can be muted with a pot holder, as it may be disturbing in a close dental clinic setting. The lid is opened after the steam dissipates.

8)   Using the slightly ajar lid to hold the instruments in the pressure pot, excess water is drained through the crack between the lid and the pot and often is poured directly into the clean water tub. Cooking mittens are used to avoid burns.

9)   The instruments are dumped onto a clean tray that may be covered by a bib or a paper towel to absorb any excess water. The hot instruments immediately dry and are cool enough to use in about five minutes. Immersion in water can rust the instruments. Some sterilization personnel prefer removing the hot instruments with tongs, but that method is slower. The instruments are removed while hot, so that moisture will evaporate to avoid rust and corrosion.

Sterilization items that are useful to bring are listed in Appendix E.

High-level disinfection (HLD) may be an option when sterilization is not possible with the pressure pot, although it is not recommended. Chemicals in HLD will harm the handpieces and will corrode instruments. These HLD items may be difficult to procure, may be more expensive, and may be more difficult to transport into the developing country. HLD takes more time than using the pressure pot sterilization method. The pressure pot sterilization does not harm handpieces. Consider these options if unable to sterilize:

   ◆   Boiling water: Instruments are fully submerged in a gentle, rolling boil for 20 minutes. White lime deposits are minimized by adding three tablespoons of vinegar to the water followed by boiling for 10 minutes to precipitate the lime. Then the instruments are added.

   ◆   Glutaraldehyde: Many HLD items contain glutaraldehyde, considered a sterilant with 10 hours of immersion. CidexPlus (J&J) is sold in a gallon jug and needs to be activated. Cetylcide-glutaraldehyde in concentrate form is not allowed on airplanes per security regulations.

CidexPlus is allowed but will be removed if there are animals (pets) in the luggage area due to its toxicity. CidexPlus, once activated, is good for 28 days, but it is very caustic. CidexPlus exposure on hands or in eyes is avoided by wearing gloves and eye protection. Good ventilation is important. It is not to be used as a surface disinfectant and is disposed of in a conventional sewer or pit toilet. Suggested technique for use includes a scrub tub using a mild detergent, then a rinse of the instruments in a second tub. Fully immerse the instruments in the glutaraldehyde solution for 20 minutes. Several tubs may be needed. The instruments must then be rinsed three separate times in fresh, purified, plain water with each rinse lasting one minute. Due to its caustic nature and staining potential, the manufacturer stresses the importance of thoroughly rinsing off the glutaraldehyde. Gallons of pure water are necessary to disinfect correctly.

* Orthophthaldehyde (OPA): An approved, aromatic aldehyde similar to glutaraldehyde, Cidex OPA is packaged in gallon containers. Once opened, it is effective for 14 days. Typical 0.55% solutions have excellent stability, are less toxic and irritating to eyes and nasal passages than glutaraldehyde, and have a barely perceptible odor. OPA solutions are faster-acting than glutaraldehyde, requiring only a 12-minute soak. Since OPA is caustic to the eyes and skin, all precautions and suggested techniques used for glutaraldehyde should also be followed for OPA. A potential disadvantage of OPA is that it stains proteins gray (including unprotected skin and almost everything else). It must be handled with caution.

* Hydrogen Peroxide 7.5%: This is packaged in a gallon container called Sporox and, after opening, is effective for 21 days. No mixing is required. Peroxide will provide a high-level of disinfection in 30 minutes and sterilizes in six hours. Since it is not irritating or stain-producing, Peroxide seems to be a reasonable HLD agent, although instruments will corrode.

* Birex: Some dentists bring the small, 1/8-ounce packet of Birex concentrate as a backup phenol-based disinfectant in the event all else fails. Note Birex is Federal Drug Administration (FDA)-approved only as

a surface disinfectant and is used as a last resort. Manufacturers state that it does kill HIV virus in one minute and tuberculous in ten minutes.

⁕ Bleach: Household bleach (5.25% NaOCl) can be diluted 1:10 for a 10-minute HLD but is not recommended, as it is very caustic and severely corrosive to dental instruments.

INFECTED DISPOSALS

Burning waste that is medically contaminated is important. In developing countries, there is always a place to burn garbage, and it is important to destroy all the infected items to avoid the spread of disease. Bags of gloves, patient bibs, and gauze come from the dental chairside where plastic, stackable, small garbage buckets have been placed. These buckets come from "dollar stores" at home. *"We used to ask for garbage containers on site, but we rarely could find enough for the clinic. We often felt we were using their treasured and functional items and didn't want to hurt their belongings in any way. We bring plastic bags to line the garbage buckets. These plastic bags have been easily collected from grocery stores at home and are used as packing materials on the way to the mission. Extra stackable garbage cans can be used to carry water to the sterilization table from outside faucets. It was difficult to find buckets in the neighborhoods also."*

Sharps containers (which might be plastic water bottles) can be carefully placed on top of the plastic, garbage-filled bags of medical waste where the heat from the flaming plastic burns very hot. The fire melts the needles and pulverizes the glass, so there is no chance for contamination or secondary use of needles by national people.

Contaminated medical waste is usually burned.

Suction containers of liquid spit and blood and the instrument-cleaning, container water are dumped into the toilets in outhouse or lavatory facilities. These liquids should not be dumped into the bushes as they may attract animals. Fluid contaminates can be buried if there is no place to dump them or if the lavatory facilities flow into commonly used water sources. *"We have given our important containers to national people to dump (who we thought understood our English instructions). We have had tragedies where they did not understand and where we lost valuable items (several containers were thrown into a deep outhouse, and one suction bottle—essential and custom-made for our dental operating unit—went into a fire). It is best to have only trusted volunteers handle the dumping of infectious liquids."*

CHAPTER 11

Paperwork Considerations

RECORD KEEPING

Simple documentation of dental care may be important as some organizations or individuals feel that follow-up care may be necessary. It is reasonable and understandable that some people need paperwork for validation and justification for support. Patient histories in developing countries may be verbal or written and may be necessary. However, this documentation takes time and resources and may not be more valid than the dentist's overall clinical evaluation and impression concerning patients' health and their ability to withstand dental treatment. Charting and record keeping is situational and organizationally dependent, based upon agreements between the team leader and the sponsors. *"In most situations we do not keep paperwork or medical histories on the patients, as we have a one-time, limited contact with them and are focused on taking care of their chief complaint."*

* *"We like to make out cards on each patient. We do brief examinations to determine the severity of their dental need, and write short descriptions on their cards. The card, which contains their name, address, age, basic medical information, and chief complaint, can be extremely helpful in giving the best care possible while making our clinic efficient."*

* *"We don't like to track comparisons amongst the team concerning numbers of patients treated. On one trip a dentist often announced how many patients he had seen and urged others to compete. If one dentist is bent on productivity as the main consideration, this attitude becomes uncomfortable for other practitioners. This didn't mesh with our philosophy of providing the best care for the most people possible without stress or pressure for everyone involved."*

Health Histories

Health histories often are not documented in austere settings in the developing world. Obtaining accurate information is time consuming and difficult to acquire. Everyone is treated as a potential source of infectious disease, and universal precautions and infection control prevent the spread of contamination between practitioners and patients. If patients appear healthy, they generally can withstand basic surgical and restorative procedures. If health problems such as hypertension, uncontrolled diabetes, pregnancy, heart problems, allergies, or obesity— which dental treatment may impact—are suspected, the dentist should question the patients or those who know the patients and obtain medical consultations or refer them to a local medical facility when uncertain that they should undergo dental treatment.

Monitoring hypertension is important and a blood pressure cuff and stethoscope are helpful in monitoring some patients that the dentist may suspect are hypertensive. *"I have deferred treatment and referred patients to a physician if the blood pressure is too high."*

Medical histories are obtained when time and resources permit. A basic medical history can generally be understood by patients and relatively easily translated into the patients' language. An example is shown in Appendix G.

Medication Information

Necessary medications generally include Ibuprofen and Tylenol for patient pain relief. For more severe infections, Penicillin (or Amoxicillin) and Clindamycin can be taken, but they are rarely needed, since local infections resolve quickly with tooth removal. Antibiotics should be used when patients require prophylactic premedication, exhibit systemic signs, have significant swelling, appear to have a spreading infection, are immune-compromised, or if it seems that antibiotics would be advantageous. *"Narcotics are generally not needed, and I don't take them as it might cause difficulties at customs."*

Emergency drugs are recommended and the following two are highly suggested: 1) an Epinephrine-pen (or epinephrine and a syringe with a needle) for both a child and an adult for anaphylaxis reactions, and 2) a medi-haler for asthmatic conditions. A practitioner may want to pack anti-histamines and other emergency drugs depending upon individual comfort levels and particular situations. The emergency drugs are easy to access with the repair and maintenance kit in a clear, plastic, divided, fishing tackle box. *"It is rare that you would ever have to use these drugs and fortunately we never have—praise God."*

EXTRACTION INSTRUCTIONS

The interpreter or someone with an understanding of the procedure and post-surgical care gives extraction instructions. The patient needs to understand what to do and what to expect. Appendix H shows an example of tooth extraction instructions. These instructions can be sent ahead, if possible, and the national host can often translate the information into the local language and reproduce it for distribution.

When possible designate a local, medically savvy person to give each surgical patient detailed instructions and to distribute pain medications. This technique saves time at the chair, allows the patient time to fully comprehend the instructions, and gives the patient someone to turn to for questions or complications when the team leaves. It is helpful, especially when working with children, to leave extra pain pills and post-surgical instructions with a responsible local person. *"Patients often do not understand our post-surgical instructions, and we find it helpful to leave written instructions (which are often in English but are better when translated) with someone responsible who can read and explain the English instructions."*

CHAPTER 12

Preventive Education

GENERAL INSTRUCTIONS

Hygiene instruction is a priority and requires a competent interpreter and engaged listeners. Large models of teeth and a toothbrush are helpful and stuffed animal props or other entertaining items can create interest. Local dental preventative behaviors can be explored and reinforced. *"In the Philippines they showed us how to floss using strands of palm leaves."*

* *"In Senegal we saw people brushing their teeth with little twigs that, when the bark was pulled off, made bristly little brushes of inner cellulose. These performed well as soft and sanitary toothbrushes, keeping mouth hygiene fresh and fun. We all joined in to support the excellent, although unconventional (to us), regional tooth-brushing technique."*

The team joins with nationals using twigs to brush teeth in Senegal.

Educate patients about why the team has come, what to expect in the dental chair, and the basics of oral hygiene. This invaluable step is as important as the dental care provided in many instances.

Flip charts for education can be created when language and understanding are a barrier. One chart example utilizes large pictures to help convey a greeting, an introduction to the dental clinic treatment expectations, and oral hygiene education. The simple text in English is interspersed with pictures on the 21-inch by 13-inch horizontal flip chart. Large rings at the top help the pages flip easily. The interpreter can listen to the team member, as well as read the words on the page. An example of the wording is shown below, and suggestions for pictures are in parentheses. The chart is illustrated with diverse people from different cultures, so it can be presented anywhere. The colored dental pictures (cut from dental and hygiene magazines) were glued around the text, and then the pages were laminated.

A flip chart is used to introduce dentistry and to
teach oral hygiene in Mozambique.

Page 1: Jesus Loves You. . . We Love You (There is a large picture of a darker-skinned Jesus helping children at the 'Feeding of the 5,000' miracle.)

Page 2: We came with dental workers and families to help you. Our job at home is to help people get a healthy mouth, so they won't have dental pain. Can you think about what may hurt in your mouth? (Pictures include multi-racial, multi-age people smiling and in dental scenes with a dentist, a hygienist, a patient, and an assistant.)

Page 3: The dental practitioners would like to hear how we might help you. You will lie in a chair and the dental workers will look in your mouth with a little mirror and a tool that just touches your tooth without hurting. The dental professionals wear special glasses and a light to see well. They and their helpers may also wear gloves and a mask over the mouth for protection against germs. (There are pictures of a mouth open with a mirror inserted, a hand holding an instrument, dentists with loupes and masks, and a gloved hand.)

Page 4: If you have a bad tooth, the dentist may take it out to stop the pain. You may take some pills so it won't hurt much afterwards. If the tooth can be fixed, the dentist may take out the bad part (with a little machine) and put good tooth materials in. So it doesn't hurt to work on your tooth, the dental workers may use something like this needle to give you medicine that makes your tooth go to sleep. You might feel a little pinch. (There are pictures of smiling teeth, a patient smiling, and a gloved hand holding an injection that is purple and attractive-looking.)

Page 5: A paper towel protects your clothes. Sunglasses can protect your eyes. The helpers use the light to see your teeth better. You can hold a toy animal or someone's hand so that your hands are out of the way of the dentist. (There are pictures of a dental light, a boy with a bib on, patients with sunglasses on, and another dental operatory scene with a smiling dentist and an assistant.)

Page 6: The person helping the dentist or hygienist holds two little machines. One sprays a small stream of water to rinse your teeth, with air to dry the teeth. One has a straw that pulls water from your mouth so the dental workers can see well. You do not have to spit. The dentist will not take long to fix your teeth. We sterilize so germs are not passed from one person to another. (Pictures are of the operating unit, the suction tips, the handpieces, and an assistant holding a tray of instruments.)

Page 7: Acid makes cavities (holes) in your teeth. Acid comes from foods you eat which are acidic, like sodas and fruit juice. Bacteria from a dirty mouth produce acids when you eat sugary foods. Every time you eat sugar and acids, your teeth decay for about 15 minutes. It takes this long for saliva to rinse the acids and sugar away. (A separate list occurs on the same page.) Drink water between meals. Do not drink or eat sugary and acidic foods between meals. Clean your teeth to keep bacteria count low, so less acid is produced. (Pictures show illustrations of how the teeth break down in cavity formation. If there is time, go into more detail on brushing and flossing instruction.)

Page 8: It is also important to brush your teeth. Try to brush two times each day, in the morning and before bed. Brush slowly and in little circles. Be careful to brush each tooth in the front, sides and back. Floss can help between teeth. (Pictures are shown of people brushing, toothbrushes, and floss.)

Page 9: Eat healthy foods: (pictures of chicken, eggs, fruit, dairy products, and vegetables) Have less of these foods: (pictures of sodas, pastries, cookies, gum, and candy) Help your teeth stay strong. (Pictures include healthy foods on the top and less healthy foods on the bottom. A food pyramid is shown in the middle.)

Page 10: We thank you for allowing us to share God's love with you. We travel to new places and enjoy making friendships around the world. We are using our talents to help others and we encourage you to use your skills to reach out to people around you. We will pray for you. (Pictures include a globe with children from many nations encircling the globe.)

Disclosing solution or tablets stain dirty areas of the teeth that aren't cleaned well. These products can be a useful adjunct to teaching proper tooth brushing and is something team members can be taught to do. The solution or tablets can be applied prior to brushing and flossing instruction. Patients can be reminded that healthy, clean gums do not hurt or bleed. Detailed information about brushing and flossing can be found at www. brushforlife.com/HiddenHygieneMobileMission/ .

Tooth Brushing

Brushing instructions may follow the acrostic S.M.I.L.E., developed by Lynelle DeRoo, dental hygienist.[46] Using a soft toothbrush and non-abrasive, fluoride toothpaste, brushing sessions are recommended twice a day for about two minutes each session.

* **S**tart brushing where the calculus (tartar) is/has been the heaviest—usually on the inside of the lower front teeth. An organized pattern ensures that all of the teeth are contacted while none are over brushed.

* **M**ovement continues after brushing the lower front teeth. Manually vibrate or wiggle the bristles of the brush back and forth, concentrating on two teeth for about five seconds at a time as movement is made around the arch. Next, brush the inside of the lower left, followed by the lower right. Brush the outside of the lower teeth from right to left. Move to the upper teeth, brushing inside the upper left and going around to the right. Brush the outside of the upper teeth last, moving in a right-to-left direction.

* **I**ncline the bristles of the toothbrush at a 45° angle towards the roots. Place the brush so that the bristles also contact and clean the gums next to the tooth.

* **L**evel the toothbrush handle even (parallel) to the row of teeth at all times, no matter where the brush is. Maintain the 45° angle by directing the bristles against the teeth and gums to maximize effectiveness of the toothbrushing, the gum line cleansing, and brushing between the teeth.

* **E**xercise caution against vigorous brushing, especially with a hard bristle brush which can cause wear on the teeth. This aggressive form of brushing also irritates the soft tissue and can cause the gums to recede. Pressing too hard quickly wears out the brush and spreads out the toothbrush bristles so only the long side of the bristle contacts the teeth. The bristle tips are the working part of the brush and need to contact the teeth and the gums to clean well. Gentle brushing will clean adequately.

Flossing Techniques

Flossing instruction involves more than just the removal of food between the teeth to prevent cavities. Flossing also prevents gum disease (gingivitis) and bone loss around the tooth (periodontitis), the most common cause of tooth loss in adults. Flossing cleans the side of the tooth under the gums where the toothbrush bristles do not reach. The technique of flossing is more important than the type of floss and requires practice in front of the mirror initially.

Flossing frequency depends on the condition of the gums. Two or three flossing sessions a week should be adequate if the gums aren't sore or don't bleed. Flossing daily is recommended if the gums are sore or bleeding.

Flossing technique with the acrostic "GPS" aids in teaching flossing.

* **"G**ood control" begins with holding the floss correctly. At least 10-12 inches of floss is used each time. The floss is wound several times around the finger (index or middle) of each hand so it does not unwind. The floss is positioned over the thumbs and fingers so it can be placed into the mouth. Minimize the gap between the fingers and thumb so they stay up against the teeth as the floss is passed between two teeth.

* **"P**roper direction" reminds the patient to properly wipe the sides of the teeth, cleaning all the way to the bottom (depths) of the gum pocket. The floss is pressed against one tooth following the contours of the tooth, and the ends of the floss are pulled towards the center of the tooth. The floss is carefully moved up and down several times (not back and forth) all the way to the bottom of the pocket where the gums attach to the tooth. The floss is now moved over (not damaging) the bump of tissue (papilla) between the teeth. The ends of the floss are now curved in the opposite direction to be moved up and down to clean the adjacent tooth always being careful not to injure the tissue between the teeth.

* **"S**imultaneous up-and-down movement" of the fingers and thumbs holding the floss both on the inside and outside of the tooth allows the floss to hug the tooth and to clean all surfaces between the teeth.

CHAPTER 13

Successful Teamwork

LEADERSHIP HINTS

God controls the mission and recognizing that it is HIS team takes some of the stress off the team leader. However, someone still needs to guide and to direct the team. The team leader, in conjunction with the host organization and the local leadership, must coordinate the trip dates and must schedule to meet the needs of the mission and the individual team members.

A team leader exists so that the group can function well and can maintain a unity of purpose and harmony within the group. Managerial responsibilities and duties are often shared, but it is advisable that one identified person coordinates and communicates the myriad of details involved. Group dynamics must be worked out and the team needs to bond together. *"Dentists and hygienists are independent operators and often desire autonomy. Working efficiently as a team on a mission trip requires each individual to adjust, to communicate needs and expectations, and to be especially tolerant of change. The leader tries to be a servant to all and must attempt to balance the individuals' needs with the purposes and goals of the mission trip, so that God's kingdom receives the praise."*

The leader communicates the responsibilities and the duties of all team members and supports the local national leadership. This dynamic process occurs throughout the trip. The team supervisor oversees administrative details, finances, time lines, transportation, food, lodging, patient treatment, dental logistics, spiritual expectations, cross-cultural basics, and many of the concerns outlined in this manual. This leader does not do all tasks, but s/he must see that it all comes together. *"Even people who are expected to be in complete charge of their composure—like leaders, dentists, or* *host national overseers—can be having a tough day. Team members need to be as supportive as possible."*

A successful leader establishes the team vision and directs by example. S/he takes care of the team and places the need of others above his/her own. The person in charge ensures that organization, priority setting, communication, and proactivity minimize unpleasant surprises. A shepherd leader challenges and stimulates others to grow while encouraging, supporting, and setting boundaries. S/he promotes fun throughout and uses humor to lubricate the gears of human adjustment.

MENTORSHIP EMPHASIS

Mentoring provides another ongoing process and a valuable aspect of a mission team. A professional relationship or friendship is developed by an experienced person (a mentor) who assists another less-experienced individual in developing specific skills, knowledge, character, and values enhancing professional and personal growth in a safe learning environment. A dynamic team is constantly teaching, learning, growing, and building relationships as the individuals fulfill God's plan for maturity and service. *"No one goes his way alone, for all that we put into the lives of others comes back into our own."*

♦ *"One of God's primary means for bringing His children to maturity occurs as we sharpen each other. 'As iron sharpens iron...'" (Proverbs 27:17).*

♦ *"The personal touch is so lacking in our techno-centric age."*

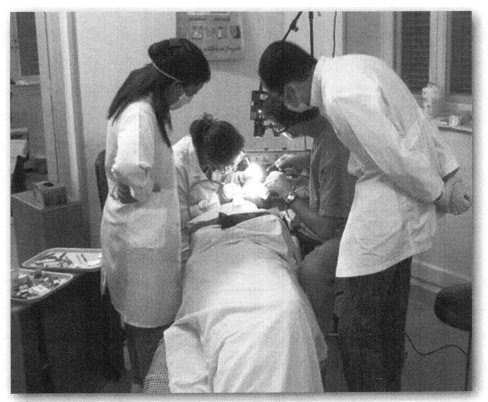
An American teaches Egyptian dentists in a portable clinic.

Formal mentoring can be more directive with group meetings, training sessions, and/or literature and handouts to convey valuable information. Informal mentoring is often one-on-one where personal relationships are built and reinforced. "For it is in giving that we receive." (St Francis of Assisi)[47] *"Some of the best teaching times are on the way to or from the clinic. Even casual conversation at God's appointed time can be a form of guidance."*

* *"Processing experiences with a friendly, knowledgeable ear allows students to learn from mistakes and provides an avenue for feedback on both sides."*

* *"Mentoring becomes a lifestyle choice. It is good to have talents and gifts and to have skills and insights, but it is better to use them and to pass them on to others."*

Dental education goes beyond the old adage of "see one, do one, teach one." Mentoring seeks to build skills and people. The process reenergizes the instructor, often providing insights and giving satisfaction in sharing expertise and beliefs. Students acquire knowledge and experience in specific skills and ideals. Learning how to focus, how to have proper perspective, and how to obtain balance are often learned by observing more mature professionals. *"The highest form of a compliment is to copy someone. The mentor truly shines when passing on assimilated wisdom to one who learns and changes."*

* *"As in all relationships, remember to say, 'I am proud of you' and 'I appreciate you.'"*

TEAM MEETINGS

Group meetings and clear communications are highly desirable before the team leaves for the mission. Meetings are not only important to discuss mission trip details, but also to build the team, to define roles, to align expectations within the group, to teach cross-cultural tips, and to pray. It is vital that volunteers are advised on how to be responsible and respectful team members and guests of the international country. It is extremely important to show sensitivity to host cultures concerning language, traditions, superstitions, and beliefs about health, as well as religious faith and practice. (See Chapter 18.) Most importantly, as team members pray together, they are encouraged to hear the heart and the concerns of fellow team members. They can pray more specifically for their needs and find that cohesion comes from sharing faith in Christ.

Cohesive teams need group interaction. People often feel led, "called," or have a desire to step out of their comfort zones and to commit to an overseas mission, resulting in a sense of significance. Volunteers come from all walks of life and in different stages of maturity—both physically and spiritually. Many personality differences may exist. *"The quality of our unity as a team and our assimilation of new members—especially nationals— may be our greatest witness."*

* *"We stress that the team merely turn the "m" to a "w"—make it not a "me" trip, but a "we" trip.*

* "*Several times when our dental team was with a construction team, we took a half day to go out and help them build or dig— to bring team cohesion and support and to take a break from doing dentistry.*"

Group dynamics must establish a mechanism through which suggestions, concerns, and thoughts can be tactfully brought forward and feedback given. Learning to know and to respect each other helps tremendously.

"***Three freebies***" *(verbally awarded) are given to each team member on our trips to be used for mistakes, omissions, or misguided actions. These "freebies" are extensions of grace and a gentle reminder that the team is forgiving and will tolerate individual problems or mistakes (for example: lateness, loss of an item, a wrong communication). We use humor and light teasing when we award a "freebie," knowing it is easy for all of us to make mistakes when we are out of our normal routines and practices. We don't expect anyone to be perfect.*"

TEAM DYNAMICS

Team Types (Hint: The work and witness model is the goal!)
* The Workaholic Team: The members work long, hard days with little or no leisure time. There are so many people to treat that it becomes all-consuming, and they avoid developing relationships with the nationals. They sometimes suggest non-patient nationals not even come to the clinic site.
* The Safari Team: Volunteers have taken vacation time to make this trip, and they are going to have a vacation. This team is mostly leisure, with little work accomplished.
* The Work and Witness Team: People labor hard on clinic days, but they stop to rest and to visit with nationals who are welcome in the clinic and often work alongside the team. They take a day or two of leisure to see the sights and to shop. Treating as many patients as possible is important to them, but they will keep a reasonable schedule. They have established good relationships, reasonable expectations, and a healthy balance of work and leisure with their host national team.

A team model for group dynamics was developed by Bruce Tuckman (Ph.D. in psychology). Tuckman teaches the stages of "forming-storming-norming-performing."[48] With diversity among individuals and the preconceived ideas and expectations each person carries, it is important to communicate as the team passes through these stages/phases. Short-term mission work is dynamic. Maintaining group cohesion is every bit as hard as the dentistry and is just as important. Discussing these steps seeks to ensure maximum harmony and efficiency of purpose as rapidly as possible.

1) The "forming" stage is driven by a desire to be accepted and to avoid controversy and serious issues. People are on their best behavior and gather information and impressions. They learn about the opportunities of the mission and the challenges involved. They agree on goals and they begin to tackle tasks. It is a comfortable stage where the leaders can be quite directive concerning the trip details and the motivation and missions' purposes.

2) The "storming" stage is inevitable; and, although conflict may be more or less suppressed, it will be present and is necessary for growth. People deal with issues and differences and often establish a pecking order. Leaders may stress tolerance, patience, open communications, and conflict resolution, as this stage can be destructive. The goal is to help everyone feel safe in sharing input without negative judgment from others.

3) In the "norming" stage, the "rules of engagement" and responsibilities for the group become established, and team members often change preconceived views. The team agrees on goals and has a mutual plan. Some volunteers do have to compromise their expectations and wishes.

4) The fourth stage is "performing," characterized by a state of interdependence and flexibility. The team knows each other well enough to work together, and everyone is trusted in their independent activities. The high degree of comfort allows the energy of the group to be directed towards the task with maximum efficiency.

Establishing harmony in the relationships on the team can be challenging between family members, friends, and team members in an unfamiliar, often stressful setting. Although dentists or hygienists are in their usual work mode of performing dentistry (although out of the comforts of their own office), the spouse, family member, friend, or team member is trying to help in a situation where s/he has little or no knowledge of the role of how to assist, to sterilize, and to comfort a patient. Dentists and hygienists must adjust their mentality not to be driven to the efficiency and productive levels of their home offices. It is helpful if the practitioners offer information, encouragement, and reassurance to those unaccustomed to clinic work. *"It is quite different using family members and friends as the dental staff, as they are thrown into an altered, subservient role. If non-dental volunteers come along, I always tell my dentists how lucky they are to have them. They are the ones who really have to work outside of their comfort zone if they are not used to dentistry and should be praised and thanked often."*

● *"My dentist husband and I worked out code words so I could signal him if I was getting overwhelmed or frustrated without the team or nationals knowing I was struggling. '1-4-1' meant 'one person is 'for' the other one,' which meant I was on his side, but not keeping up. When I told him 'It's getting hot in here,' I really meant, 'I'm getting provoked.'"*

Assign everyone a job on the team so s/he feels useful. It is essential that everyone feels included. Sometimes people get oppositional on no other basis than the unspoken question, "Why wasn't I included in this decision?"

● *"One spouse had nothing to do, but then we found out she had everything along to give manicures and pedicures. We became a full-service salon doing teeth and nails!"*

● *"One missionary praised liberally and knew the value of motivating those around her. She said, 'Everyone has an invisible sign hanging from his or her neck that says, Make Me Feel Important.'"*

● *"While on a weekend, small-plane trip to Baja, Mexico, a pilot's wife hobbled into the dental clinic with a cane in one hand and a large paperback book in the other. She half-heartedly asked if she could help, while stating she knew nothing about dentistry, could hardly walk, and could not speak the language. Each of the five dentists had an assistant, but we had no one to do sterilization. We showed her how to sterilize. As she became part of the dental team who helped so many, she became a changed person. She discarded the cane and book and evolved into an enthusiastic encourager in joyful service."*

CHAPTER 14

Student Involvement in Short-term Dental Mission Trips

Dental students bring a blessing to a dental mission team and have positive potential for all involved. The students are likely to receive more hands-on experience in the mission field than they would obtain in a similar time frame in dental school, especially in the area of extractions. Dentists have the satisfaction of passing their expertise to benefit future generations. More needy patients will receive the care they so desperately need, and it is highly unlikely that patients will be concerned that those treating them are students. Bringing dental students to the mission field often "hooks" them. They may become future trip leaders as they develop the confidence to branch out on their own. If experienced team leaders want missions to continue beyond their own lifetime, then investing in the development of dental students is vital. Working with young dental students has an energizing effect on the older leaders that is contagious and addictive. (See "Mentorship" in Chapter 13.) *"Success with students lies in a strong leader at the helm and unquestioned guidelines for trip rules and ethics."*

School administrators of the dental teaching programs do not necessarily sanction the trip for student participation. Some trips are held under the authority of particular dental schools, but most are independent of any institution. Both arrangements can result in successful trips. Some dental schools distance themselves from dental mission trips due to liability, religious, or other official concerns. *"If trips are not under the authority of a particular dental school, they will generally be more beneficial, with less unnecessary red tape."*

    ❋   *"Asking a dental school to assume responsibility for a dental mission trip is like putting the federal government in charge of a neighborhood lemonade stand. Too many restrictions and precautions can unnecessarily increase the cost of the trip, decrease the number of patients who are seen, and greatly limit the opportunity for participants to serve the unmet needs of their fellow man."*

    *   *"Certainly nothing that occurs on the trips should be purposely hidden from a dental school's administration; but when the school assumes administrative oversight of the trip, it gets messy. The best trips are done in cooperation with a dental school, but not under the school's authority."*

    *   *"At our dental school, students are not allowed to participate on overseas trips without a fairly complicated application process through the international travel office. We have had trouble getting permission for students to travel to Africa, Honduras, and Haiti. It would be nice to avoid this hassle, but we have been warned against trying to circumvent the system."*

The treatment repertoire of students should generally be limited to only those procedures that they have previously accomplished in dental school. Strong opinion exists on both sides of this question, and a good case can be made each way. It is better if students only perform procedures, with the exception of extractions, that they have received the necessary training in dental school to do well. With extractions, although some basic knowledge is certainly required, experience is a far greater teacher than a textbook. One good approach is to pair trip members with regard to experience— the more experienced dentist or students work with those who have less experience. Volunteers gain insight through discussion of the treatment needs they encounter. If the patient has a periodontally involved, lower incisor, this is an excellent opportunity for the less experienced student. The more experienced practitioners remove challenging teeth. There will be other teeth that require the expertise of seasoned dentists, who should be present in sufficient quantity, and ready to share their skills and knowledge. *"Our experience over the years, on perhaps 100 trips involving students from 15 different dental schools, tells us that participants should only perform those procedures that they have practiced, except for extractions."*

    *   *"We instruct pre- and early clinical students in local anesthesia, but limit extractions to third- and fourth-year students. We usually have one dentist overseeing no more than three learners who are doing extractions."*

    *   *"Removing an easier tooth under supervision on a trip can be the highlight for a student and be the most motivating experience for him/her to continue and to excel in school!"*

Student involvement can be primarily from one dental school or from multiple schools. Each of these scenarios has inherent benefits. Participants from multiple dental schools can compare their dental school experiences and learn different approaches to mastering their chosen profession. Volunteers coming from one school enjoy an immediate sense of camaraderie, since they will have at least some knowledge of their trip mates. If young adults from multiple schools are represented on the same trip, then some sort of ice-breaking activities should occur early on to help build the cohesiveness that facilitates a great learning and serving environment. *"Although both situations have provided productive environments for our varied 100 trips, there may be a slight advantage to having all—or almost all—participants from the same school."*

* *"My trips involve two dental schools. The synergy of mixing students of like minds is exhilarating and has led to long, permanent friendships."*

* *"When volunteers are from different states or other countries, logistical challenges arise with flight delays, so it makes it easier if everyone travels together. However, these are minor hurdles, and God works it all out, often as a faith-building exercise."*

Instructors/professors from the students' dental school(s) may or may not be encouraged to participate in the trips. Distinct differences occur between the learning environment of a typical dental school and the educational opportunities of a dental mission trip. Dental schools will have superior equipment and supplies, a controlled climate, better opportunities for medical evaluation, more complete infection control procedures, and increased clinical oversight designed to facilitate learning. If dental school clinicians are to be a true asset in the mission field, they must be aware of the differences between the two environments, and they must have realistic expectations regarding what can be accomplished on the mission field. If this is the case, then professional clinicians can be a wonderful asset on the trip; and the benefits of their participation can continue after the trip in the relationships that have been developed with the students and with future teams. On the other hand, if instructors expect the mission trip environment to be an extension of the same criteria for success that exists at the dental school, then perhaps the mission field may not be the best use for instructors' time and abilities. *"I wish faculty would participate, but I have only had a few express interest."*

"Seldom does an instructor want to spend a week with students when on faculty vacation—after spending most of the year with students. It is a different set of relationships."

Dental students worked in Jamaican clinics.

Leadership duties executed by students should be a central goal for leaders of dental student mission trips, in keeping with Biblical mandate: "The things which you have heard from me in the presence of many witnesses, entrust these to faithful men, who will be able to teach others also" (2 Timothy 2:2). Usually leadership would not be beneficial for students on their first trip, as they can be overwhelmed by the differences in culture and treatment modalities, as well as the need to learn dentistry skills. However, trip leaders have a great opportunity to develop leadership skills among team members who participate in repeat trips. The more leadership responsibility that team leaders can delegate to students, the more likely the work is to continue and to expand in future years. The extent to which responsibilities can be delegated will depend on the makeup of the team—the level of experience, know-how, and initiative. If the student is a committed Christian, this helps set the tone of the trip early on. These tasks that can be assigned to students which can serve to develop their leadership skills:

- Collecting payments from the trip participants
- Answering most questions from prospective team members, while passing the tougher ones to the professional team leaders
- Verifying that paperwork responsibilities have been fulfilled
- Collecting and transporting dental supplies to the mission field
- Making clinical assignments, pairing experienced students with less experienced students
- Leading Bible study/devotionals and prayer times
- Providing insightful feedback regarding the students' experiences on the trip
- Presenting information about a future trip to interested students at their school

"As I try to attract more natural leaders, the more I realize that the dental profession is filled with quiet, soft-spoken, not-wanting-to-be-in-front dentists. Mission trips are the ideal place to identify potential and to develop leadership. It may be the first time someone has been offered to be a leader with a cause!"

Alcohol use is controversial. A difference of opinion exists on whether alcohol should be allowed during student trips. A definitive answer applicable to all cases cannot be provided. The simplest approach would be to ban alcohol, thereby (hopefully) eliminating the potential for abuse. This will also make it less likely that the team might incur a bad reputation in the community in which they serve, either justly or unjustly. If alcohol is allowed, team leaders have a responsibility to both team members and the community in which they serve to do what is necessary to verify that this privilege is not abused. *"Most professionals are aware that alcohol use in any form is the main entry point for most drug abuse. To allow it on a Christian Dental Society-sponsored trip is counter-productive and will lead to conflicted signals to both participants and patients, not to mention the family of faith sponsors. To yield to the allowance of alcohol use on CDS mission trips is to capitulate to the weakness of human nature rather than focusing on the power of our faith and witness!"*

- *"I would have to vote on the side of no alcohol. I am not opposed and drink occasionally myself, but my personal opinion is that it's too easy to be misunderstood by either the local Christian community or students who don't drink. I have had team members on previous trips consume alcohol (against my wishes) and felt that it was a distraction to the group. Time is better spent in sharing, rest, or study rather than what could be perceived as 'partying.'"*

* *"Most of the student trips in which we have participated have allowed alcohol, and we have attempted to keep its consumption to moderate levels, which has usually been successful."*

Unruly students during trips may need discipline. Mission team members have a right to know what type of behavior is expected of them during their trips, prior to their decision to become part of the team. Student trips that occur under the umbrella of the Christian Dental Society include behavior that is consistent with the calling of Christ, as taught in the Bible. Examples of acceptable behavior are spelled out in the "Code of Conduct" examples in Chapter 3. They are not a comprehensive list, but the message is communicated that there are standards to be respected. All student team members do not need to be Christians; but for the time of the trip, they must agree not to harm the reputation of the faith-based group. The team is informed that violations of agreed-upon team policies may result in team members being counseled and possibly being removed from the team, with the requirement of returning home immediately at their own expense. It is important that the chosen "Code of Conduct" be reviewed during the first meeting in the country of service. If it is in an area served by previous teams, the students can be informed of the blessing they have of instant credibility and respect within the community, because of the service and behavior of those preceding teams and that they are setting the stage for future teams. *"Team leaders can extend both law and grace in penalties. This is a perfect opportunity to share with offenders that we are all in need of forgiveness and greater righteousness, and that Jesus Christ came to earth with these two goals in mind.* The Lord's bond-servant must not be quarrelsome, but be kind to all, able to teach, patient when wronged, with gentleness correcting those who are in opposition, if perhaps God may grant them repentance leading to the knowledge of the truth' (2 Timothy 2: 24-25). *It is exciting to see how the Lord can even use disobedience, when properly managed, to accomplish His purposes!"*

❖   "I sent three students home who were drinking before arriving at the airport. Years later, one of them called me and donated lots of equipment and supplies. They respected my handling of the issue. Those are a part of life lessons learned as a student— rather than after becoming a licensed dentist!"

Undergraduate students who are pre-dental candidates can be allowed to participate on trips. Several pre-dental students may accompany a dental trip, but what they can do is rather limited, primarily in the role as helpers, not clinicians. They can assist, sterilize, or organize supplies, but these tasks dental students can also accomplish. Pre-dental students may confirm their desire to continue in the dental profession through what they see on the trip, or others may conclude that dentistry is not for them, making these trips a valuable learning experience for either outcome. *"One former pre-dental student team member later went on to dental school, and while there he helped to lead three subsequent trips; and I have no doubt that he will continue to lead trips throughout his professional career."*

❖   "On one trip where we had over 100 participants, we took 11 pre-dents. More than half of those are now practicing dentists today. Do not limit God in how many want to go—just do your job of preparing for the ones He sends your way! Everyone will be blessed from your thoughtful leadership."

Parents/family members of dental students can attend the mission. Family participation is an invaluable experience as they work together, furthering the student's education and, more importantly, serving Christ together on the mission field. This experience speaks loudly to the patients, other students, and the community as they answer the call to serve as a Christian family. *"We often have dentists who want to bring their own children on the trip. I took both of my sons through the years. It is a wonderful parent/child mentoring of lifestyle!"*

Non-dental volunteers are welcomed on student mission trips. Due to space limitations, often teams are primarily dental professionals. Non-dental volunteers/spouses/family members can play important roles in the success of mission trips by helping with assisting, equipment repairs, sterilizing, crowd control, oral hygiene instruction, and supervision of on-site brushing/flossing before being seen by the hygiene team (who can then clean, polish, varnish, and seal teeth). Sometimes these volunteers may witness and evangelize while the patients await treatment. A willing servant will always be welcome and will find a place to serve in Christ's vineyard.

Post-mission trip sightseeing in the developing country may interest some students. As this may be their first visit to a particular country, many volunteers desire vacation time. This extended time is allowed as long as students realize that they are on their own, responsible for themselves, and make all of their own arrangements. They must share those plans with the team leaders in advance so that all are aware of the varied itineraries.

Raising funds for student mission trips must be accomplished by each student. Unfortunately, the cost of dental school is in the stratosphere, and the students already have debt. (See the hints in Chapter 19 on raising funds and preparing support letters.)

CDS' benefits for student trips encourage continued service.
* Students are eligible for a free CDS student membership for the duration of their dental school education.
* A CDS "designated funds" program aids in tax exemption.
* The trips are tax-deductible for students and donors who itemize deductions.

CHAPTER 15

Sponsoring Organizations

LEADERSHIP ROLES

A sponsoring organization may be familiar with medical or dental teams at overseas locations. These groups may have many of the protocols, the details, and the logistics of the trip worked out so that the team can arrive with minimal preparation. Other organizations have been impacted by short-term teams, but they have never tried to sponsor or to utilize a dental team. Other opportunities abound where the ministry has never sponsored a team before. *"In India we went to a village where one lady had prayed for 30 years for a missionary to come to her village and we were the first!"*

Host responsibilities include the spiritual welfare of the patients and the outreach to the communities. The team is there for them, and they are orchestrating the priorities of which dental clients to see and the evangelism. The spiritual follow-up is their task.

Budget planning is usually the sponsoring organization's duty. Although the volunteers supply the funds for the stay, the locals inform concerning administrative details, airport fees, visas, trip/travel insurance, immunization requirements, and cultural customs. They set up transportation, lodging, food, water, and sightseeing opportunities.

Team expenses should be paid ahead as much as possible, since the locals usually don't have reserve funds to cover costs. *"One of the host country leaders was very shy and disturbed about asking us for more funds. Without our knowledge, our costs totaled more than we'd sent ahead. We'd planned to settle up later, but the local budget leader agonized over telling us he needed the money to continue with our needs. We felt sad we'd put him in an* *uncomfortable situation, and now we check frequently with the national person controlling the money."*

Patient groups must be established for the dental team. The patients are the responsibility of the host organization, as the dental needs are usually overwhelming for the visiting team's capabilities. The dental team's time must be aligned with patient numbers and expectations, and the host organization normally takes responsibility to identify those who will be treated. If patients who expected treatment are not seen, it may damage the reputation of the host organization or cause negative feelings and animosity towards the mission goals. *"We like to go where they are planting churches or working on outreach. We consider ourselves bridge builders and door openers, an attraction or side show that gives credence to the church endeavor."*

✦   *"We like to serve pastors, seminary students, medical practitioners, and other servants of God who are doing the Lord's work. We do outreach to others as time permits."*

Advertising/informing potential patients at the local level is the host's duty. The national leaders make local contacts and disseminate information in the clinic's neighborhood. The host should be attuned to maximize the impact of the dental team.

Accommodation Considerations

National sponsors arrange appropriate accommodations that will fit the team's needs. Since married couples or family members usually like the option of privacy and the chance to stay together, same-gender, dorm-like settings may not be desirable for them. When local homes are used, acceptance of challenging sleeping arrangements may be required. *"We have had team members request private rooms, but that is not always possible. We accommodate when we can."*

Ideal housing qualifications include facilities that are reasonably clean, safe, moderately priced, close to the work site, fairly quiet at night, and have breakfast provided. It is always preferable to have rooms with bathrooms and water heaters and heat or air-conditioning according to the seasonable needs. Since this is a lot to ask, teams are warned to accept and adjust wherever they are placed. *"We are here to serve, not to be served."*

Larger teams often stay in local hotels. Often the accommodations are an adjustment for teams. Upon arrival, the team members check whether everything in the room is working—lights, sink, tub, and shower. Problems should be reported immediately. Requests for pillows, towels, or extras are usually granted. *"There are usually no toiletries offered as in American hotels, so take shampoo, etc."*

Identify uncleanliness. Many hotels still use fancy-patterned bedspreads that can't take the wear-and-tear of regular washing, so it may not have been washed recently. It might be wise to cast the spread into a closet. It is best to use water bottles rather than glasses that may have been washed in unsafe water. *"Some hotels do not provide top sheets, so we take a sheet in case they are unavailable or dirty."*

Fire emergency instructions and exits should be noted.

Smart travelers don't leave valuables in the room. Since hotel safes may be questionable, it is advisable to keep valuables (passport, money, phone, and camera) on team members at all times. Waist and neck wallets work well. If asking the hotel to lock valuables in the hotel safe, it is best to have a staff person sign an itemized list.

Brief stays in one location motivate organized travelers to put anything taken out of the suitcase in a single drawer so that packing will be easy and complete. (Some teams move after a day or two to a different location.)

Noise irritations at night sleep times are frequent occurrences. Vehicle noise, hotel activity, loud talkers, babies crying, noisy fans, barking dogs, crowing roosters, snoring roommates, and unfamiliar sounds disrupt. Ear plugs help or a request of a hotel room on a quieter side of the complex may be granted. *"Several times we have had roommates who were loud snorers. We moved them to a separate room, if possible, or used ear plugs."*

Adaptors/converters that are appropriate for the plug-ins for the hotels or homes will be needed.

Personal needs should be considered. Some team members may bring small air mattresses if they expect difficult times with unknown beds, and a small pillow is advisable. Plan ahead for special diet considerations. *"We have been many places where the pillow seems impossible to sleep on. We even had blocks of Styrofoam in Africa. I have a small, feather pillow that compresses easily into my luggage that I now take everywhere. I sleep so much better."*

LEISURE OPPORTUNITIES

Relaxation opportunities promote rest and enjoyment of the people and the culture. Dentistry is hard, demanding work. The backs of dentists, hygienists, and helpers are often compromised with less than optimal ergonomic methods for doing portable missions. The team leader advises the sponsoring organization that a balanced experience with work, outreach, rest, relaxation, and some shopping and tourism are non-negotiable. The country hosts, along with the trip leader, understand that if the team is too tired or sick, the members will be ineffective. Since each country has many interesting sights, the schedule should allow at least one day for sightseeing. The host nationals can arrange to take the team themselves or can help set up a tour with a local company. Cars or vans can be rented that give more freedom to the group in stopping when desired. *"The local nationals have always taken great care of us to ensure our health, safety, and general comfort within the restraints of the setting. It is important to communicate needs between the team and that of the locals."*

⁕ *"We find it best to work no more than two or three days in a row before taking a break to transition between work sites and to experience local activities, shopping, and/or tourism. We want to be as useful and resilient as possible, but we also want to preserve our backs and experience the blessings of serving without becoming too exhausted or physically debilitated."*

✦ *"Fishing, hunting, diving or exploring may be an interest to pursue while working in another country. By all means take some time to see the natural beauty of the country. Smell the roses along the way to make the trip relaxing and rewarding. No one expects the team to be all work."*

A team rode camels around Egyptian pyramids.

Sponsor Appreciation

Helping missionaries is an important aspect of all trips. It is essential to honor and to respect local missionaries and nationals who are taking time from their responsibilities and busy schedules to host the team. As visitors, the team members may not be aware of what the hosts are facing or going through, and volunteers want to help them carry their load. The team must show flexibility to changes in daily schedule and varying needs of the host-sponsoring organization. *"Look for opportunities to help the missionaries. These might include doing the dishes after a meal or watching their kids for an evening so they can have time alone. Ask frequently, 'How can I help?' Try to do more than your share."*

Guest behavior is important since the dental team members are visiting the mission field at the invitation of the national church and the missionaries. No one has come to take over the work or to tell them how to do it. The group is there to lend a helping hand. Although the team's way of doing things is personally and culturally based, it is not the only way a job can be accomplished. It might be necessary to perform the task "their way" with a cooperative spirit. No job is beneath the volunteers' dignity. *"We do not feel we are better than the nationals or anyone on our team because we may have more resources, more education and skill opportunities, and possibly even a more spiritual background. We seek to follow the example of Jesus who "taking the very nature of a servant...he humbled himself"* (Philippians 2:6-11). *Any good we do is because of the grace of God and is for His honor and glory, not ours."*

Volunteers learn the purpose and the long-range strategy of the mission. How does the team's presence fit into the broader strategy of the missionary on the ground? How will the group help with the work already done and the work yet to be done? Is this a "planting field" where the Gospel is exposed to many non-Christians? Is it a "harvest field" where many people are ready to become Christians? Is the team helping Christians who are planting and harvesting? Are there specific restrictions on mission activities (or even using mission-related phrases) in the country? The sponsoring organization introduces the team to the local mission, and each group symbiotically encourages and strengthens each other. The team's presence and attitude of service is a witness to Christ's love and is a special tool to be used by the local pastors and religious organizations to further God's kingdom. When and how is it acceptable to preach, sing, pray, witness, and give testimonies? *"Although I am a dentist, I am often asked to give a Sunday sermon or a testimony in an international church. I do dentistry with few qualms, but a speaking gig causes me the most anxiety on any trip. God helps me when I am out of my comfort zone."*

Local ownership is important since the nationals are ultimately responsible for the clinic. No matter the situation, someone needs to coordinate and to communicate so that realistic expectations on both sides are understood for a successful mission experience. The team leader is responsible to communicate what the dental group can do. *"We go overseas with good support from local nationals within the country. The* *sponsoring leaders know the political, the spiritual, and the safety considerations and strive to use the team to the maximum benefit possible. We are usually protected and provided for from the time we arrive at the airport until we are dropped off to return home."*

Judgmental attitudes by the team should not be made concerning how the missionaries live. There may be surprises in the "luxuries" the missionaries seem to have. It may be difficult to understand some of these situations. For example, volunteers can't conclude that the missionaries' salaries are so good that they can afford hired help, or that the church is wasting money on this service for the missionaries. Actually, many missionaries would rather do their own work, as it might be of higher quality and take less time. Maybe the missionaries must have help to free them for mission duties. Often the national people are given the jobs so they can go to Bible School or can support a family.

Gift giving should be discussed prior to traveling. The team should discuss if and how gifts will be collected, prepared, and packed. It is best to refrain from giving individual gifts to locals, whether during home visits or at mission sites. Instead of bringing gifts for missionaries, one appreciation card to give as an encouraging sentiment from the group is thoughtful. Communication ahead of time with the missionaries or local leaders may reveal much-needed gift ideas. Trip leaders can work with the team on disbursement of the items to make sure this happens appropriately and equitably.

Offering help to individual nationals must be handled with care. Even with the best of intentions, team members must be very careful about encouraging nationals to leave their country to go to school or to work abroad. Usually, government restrictions and quotas make this difficult or impossible anyway. But even if it's an option, it may be unwise. Bringing a young person out of his/her culture into a more affluent one can ruin his/her usefulness to the country, the mission, and the church. If confronted with any unusual requests, the member can discuss concerns with the local host to determine the best response.

Dental Capabilities

Dental capabilities must be communicated to the nationals. The following is an excerpt which can be modified appropriately and sent ahead to share with the sponsoring organization and country hosts to instruct on the team's abilities, limitations, and needs:

* Concerning dental care, we attempt to do the greatest good for the greatest number and try not to make promises we cannot keep. Your role in explaining this is important as we do not want disappointed patients or angry feelings from those who might have expected treatment and did not receive it.

* We sterilize all our instruments, and patients need not worry about getting diseases from other patients. Since we use anesthesia, there is little pain with the procedures.

* We want to teach dental hygiene (brushing, nutrition, prevention of tooth problems) to groups, as this is very important. We may bring a hygienist to clean teeth full time.

* As dentists, we can do extractions and fillings, which most patients need. Dentists can do cleanings, but that takes much time and then we cannot treat as many who are in pain. We can treat the patient's one, main problem in about thirty minutes. This usually means removing several bad teeth or completing a few fillings. We find that patients come with many dental needs, and we cannot fix them all without leaving other patients with no care.

* The person who allows patients into the clinic has the most difficult job. We call him/her the "Gate Keeper." Because a dentist or a hygienist can treat only about 15-20 patients a day when doing extractions, fillings, or cleanings, someone has to decide whom we see without upsetting all the others who would like to be seen. We must make it clear that the dentist is only treating one problem area and not the whole mouth, unless the sponsors want us to spend hours treating all the dental needs of just a few patients. People with pain and swelling should be seen first.

* We often have used sign-up lists with patients coming every 30 minutes or cards with numbers for those we can see. These can be given to leaders to hand out. Pre-screening patients (especially children) by medical staff or national hosts who select those most needing care helps maximize

the efficiency of the dental care. The "Gate Keeper" is an important and respected local person who can make the important decisions about who will get to see the dentists.

* Dentistry is very hard on the workers' backs, so we will need a day of rest from dentistry in the middle of the week. Examples of activities for a rest day include relocating to another work site, visiting and evangelizing within communities, sightseeing, and shopping.

* To operate, we need a source of adequate electricity, several tables, three or four chairs per dentist, and water, both bottled and regular community water. We will need a source of electric power for our sterilization pressure cooker. We can use a propane burner or whatever is used to safely boil water. (See Chapter 4: Electrical Considerations.) We will bring the dental patients' chairs, lights, dental operating units, sterilizer, instruments, and all the supplies to do dental care. It takes about an hour to set up the clinic and an hour to repack it.

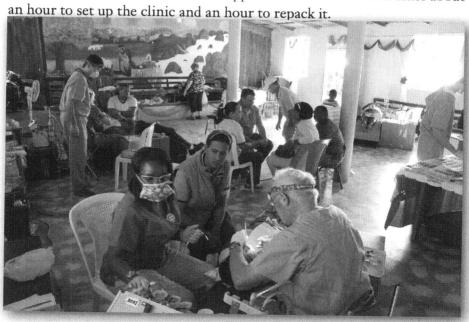

Dental chairs are placed in the four corners of a
church in the Dominican Republic.

* It is very important that we have an interpreter for every dentist and hygienist. Dentistry can be frightening for the patients, and we need to

communicate well to treat them best. We must understand what the patient is saying about their problems. The interpreter must learn dental terms, quickly translate the problem to the dentist, and show compassion and care to the patient while the dentist gives anesthesia and removes or fills a tooth. The interpreter must be able to watch a bloody procedure. It is important for the interpreter to give clear instructions after the treatment. It often takes a day of working with a dentist or a hygienist for the interpreter to understand the terms needed and how to best care for and to teach patients. We prefer the same interpreter to be with the same dentist and hygienist each day, as it makes it easier for both. We always pray earnestly that God will give us good interpreters. If the interpreters have any questions at all, or if they become confused, they must be comfortable with asking questions right away. Getting it right is more important than speed.

✳   If possible, it is best to have the noon meal near the dental clinic to allow for a short rest period and to give the dental practitioners more time to treat patients. The team is careful, however, to eat "out of sight" of patients who may suffer from chronic hunger or malnutrition. Otherwise, some team members feel sad and give their food to the patients or their families.

CHAPTER 16

Spiritual Preparation

———◆———

CHRISTIAN VIEWPOINTS

A Christian understanding of missions is based on the belief that peace with God is humanity's deepest need and that all people need to hear and to accept God's plan of salvation to meet that need. (See Appendix J.) A good biblical foundation instructs, ". . . Everyone who calls on the name of the Lord will be saved. How, then, can they call on the one they have not believed in? And how can they believe in the one of whom they have not heard? And how can they hear without someone preaching to them? And how can they preach unless they are sent? As it is written, 'How beautiful are the feet of those who bring good news'" (Romans 10:13-15).

"The Christian majority are young, poor, theologically conservative, and female. The largest Christian communities today are not in the United States Bible Belt but in Africa and Latin America. The story of Christianity represents a fundamental and a historical shift in worldwide religions. Christianity is not held captive by any particular culture. In fact, more languages and cultural expressions are used in Christian liturgy, devotion, worship, and prayer than in any other religion."[49]

Short-term missions are spiritual, where even the most seemingly insignificant aspects of a trip can impact the team members. For instance, poor food preparation could cause individuals to become sick and to miss out on parts of the mission. However, proper spiritual preparation beforehand can enable those same team members to still grow from that experience. Good spiritual preparation creates the fertile soil for spiritual growth that can occur on the project. "The greatest challenge is to live and work out of gratitude on the mission field, because the two most damaging motives in the makeup of missionaries seem to be guilt and the desire to save, neither of which are beneficial motivations for going. If we go to a poor country because we feel guilty about our wealth, it will bring trouble. Guilt is not taken away by work. Also, the desire to save people from sin, from poverty, or from exploitation can be just as harmful, because one becomes confronted with one's own limitations, which can lead to a destructive and depressive loss of self-worth. If we work out of gratitude to God, we are showing that the Lord took on our guilt and saved us. In Him, the Divine work has been accomplished. Then we are free to serve and live truly humble lives. Clinging to guilt is resisting God's grace, wanting to be a savior, and competing with God's own being. Both are forms of idolatry and make missionary work very hard and eventually impossible." (Henri Nouwin, theologian)[50] *"A short-term mission is successful if, at its end, the participants know Jesus more fully than they did before."*

Evangelism responsibilities are carried primarily by the local national group leaders and the full-time missionaries. Many dental teams ask them to be responsible for the spiritual outreach. The dental team has come to help people and to draw them into contact with the local ministry, but the nationals are much more adept at the language, the use of their outreach programs that are already in effect, and the follow-up strategies after the U.S. team has left. The dental team is glad to help, whenever possible, with prayer, conversations through interpreters, and excellent dental care; but the team is often not as effective at evangelism as the host nationals are.

A healing focus is an important part of the Gospels and of ministry services in many countries. In many churches faith healing and prayers for healing are integral parts of the worship service and of popular aspirations. The proportion of the Gospels describing how Jesus and the apostles healed the sick may outweigh the proportion of the Gospels where Jesus talked about doctrine or issues that many associate with Jesus' ministry.

SPIRITUAL EMPHASIS

Bible studies or short devotional lessons are applications of the Bible that team members have prepared with personal or researched commentary. Through team member's planned thoughts, the team can experience inspiration, encouragement, and instruction concerning biblical principles, the Christian faith, a team members' favorite verse(s), or personal stories with faith applications. Some teams may be composed of Christians and non-Christians, all with varying levels of understanding and spiritual maturity, so this can be encouraged, although optional. *"We follow the Bible's advice on our trips.* 'Do not let this Book of the Law depart from your mouth; meditate on it day and night, so that you may be careful to do everything written in it...'(Joshua 1:8)."

* *"We encourage all team members to lead a short devotional or Bible lesson, as it provides opportunities for individual growth and builds up the team when all participate."*

* *"Singing adds a fun and engaging way to worship for the team and the national hosts."*

Devotional lessons or daily Bible studies unite the team in spiritual focus. These messages are often given in the morning, the evening, or whatever time works best for the team. They may be followed by team announcements or discussions about daily events and can include a prayer time.

A Bible study is shared with an international dental team in Cambodia.

Bible references for devotional lessons may use scriptures such as these:

* www.emiworld.org/volres.php under "Trip Guide" has "Devotionals" for fourteen Bible passages, complete with excellent questions and answers for discussion or quiet times. References include: Psalms 10, 73, 103, 139; Jonah 1-4; Matthew 10:26-33; Mark 12:41-44; Luke 10:38-42; John 13:1-17; Acts 8:26-40; 1 Corinthians 3:5-11, 9:19-23, 12:12-31; Philippians 2:5-11.

* *Mission Trip Prep Kit*[51] has Bible passages and discussion questions that work well for devotionals, such as: Matthew 22:37; John 1:1-14; Acts 26; Romans 8:38-39; 1 Corinthians 5:14-15, 12:14-26; Galatians 5:22-26; Ephesians 1:17, 4:2-3, 4:11-13; Philippians 2:1-8; Colossians 3:12-14; James 2:1-9; 1 John 4:19.

* *Mission Trips from Start to Finish.*[52]

* Internet or church libraries.

INSPIRATIONAL PRAYER

Ongoing prayer is an essential and inspiring part of time spent with God and especially necessary when doing His work. Communication with God helps all to understand His will, to give peace, and to relieve participants from putting the burden of the mission outcomes upon themselves. Dr. Tim Dearborn (World Vision International associate and theologian) says, "We cannot minimize the significance of prayer. Note what Paul says we are to do once we are fully clothed with the armor of God: stand, pray, and proclaim Christ. If we are to participate in God's mission in the world, we need to be equipped as intercessors. One of the most significant ministries we gain from our short-term service is the ability to pray more intelligently and passionately for the region of the world we visited."[53]

Contemporary Christians stand in the tradition of the biblical prophets and the Reformation, which sees prayer not as recitation (as in formalistic religion) or meditation (as in mysticism) but as dialogue between a living God and the one who has been touched by His grace. Dr. Donald Bloesch (a noted evangelical theologian) states, "The primary aim of prayer is to be conformed to the will of God; however, this should be seen as the realization of true humanity made possible only by the outpouring of unmerited grace."[54]

    ❖   Dr. Bill Hybels (pastor of Willow Creek Community Church) says, "Prayer is alien to our proud human nature. From birth we have been learning the rules of self-reliance as we strain and struggle to achieve self-sufficiency. I didn't want to get off the fast track long enough to find out what prayer is all about...but the Holy Spirit gave me a leading to explore, study, and practice prayer until I finally understood it. I have been transformed."[55]

    ❖   Pastor Dutch Sheets of Springs Harvest Fellowship says, "Prayer is 'communion with God.' Through prayer we actually experience a relationship with God. Prayer is talking and listening to God and enjoying His presence. God is looking for a heartfelt relationship. Loving relationships built around true communion and the pleasure of friendship result in the serving of one another. Paul said his love for God, not duty or reward, constrained him to serve God."[56] *"For Christ's love compels us, because we are convinced that one died for all...that those who live should no longer live for themselves but for him..."* (2 Corinthians 5: 14-15).

Prayer partners benefit short-term missionaries. Each member can ask five to ten people to pray specifically for the individual, the team preparations, and the mission trip. Establish specific guidelines on what the prayer needs are and the dates when prayer is especially needed. Consider meeting regularly with prayer partners for a one-on-one or group prayer time. The emphasis placed on prayer during this process will reflect faith and trust. Many of the partners who share in this mission will be ones who remain home or will be long-forgotten friends and mentors who helped team members arrive at this point in their lives.

A "Prayer Commissioning" by those staying behind can be powerful. An evening meeting or a portion of a worship service can be devoted to this. At the meeting, a brief overview of the trip purpose, schedule, and prayer needs should be addressed. A media promotion from the organization (or a movie clip related to the cause) will help guests connect visually with the mission. The team gathers in an area where others can surround them to pray. (It is often helpful to ask only a few people to pray and to designate someone to end the prayer time.) These are other ideas to extend the event:

* People pick a member not related to them to pray for.
* Team members can give testimonies and can tell what they are most looking forward to experiencing.
* The senior pastor or an elder can share words of encouragement and blessing.
* There can be a question-and-answer time.
* The time closes with a prayer of commitment to Christ, that the group would be His servants.

Pray silently throughout the day. By consistently bringing requests to the Lord, the team is showing that they depend on Jesus Christ. The consistency of prayer demonstrates submission to and dependence on

Christ. *"We try to make it a priority to pray in a group with the nationals before each clinic day. It can be hard to remember to do this, as often patients are waiting and there are many details and routines to get the day started."*

* *"A designated team member can be asked to remind everyone of prayer times."*

Prayer requests for these concerns are often needed:
* practical arrangements of the trip
* spiritual preparation for all involved
* positive attitudes for all team members
* team unity for each aspect of the trip
* special needs for each member
* concerns of the family and friends left at home
* financial considerations and employment concerns
* the people who will be met on the mission field
* the leaders of the team and the local missionaries
* the sponsoring organization and the host nationals
* all who have helped team members during their faith journey
* the team's ability to have service-oriented minds and heart
* the appropriate numbers and the dental care of the patients who will be treated
* the impact of the Gospel on the patients' and the national peoples' lives
* safety during the mission trip for everyone involved

EFFECTIVE EVANGELISM

Sharing opportunities arise to speak of Christian faith while providing dentistry at home and around the world. Also, portable dentistry can be taken to remote areas with those who have never before heard the Gospel message. For some health professionals, it may be the first opportunity they have taken to witness to others. Each health care practitioner or worker should attempt to project a Christ-centered life and to share God's love and Christian hope as they are led and when opportunities present themselves.

"When I first introduce myself to a patient through the translator, I tell him or her, 'Jesus sent me to help you. How can I help you?' Lost people will give a bewildered look, and the believers realize their God can send a 'gringo' to meet their need."

An American shares her Christian testimony using a translator in Mongolia. They were showing the Jesus film on the side of a van.

Church attendance can be an exciting experience. Sunday services in an international church are a highlight and should be attended whenever possible. Often these meetings are lengthy, with multiple sermons, meals, singing, and healing times. The team can agree on how long to stay at the service.

Offering donations will be taken in each church service normally, and team members can use these opportunities to donate. To be in keeping with the individual, national person's offering it is better to contribute only a small amount. Even though a team member may be able to afford much more, it is better to "feel the need" and then to give mission support in a more balanced way. The host leader can advise.

Giving testimonies and/or devotionals are often available opportunities for team members. The nationals usually enjoy hearing from the team as their sisters and brothers in Christ. They look for examples of Christian life. What an important way for God to use the team! *"We like to use items found at www.e3resources.org that include "evangecube" manipulatives that present the gospel visually. They have large cubes with pictures and a biblical script that shares the plan of salvation in pictures, scriptures, and explanations for groups or individuals. We also buy evangelism "e-cards" in packs of 50. These are square, three-inch cards that can be stored in a pocket or a wallet to share the gospel similarly to the large cubes. Since these products are reasonable to buy, they make nice gifts for the pastors, Christians, or new converts."*

* *"We are often asked to share our story of why we are there. 'Always be prepared to give an answer to everyone who asks you to give a reason for the hope that you have' (1 Peter 3:15). We instruct and encourage everyone to be ready with a testimony as a good 'door opener.'"*

* *"We try to attend church services with our country hosts and patients and are regularly asked to speak and even to bring a message during their services. This is a great opportunity to encourage the nationals, many of whom have never seen an international speaker. We share the living hope we have in Christ and encourage the team to be prepared to speak."*

Christian conservatism is often found in other cultures. Trying to advocate vocally "enlightened, Western, liberal" approaches to social issues like women's roles, abortion, homosexuality, governmental policies, and others may be not only inflammatory, but also they may put the host Christian community in danger. Local values are often strongly held, and offense is taken if they are considered threatened. If asked about such issues, missionaries can calmly advise the questioner that even in America or in Europe opinions are divided on these issues, that everyone respects other traditions, and that Americans are not suggesting their opinions are better than those of others. The subject should be gently moved in a different direction.

Personal Testimony

When speaking in public services or with individuals on a one-on-one sharing opportunity, it is best to exalt Christ and His power in the team member's life. Pray for wisdom. These guidelines may help.[57]

* Avoid comparisons between a developed country and that of the nationals.

* Treat the people as equals. (They might be our superiors!)

* Avoid references to the military, political issues, or to other religious groups.

* Refrain from jokes about the local food or customs or personal likes and dislikes.

* Praise the beauty of the local country, the warmth of Christian fellowship felt in the church, the national people's wonderful testimonies and singing.

* Check with the interpreter beforehand on any anecdotes planned as illustrations in the message. (For example, a story with a setting in an elevator in a mall would not have much meaning to those who have lived all their lives in a one-room house in a mountain village.)

* Share about what happened to you, without preaching about what should happen to them. Say, "I" and "me," not "you," as it keeps the testimony warm and personal.

* Make it sound conversational. Avoid literary-sounding statements. Use informal language.

* Avoid religious words, phrases, and jargon. The listener may not know what is meant by terms like "accepted Christ" or even "Christian."

* Simplify and reduce "clutter." Mention a limited number of people and use only their first or last names. Combine information when you can. (Examples: Martha and two other friends talked with me at work one day…" or "After living in five states and attending six universities, I finally graduated and got an engineering job…")

* Generalize information so that more people can identify with your story. Avoid naming specific churches, denominations, or groups. Avoid using dates and ages. Deglamorize the sin portion of your life and keep the "before" not overly dramatic or exciting.

- Include some appropriate humor and human interest. When a person smiles or laughs, it reduces tension. Humor is disarming and increases attention.

- Share word pictures to increase interest. Expand on, "Bill shared the gospel with me." You might briefly describe the setting so that a person listening can visualize it.

- Explain how Christ met or is meeting your needs (and working to remove your sin), but acknowledge that not all the struggles and problems ended at conversion.

- Reflect an adult point of view, even if you were converted at an early age.

- Avoid dogmatic, strange (especially to internationals), and mystical statements that skeptics can question, such as, "I prayed and God gave me a job" (*That is hard to understand.*); "God said to me…" (*He's hearing voices?*); "I love our worship services—they're filled with passion!" (*Hmm. What kind of loose place is that?*); "Since I was saved I've lived a victorious life." (*She suddenly became thrifty and now wins all her conflicts?*); "I have constant peace." (*Nothing bothers him?*); "I'm really getting into the Bible." (*Where is that?*)

- Be careful not to condemn others for living as non-Christians. The objective is to share the personal story of having found a better life in Christ.

- Caution is advised when using "religious" statements or clichés. "Jesus is the answer to all your problems." He is, but they might not know much about Him, much less what He can do in their lives.

- Speak loudly, clearly and concisely, in a natural and relaxed tone of voice. Avoid assuming a "ministerial twang."

- Watch mannerisms such as rubbing a part of the body, jingling coins in a pocket, saying "uh," or swaying.

- Look at the audience. Refrain from staring at the floor or looking only at one person.

- Be humble. Let people know the limits of your eloquence and that your experience is just one example of an infinite God working.

- Try to memorize the main points so the talk can be delivered naturally and confidently.

* Bible references and Bible stories or illustrations can be powerful, especially from the possibly new and different perspective of a person from a different nationality.

An effective tool for sharing faith follows the example used by the Apostle Paul as he stood before King Agrippa. Paul spoke simply, logically, and clearly about his life before salvation, how he met Christ, and what his life was like after conversion. Paul's testimony (in Acts 26) takes 3-4 minutes to read aloud in a conversational manner and is a biblical model that can be followed in writing personal testimonies: lead-in— verses 2-3; Paul's life before meeting Christ—verses 3-11; how Paul came to Christ—verses 12-20; Paul's life after meeting Christ—verses 21-23; closing—verses 24-29.

Personal testimonies can be developed using these practical suggestions for the before, how, and after section in a presentation:[58]

1) Before meeting Jesus, what happened? Describe that period of life. This might include one's unsatisfied, deep, inner needs: lack of peace, fear of death, something missing, no meaning to life, desire to be in control, loneliness, lack of security, lack of purpose, lack of significance, no real friends, no motivation, or other needs. The unsatisfactory solutions (either positive or negative) that were used to attempt to meet these needs may be discussed: marriage/family, work, drugs/alcohol, sports/fitness, money/education hobbies/entertainment, wrong friends, or other ideas.

2) How did Jesus become personal? Describe the circumstances that caused Christ to become the solution to those needs. Identify the events leading to your conversion. In some cases this may have taken place over a period of time. State specifically the steps involved in becoming a Christian, including a paraphrased or actual passage of Scripture that applies here, if possible. Include the gospel clearly and briefly. The gospel includes the thoughts that all have sinned; death is the penalty for sin; Christ paid the penalty; and the importance of receiving Christ as our sacrifice and Savior.

3) After accepting Jesus, how did life change? Talk about how Christ filled or is filling deep, inner needs (and how He works to take away sin and the punishment deserved). Since the "before" section showed

needs and unsuccessful solutions, now it is important to show briefly the differences that Christ has made in one's life. Conclude with a statement similar to this: "The greatest benefit is that I know for certain that my sins are forgiven and that I have eternal life."

Testimony formats are varied, and one of these may fit a given individual.

* The Adult Conversion. Christ was discovered and accepted in adult life. There is a clear before, how, and after.
* Early Conversion and Full Commitment Later. A decision for Christ was made as a child, but life was characterized by spiritual immaturity and a lifestyle similar to that of a non-Christian. Then there was a point of crisis and recommitment to Christ. If the early conversion experience didn't seem to be genuine, then use the "Adult Conversion" format.
* Early Conversion and Constant Growth. This format is for those who have grown up in a Christian home with a strong church background. There may be very few "before" experiences.

Team members share testimonies in a crowded church in India.

Practicing articulation of the testimony is wise. Ask a team member or another respected Christian to read the content, to make suggestions, or to point out areas that could be explained more clearly. When the final draft is completed, outline the thoughts on a 3" by 5" card. Giving the testimony to a small group would be an excellent opportunity to practice and to receive feedback.

Individual sharing of a testimony informally, with a small group or a one-on-one opportunity, is led into more carefully. The following suggestions may be helpful when working with one individual:

* Include some "small talk" before discussing spiritual matters. Mention family, job, hobbies, and interests.

* Stay alert for expressed needs, such as family problems or stress on the job. Use these connections to show how Christ has helped you through some of the same areas.

* Discuss past concerns and needs in your life. "We used to struggle with that…" or "I used to let the pressures of work get to me…then I discovered what makes a tremendous difference…"

* Discuss contemporary situations in the news or in a given area. "I saw on TV that drugs are epidemic in our country. It seems that people are trying to find satisfaction so they are turning to drugs…"

* Build relationships with others. It may take ten minutes or ten hours or ten days or ten years—but build relationships.

* Forgo arguments on moral issues. Expect non-Christians to have conflicts with clear biblical teaching. Remember, they do not have a valid base from which to make correct moral decisions.

* It is important to assess if the timing is right before presenting the Gospel of Jesus Christ to an inquirer. The non-Christian must be ready to acknowledge a hunger for God and be receptive to the idea that God is the Creator and the Savior of the world. When a person is truly seeking to reach out to God, the way to lead him/her to a saving faith in Jesus Christ is outlined in Appendix J.

Closing conversations after sharing a testimony will depend on the response received.

* With a positive response, say, "Has anything like this ever happened to you?" or "Mary, do you know for certain whether you have eternal life?" Carefully ask, "May I share with you someday how I know for certain that I have eternal life?"

* With a negative or neutral response, say, "If you're interested, I would like to share more with you sometime." Another approach is to ask, "Do you have any questions on what I have just shared with you?"

Productive Journaling

Journal writing on a short-term mission project is intended to record experiences, emotions, and insight from one's interactions, observations, and Christian walk. The purpose is to bring remembrance of the day's experiences, growth with God, life's lessons, and personal feelings during the project. Writing can include these suggestions from Pastor Borthwick, a minister of missions.[59]

* Notes and daily prayers from quiet times: What attributes of God were evident today? What is He teaching? What are the prayer needs that require attention? Who should be remembered in prayer?

* Spiritual lessons and insights. Where was God seen at work? Where was the Gospel proclaimed? What signs of hope were seen?

* Clinicians and others may note what works well and what they need to bring or not include on the next trip.

* Impressions and observations of people met. What visual images made an impact?

* Areas of struggle and confusion, as well as new insights. What kinds of poverty were seen? When was failure or discouragement experienced?

* Interesting observations of animals, plants, birds, or food.

* Observations or experiences of cultural differences and entertaining moments. What gifts and assets were encountered within the community? Where was hospitality offered and received?

* Language phrases learned.

* Keep a record of thoughts, impressions, feelings, and prayers, contemplations about whether God is calling you to be a short-or

long-term missionary. What is being learned about missionary service?

    ⁕   One excellent exercise is to spend an hour or so the day before the trip to detail hopes, fears, dreams, and expectations. Then pray about each of these issues, giving them up to God. Soon after the mission trip, spend another hour or so reviewing the trip. How did God answer prayers? Were hopes fulfilled and fears relieved? What were the differences between what was predicted and what actually happened?

Journaling tips are offered:[60]

    ⁕   Avoid journaling as a duty. Rather, approach it as writing a letter to a beloved friend.

    ⁕   Begin with "Dear Lord," and then write a letter to God sharing thoughts, fears, joys, and concerns.

    ⁕   Don't worry about being profound. Journal entries are not your memoirs but a private dialogue with God.

    ⁕   Incorporate reflections on the Bible. This makes it a true dialogue. Choose one section of Scripture to study throughout the short-term mission trip.

    ⁕   Conclude by listening to God and expressing thankfulness. Think about what God may be seeking to say to you.

    ⁕   Experiences do not make an individual a good short-term missionary. Rather, *evaluated* experience makes one's mission time meaningful. Analyze what has been learned and record growth.

Realistically, journaling on a busy mission trip may be difficult. It can be challenging to achieve privacy, personal time, and energy at the end of the day. Quick notes jotted down in a small notebook to be reflected and expanded upon later may be the most reasonable journaling technique. Often journaling or trip write-ups are completed at home, although waiting too long after the mission may lead to forgotten details.

CHAPTER 17
Safety Issues

———

GENERAL SAFETY

Safety considerations are not just a good idea; they are included in scriptural principles, and are in the will of God. "When you build a new house, make a parapet around your roof so that you may not bring the guilt of bloodshed on your house if someone falls from the roof" (Deuteronomy 22:8). Therefore, out of love to God and to neighbors, the work and the clinic sites must be safe.

The host nationals are trusted to keep the group safe. They live there and they will know how to avoid dangerous situations and how to advise the team on local safety concerns. The host nationals should be listened to and their wise advice heeded.

Buddy traveling (in pairs) is a smart idea. Each team member should pick a "buddy" who will check for his/her presence when transporting, at meals, and in the clinic or hotel. A "buddy check" can occur frequently when traveling. If buddies leave the group, they must let someone know where they are going and when they plan to return.

Meeting times and places must be arranged when splitting up to eat, to shop, or to sightsee.

Respecting laws of the land is important.

Watching actions and limiting loud, obnoxious behavior and large groupings in public is important. Team members are reminded that they are guests and that any demanding or imposing—as an American with rights and entitlements—is not appreciated.

Dressing appropriately for the situation is important. **Walking carefully** is advised, as uneven terrain, open sewers, and large holes in streets or sidewalks are an ever-present hazard.

Surrounding awareness at all times is important, especially in crowded, common areas. Since tourists are often targets for thefts, alertness is required for potential dangers. Wariness is key if an individual is bumped in a crowd, if a stranger points out something in a distracting way, if people drop to the sidewalk in a faint nearby, or when approached with a flower, a map, or a baby. While catching the attention of travelers, thieves may attempt pick-pocketing.

Hiding wealth—flashy jewelry, large amounts of money, or fancy luggage—is advised. Expensive items should be left at home.

Nighttime activities are best avoided anywhere. The women-and-children rule is helpful—if women and children are present, there is less to worry about. If only men are present, women should leave quickly when alone or outnumbered.

If thieves approach, it may be life-saving to give them what they want. It may help to yell "thief!" if pickpocketed with others around. *"Everything but your life can be replaced."*

Travel Insurance

Medical plans from home will not usually cover a team member overseas. The host nationals or the team leader needs to have ideas in place for a medical evacuation or emergency. Volunteers who are sick or injured may not want to trust their health to well-meaning but poorly equipped or inadequately trained national health-care personnel. Hospital locations or medical clinic areas should be noted in case of team member emergencies in the developing country. The hosts should know this information, but the team can ask about these locations after arriving on-site.

Travel insurance is often required and purchased by the sponsoring organizations for their participants. However, if the team is not covered, individuals should probably purchase travel insurance coverage. Buying insurance individually is relatively inexpensive (usually a few dollars per day) when compared with having to pay costly medical evacuation bills that may be payable in advance if a person does not have insurance. This is an individual decision based upon each one's risk tolerance, the medical resources available in the developing country, and the cost and the effectiveness of the amount of insurance each individual desires to purchase.

Common risks covered by travel insurance plans and outlined in detail on the individual policies often include:
* medical emergency (accident or sickness)
* emergency evacuation
* repatriation of remains
* return of a minor
* trip cancellation or trip interruption
* visitor health insurance
* accidental death, injury, or disablement benefits
* overseas funeral expenses
* lost, stolen, or damaged baggage, personal effects, or travel documents
* delayed baggage (and emergency replacement of essential items)
* flight connections missed due to airline schedule or hi-jacking
* travel delays due to weather

Insurance options for travel are offered by numerous companies which are listed with the Department of State www.travel.state.gov/content/passports/english/go/health/providers.html. Medical expense coverage can be "per occurrence" or "maximum limit."

Purchasing insurance for dental equipment, instruments, and supplies can be costly and a hassle but can be obtained from some of the travel insurance companies. *We lean on prayer and, in fifty missions, we have not lost anything. Thank God."*

Immunization Information

Preventative immunizations are an essential part of planning before a trip. Travelers should consult with a physician, a preventive medicine or travel specialist, and the local sponsor organization or host nationals. There are many inoculations available through local health departments at reasonable prices. Complete information about individual needs and U.S. and host government requirements, as well as a 24-hour helpline, can be obtained by calling 1-800-CDC-INFO or by going online and reading the CDC General Recommendations on Immunization at www.cdc.gov/mmwr/preview/mmwrhtml/rr5515al.htm.

Immunizations dental personnel find essential include hepatitis A and B (to protect against blood-borne pathogens), tetanus and diphtheria boosters every ten years, a flu shot, and vaccinations for measles, mumps, rubella, polio, and varicella (chicken pox). Hepatitis B protection requires three shots over a period of six months. If pressed for time, the first two are given within a month of each other before the trip, and the third can usually be administered after the return home. A polio booster is important if individuals have not had one. Multiple doses are needed if a volunteer has not had the primary polio series. Other immunizations may be recommended depending on the destination country.

Health certificates that are "international" are yellow, multi-page documents that record vaccinations received. It is suggested that copies be taken along for travel to many countries. An International Health Certificate may be obtained at a local public health office. There are spaces to record allergies, blood type, health problems, eyeglass prescription, or any other health history that may be necessary for international travel. In case of an accident or loss of consciousness, many things could be determined immediately by reference to this certificate.

A Cholera Certificate of Immunization is required by some countries (for example, Senegal) before entry. If after being there for a time, entrance to another country is sought, that country will also want to see the cholera immunization proof because of a recent presence in a country with cholera risk.

U.S. Control Center of Disease (www.cdc.gov) prints a "Blue Book" every two weeks listing the diseases to be concerned within each country of the world and the precautions to take.

HEALTH CONSIDERATIONS

Infectious diseases caused by bacteria, viruses, protozoa, and worms are numerous and potentially dangerous especially in the developing world. Sanitation standards and controlling vectors of transmission are often lacking. Some developing countries use raw sewage to irrigate rice and corn fields, and disease can cycle repeatedly in this unsanitary environment. Most countries teach healthcare and prevention, but the people do not always practice it. Travelers must use common sense and must observe universal precautions. Visitors may not be able to eat or to drink what the local people do.

Health personnel are at increased risk for infectious disease. All clinic workers should be informed about basic safety rules and recommendations prior to starting any clinical work. Exposures to avoid might include body substances, contaminated supplies, environmental surfaces, or contaminated equipment, air, or water. Important information is available at the Organization for Safety and Asepsis Procedures (OSAP) website at www.osap.org. OSAP is dedicated to promoting infection-control and safety policies and practices supported by science and research to the global dental community. *"We are careful to use people in our sterilization area that have some medical training or who can quickly process the dangers. Not everyone is able to follow safe practices."*

Altitude sickness can occur when heights exceed 9,000 feet and quickly can affect an individual's quality of life upon exertion. Elevation can be a significant consideration for people compromised with emphysema, blood pressure issues, or heart problems. Sometimes it takes several days for red blood cells and the body to catch up with changes in elevation. The faster an altitude is reached, the more likely symptoms can occur.

Challenges include headaches, loss of appetite, resting pulse over 110 beats per minute, decreased urine output, nausea and vomiting, sleep apnea, pulmonary edema, and cerebral edema. Physically fit, confident people may be the first to experience symptoms as they may climb too fast. Travelers with serious health problems should check with their physician before going on a mountain mission. Prevention includes a slow ascent with a night's sleep at a lower altitude, followed by a gradual acclimation to significant elevation gain. A high carbohydrate, low fat diet and avoidance of overexertion helps. Medications include Acetaxolamide (Diamox) and Dexamethsone under a physician's direction. *"Elevation changes have been a real health factor for some team members on past trips."*

Malaria risk is a significant consideration in endemic areas and 250 million people are affected annually. Malaria in humans is caused by 1 of 4 protozoan species transmitted by the bite of an infective female *Anopheles* mosquito. Africa missions hold the greatest risk. The national host should inform the team when malaria is a concern at the time of the trip. Mosquito transmission of malaria is most likely to occur between sunset and dawn. Personal protective measures include:

* wearing body-covering clothes
* applying DEET insecticide (at least 15%) to exposed body parts
* treating clothing, hats, shoes, bed nets, jackets, and camping gear with permethrin will last through several washings (Permanone and Sawyer Permethrin are registered with EPA as they kill insects on contact.)
* spraying rooms with nontoxic insecticide or foggers
* screening windows if left open
* surrounding the bed with netting

Antimalarial chemoprophylaxis should be taken by all travelers before visiting areas with endemic malaria. These medications do not prevent infection of the malaria parasite but kill it in the blood stage of its life cycle. That is why prophylactics must continue to be taken for four weeks after leaving the area of risk. A preventive medicine doctor or national host can advise concerning when and how to take appropriate drugs. Medical attention should be sought immediately if flu-like symptoms develop. The most common anti-malarial regimes include:

* Doxycycline 100 mg once daily (started one day before travel and continued for four weeks after returning)

* Mefloquine 250 mg once weekly (started two-and-a-half weeks before travel and continued for four weeks after returning)

Traveler's diarrhea (TD) is the most common irritation on mission trips. This ailment is caused by contaminated water and food ingested by people lacking natural immunity to the local germs. E. coli is the most common causative agent of TD. Shigella, Salmonella, Campylobacter, viruses, and parasites can also cause TD. Most TD cases begin abruptly, are rarely life-threatening, are self-limiting, and resolve without specific treatment in a few days. A traveler with TD experiences three or more loose or watery bowel movements each day.

* With mild TD, traveling is not recommended while feeling ill. The patient should rest, drink plenty of fluids, take acetaminophen for fever, and wait for the illness to pass. Avoidance of acidic fluids, citrus fruit juices, aspirin, and milk products (due to lactose intolerance) is helpful. For mild cases of TD, Pepto-Bismol tablets two to four times a day may help.

* Severe symptoms of TD include nausea, vomiting, three or more loose stools in eight hours with abdominal cramps, fever, or blood in the stools. These patients may benefit from antimicrobial therapy. Ciprofloxacin 500 mg tabs twice a day for three to five days is recommended. Anti-motility medications (for example, Loperamide) may reduce diarrhea by slowing transit time in the gut and allow more absorption. However, using anti-motility medications with fever or bloody diarrhea can delay clearance of the causative agent and increase the severity of the disease. If symptoms worsen or do not clear up in a few days, travelers should seek medical assistance.

* Sensitive stomach tendencies may prompt travelers to ask their physician about taking—or carrying along—preventative antibiotics for TD. Avoiding spicy or questionable food and drinking large quantities of safe water may help. Taking two Pepto-Bismol tablets three times a day

can be helpful in overcoming the mild upsets which come from a change in eating habits.

Foot protection is often necessary, and it is prudent to wear flip flops in unclean showers to prevent fungal and parasitic infections, as well as to minimize the chance of foot cuts and injuries. Smart travelers keep feet clean and dry.

Water creatures are important considerations. It is important to know if piranhas, hippos, crocodiles, snakes, leaches, or infectious disease causative agents are present in or around a pool of water where the team might swim. Animals and insects can be carriers of serious diseases endemic to the region. Fresh-water swimming is not recommended. The ocean and the swimming pools are usually acceptable for swimming.

Animal handling can be risky. A bite from a dog or a cat that may seem clean and friendly could lead to a serious disease such as rabies. It is wise to avoid any contact with animals. *"I fed a cute and scrawny dog some scraps from the table and found I'd offended the cooks!"*

Local dangers can exist as there are few regulations and inspections in many developing countries. *"In some places we were advised to be careful under the gigantic mango trees, as mangoes could fall from a high distance and cause injury with contact. In Africa, we were told not to stand under trees where snakes might dwell."*

    ✢   *"In Cambodia, stay on the beaten path. Land mines laid during the civil war have been removed from most major tourist destinations, but unexploded ordnance exist in many places in the country."*

Skin punctures may occur during manicures, haircuts, acupuncture treatments, or piercings which may be inexpensive and tempting in a developing country. These services can pass hepatitis B or C or AIDS in some countries though nicks of a razor blade or other sharp, infected items.

Septic systems are often fragile in the developing world and may easily clog. Toilet tissue is placed in a side basket or garbage can in most places. Local personnel can advise on toilet tissue disposal. Some travelers carry extra baggies to help with sanitary disposal.

Transportation Tips

Transportation safety is important in any international country. Carry a two-way radio, a mobile CB radio, or an in-country cell phone that can be used to call for help, especially in remote areas. If there appears to be a civil disturbance, travelers should steer clear and find a temporary safe haven until the situation calms. Travelers should use the same common sense when traveling overseas as they would at home.

Vehicle accidents account for a significant number of travel-associated injuries and deaths each year. Though there may be pressure to press on despite adverse weather or road conditions, it may be an invitation for catastrophe. Riding in an overloaded, poorly maintained vehicle at night in the rain on a twisting mountain road is definitely not advised. Common sense is important. Seat belts should be used, if available. It is acceptable to ask whether drivers are rested and alert, especially for long excursions. Consideration of those who watch over the team is appreciated, and drivers should be encouraged to take appropriate breaks with adequate food and water intake. Short-term hard feelings can heal, but accidents may have permanent results.

Road rules vary in many countries. It can be unbearably unnerving to watch traffic maneuvers until an understanding and acceptance of the system occurs. Passing almost anywhere is usually acceptable, as long as oncoming traffic can slow down enough to allow passing—often with inches to spare. The right of way is given to drivers who get the nose of their vehicles slightly ahead of others. Headlights are often not required at night. Motor bikes can be present wherever there is space. Pot holes and road conditions determine speed limits. Many pedestrians, bikes, and animals are close to high-speed traffic. Two-lane roads turn into four or more lanes of traffic. *"One time in India we drove over piles of wheat upon the road and threshed the grain with our tires and seasoned them with our oil."*

A honking horn (several times a minute) constantly announces the vehicles' presence and demands others move aside. *"The more crowded and less-developed the area, the more irritating and useful horns seem to be. Our Bangladeshi driver could not continue safely when his horn malfunctioned, and he immediately sought a mechanic to fix it."*

Luggage on top of vehicles is often standard protocol, with resulting worries concerning theft or falling luggage. Good advice is to relax and to go with the local customs, while saying an extra prayer. *"We have had bags drop off moving vehicles and fortunately nothing critical was damaged."*

Street crossings are dangerous in many places. Although some major cities have traffic lights, red lights are often ignored, especially at night. One-way streets can have a trickle of traffic flowing the wrong way. Pedestrians do not have the right of way in most places. Numerous vehicles, bikes, carts, and miscellaneous creatures clog roadways and require extra caution with the unpredictability of their paths. *"I always try to walk evenly across the street, so the oncoming traffic can predict my speed and position better."*

Left side of the road driving is standard in some countries. In this case, tourists must look carefully both ways before stepping into the street. Stepping off a curb can be dangerous if normal instincts are to look left due to the orientation of right-sided driving.

Public transportation is the norm for many places in the developing world. In some places, the public buses are known for thefts. Nationals can advise about various transportation options.

Taxi costs should be set before traveling so that there are no surprises or exorbitant charges upon arrival.

Travel days take special preparations. Team members should take along sealed bottled water and snacks as meals are often off-schedule. Toilet paper is important to have in a pocket or pouch, since it is non-existent in most places. Sometimes attendants sell a few sheets of toilet paper at high prices.

Without a road for vehicles, they biked with a
dental clinic into a Bangladesh village.

WATER PRECAUTIONS

Water considerations should be the highest on a priority list of key points to know before going to a country. The hosts usually monitor this. Local water is often unsafe to drink, no matter how pristine and inviting it may look. Water can contain harmful micro-organisms, and parasites that may cause a variety of ailments, such as giardia, dysentery, hepatitis, and hookworms.

Water safety includes these five suggestions of how drinking water can be purified.

* Boiling water for ten minutes is the easiest way to purify water, provided there is equipment and time. Since water boils at a lower temperature at higher altitudes, boil for an additional minute at elevations. Boiling water removes the oxygen, and the water ends up tasting flat. The quality of boiled water can be improved by pouring it back and forth between two containers to replace oxygen or simply by shaking it.

* Chemical purifiers like iodine, chlorine, halazone, potassium permanganate, and other chemicals can purify water. It is imperative to follow directions on products specifically designed for this purpose. Typically they need to be mixed, and then must sit for designated minutes. For example, place 2.5 ml (one-half teaspoon) of regular strength Clorox in 20 liters of water (about 5 gallons) and allow to stand 20 minutes prior to drinking. Although chemicals are required, this method is often the most convenient, since carrying a few pills is simple. If the thought of chlorine is bothersome, consider that Americans have been drinking chlorine in tap water all of their lives. Some battery-operated systems work with salt and electrolysis, producing chlorine. With iodine kits, a second tablet is available that drastically reduces the chemical smell and taste of the iodine.

* Filtration is as simple and quick as pumping the water through a filter. Each filter is different, but typically the charcoal or ceramic filter removes 99% of bacteria. It does not remove viruses, unless a chemical is contained in the filter (which makes it a purifier). Filters have become much smaller, more effective, and less expensive. Parts will have to be replaced periodically, and the system must be kept clean. Overall, filtration is quite convenient.

* UV light water purification uses battery-powered SteriPens to produce UV light that kills everything, including viruses. This conveniently works in less than a minute and is only moderately costly, although the SteriPen often needs fresh batteries. A wide enough bottle neck for the SteriPen is required.

* Distillation is a method that can be used for either collecting water or gathering fresh water out of salt water. A basic "solar still" works by

digging a hole, placing a collecting container in the center, and covering with a clear sheet of plastic weighted in the center. As water evaporates it hits the plastic and runs down into the container. Salt water can be distilled by boiling, and the fresh water will need to be collected as it evaporates. One method involves using a large pot to boil the water, with a smaller, container placed inside. When the cover of the larger pot is inverted, the center points down; and water droplets will drain into the smaller pot.

Bottled water in an international country is a mandatory safety rule. It is the only acceptable drinking water unless water purification methods are instituted. Bottled water should be received only if it is opened in front of the buyer or if it is known to come from a safe source. When buying bottled water, look at the bottle cap to see if the seal is still intact. Sometimes enterprising people refill empty water bottles from the tap and recap them, selling them to thirsty tourists. Since reusable bottles may not have been thoroughly cleaned, it is prudent to check the top.

Water glasses may be dirty, and it is best if team members drink directly out of water bottles. It is wise to wash and to rinse dishes in sterile water (either boiled or chemically treated).

Coffee/tea are usually not a problem because the water is boiled during brewing.

Bottled sodas are generally safe and can be used if a source of safe water is not found. Canned foods, packaged drinks, canned juices, or any sealed product from the grocery store should be safe to drink and to carry along. A smart practice is to wipe or to wash off the possibly contaminated tops with a napkin or to use packaged straws.

Ice cubes are an easily overlooked source of pathogens. Ice that is frozen with treated water is probably safe.

Tooth brushing is accomplished using bottled water. When showering, it's best to frequently spit out any drops of tap water that sneak into a closed mouth.

Covering the faucet handles in the hotel bathroom with a towel reduces the risk of accidentally using tap water when half asleep. The toothbrush can also be marked with a tag that can be a reminder not to drink the tap water.

Staying hydrated is important to health. When travelling, savvy tourists carry a bottle of water and drink from it throughout the day. Thirst is not the best gauge of whether more water should be drunk. By the time thirst is felt, a person is behind in fluid intake. If urination is occurring several times a day and the urine is clear or light yellow, then hydration is adequate. Hydration can roughly be gauged by pushing fingernails to see venous return or by lightly pinching the skin on the hand which should rebound quickly. (Practicing this technique before leaving ensures knowing what a normal rebound should be.)

Water ingestion can be monitored by a "buddy system." Team member buddies check and remind each other to drink. Heat illness can progress from mild to serious in a very short time. Buddies should watch for symptoms of heat exhaustion: mild confusion, fatigue, nausea, vomiting, lightheadedness, dizziness, fainting, headache, copious sweating, muscle cramps, abdominal cramps, rapid heart rate, rapid breathing, pale and/or clammy skin, fever over 102° F. Cool or dry skin with "goose bumps" is a late sign.

Food Pointers

Dietary restrictions may affect some individual team members. It is wise to check on the availability of specific foods and to plan on taking a back-up stash of foods they can eat.

Local hosts are quite proficient at knowing what internationals can eat or drink safely, and they will discuss this with team members. The nationals often provide meals to volunteers. In most situations, team funds for meals will be necessary.

Local food is affected by how it is grown in developing countries. Many rural areas use untreated animal or human manure as fertilizer. Organisms such as amoebae, giardia, E. coli, and intestinal parasites are common in areas where people fail to separate their human solid waste from the water and the food supplies. Each meal must be observed carefully before taking the first bite. Avoiding pastries, raw vegetables, salads, cabbage, or fruits that cannot be peeled (or are punctured) is important. The tip of a banana should be cut off before taking a bite because little flies or worms could be residing in the exposed end of the fruit. Seafood and shellfish are difficult to preserve without spoiling and should not be ingested. Eating undercooked beef, pork, lamb, poultry, unpasteurized dairy products, or raw eggs is not wise. Silverware is best wiped with a napkin before using.

Vegetables/fruits should be purified before eating. Evident dirt is washed off first with tap water. A soaking solution of chlorine or iodine (several times more concentrated than that used to purify water) is used for fifteen minutes to ascertain good penetration. The manufacturer's directions for the chemicals and the purification products should be researched before the trip. The developing country populations often lack good toilet and hand-washing facilities. Only a few volunteers have experienced such problems in developed countries because of carefully maintained sewage treatment facilities which break down the harmful germs before they can recycle into the food and water supply.

Kitchen work requires caution. Helpers should rinse hands frequently in purified water (boiled or chemically treated) so as not to draw microbes in the tap water back to the food supply that is being prepared. If cooks are sick, others should take over the cooking.

Unclean fingers can bring contamination or germs to mouths, noses, and eyes. Travelers should not touch faces.

Normal eating habits should continue on a trip as much as possible. Travelers often joke that "on the road calories don't count." If only that were true! If a usual home morning meal is a bagel and juice, a solid week of large breakfasts could cause significant weight gain. Fitness goals can be sabotaged if one doesn't ask 'Is this what I'd do at home?' Normal eating routines should be followed while still allowing for opportunities to sample local cuisines.

Food unavailability can be an issue. It is smart to carry snacks of nuts, dried fruit, or energy bars. A plastic jar of peanut butter is easy to pack in a checked bag, since it doesn't need refrigeration, is a great source of protein, and makes a quick, cheap meal when coupled with crackers or local bread. (A plastic knife must be packed.) Since in many countries there are no decaffeinated beverages available, travelers may want to take along herbal teas or instant coffee.

Food self-preparation by the team can be convenient and money-saving. Basic food supplies can be procured locally, and some items can be brought from home. These items could include prepared mixes of all kinds, powdered milk, canned foods, dried foods, peanut butter, puddings, cereals, mayonnaise, tea bags, and coffee. Paper plates, plastic wrap, aluminum foil, and plastic bags might be helpful. Local hosts can advise. *"With large teams we brought a cook (this was her ministry) who spoke the local Spanish language, and a kitchen facility was available for her to prepare our meals. Food supplies were purchased at a local market, and the cost of meals was greatly reduced. They tasted better, were safely prepared, and much more convenient for the team."*

Food stalls are not recommended eating venues in developing countries. The meat must be well-cooked, and the soup must have a lengthy boiling time before eating. *"Many of my seasoned travel friends say they wouldn't miss eating the mouth-watering local specialties available, at very reasonable prices, at food stalls. Others never go near them. One must size up a stall, the clientele, the vendor, the food offered, and how it is cooked."*

 • *"We were taught in Army training that bread is safe. The baking temperature kills the bad bacterium inside the loaf, and the crust protects after baking—just don't eat the crust."*

 • *"Newbies on the mission field often want 'authentic food.' The reality they soon face is how difficult that is to accomplish without getting sick. Usually it's after adventurous forays into a forbidden eating venue that the lesson comes home to these rebellious eaters in the form of an 'episoodie of the booty' as we have lovingly declared the 'end' results of unwise eating."*

      ✻   "As a veteran of a hundred trips, I have been very sick several times, so I'm naturally cautious."

CHAPTER 18

Cross-Cultural Information

CULTURAL DIFFERENCES

Culture definitions refer to the total way of life for a particular group of people. It encompasses their assumptions about the world, the customs, the traditions, the language, the belief systems, the social structures, and the norms. People look at the world and process experiences through their own cultural lens. People see the world and make moral judgments in many different ways.

Local hosts help with cultural understanding and differences and are often accustomed to having teams that need assistance with local cultural do's and don'ts. *"Culture is like the air we breathe: taken for granted, but impossible to live without."*

    *   *"Listen to the local nationals! They live in the culture and the environment and know where the dangers are and aren't. In Brazil, on a tributary of the Amazon, our dental clinic and Vacation Bible School site backed up to a lagoon. The piranha's red bellies flashed in the afternoon sun. When the village kids kicked a ball into the lagoon, I started yelling at them, certain they would be nothing but bones in a matter of minutes. Then I noticed no one in the village showed any concern for the kids who swam in the lagoon all the time, only for the 'crazy gringo' who was screaming. We are very presumptuous when we enter a culture and environment we have never been in before and think we know more than the locals."*

Local differences in customs, culture, values, dress, and food can be celebrated. God has led the team here to open hearts and minds to the ways of others. The diversity encountered can be experienced without judgment. It is important not to make political statements or to criticize local facilities, volunteer and local healthcare professionals, patients, and others in the community. Even though all people are different, God allows everyone to be one in Him. *"People are more alike than their cultures. In cross-cultural encounters we are meeting long-lost, distant relatives."*

This dental team learned diverse traditions from the Maasai in Kenya.

Local issues may bring sensitivity. Not all countries are as open or as argumentative as the visiting team may be. Questions about specific areas—such as opinions of government policy or the country's history during a stressful time—can be dangerous and sensitive for the local national or interpreter. *"I am prepared to notice rapidly when I have overstepped boundaries and drop the subject with a quick, 'Sorry, I am just a stupid foreigner,' or even encourage interpreters to point out when I am inappropriate. For example, asking about police practice can open wounds if a local national has had relatives with bad experiences."*

The Internet is a good source of information, as all countries will have their own unique set of cultural and physical differences. The team can research the customs, the beliefs, the social strata, and the physical setting. The history of that culture can be traced to obtain understanding.

Homework assignments by the team prior to going will help everyone learn more about the country. These reports could be given at a meeting, where everyone has made copies of his or her research for other team members. Topics may include information about the target country:

* Brief historical summary
* Population, size, bodies of water, and resources
* Major religions, strength of the Christian faith, toleration of Christianity
* Form of government, names of important leaders, and relationships with the international community
* Family, social structure, current social issues
* Associated languages, simple phrases and greetings (See suggestions under "Interpreters.")
* Five major cities and team target locations
* Financial backdrop, currency, exchange rate, poverty level
* Interesting cultural ideas, cross-cultural sensitivities, body language, and communication appropriateness
* Interesting lifestyle differences, food, indigenous plants, animals, and birds
* Tourism, entertainment, shopping, and fine arts availability for the nationals and tourists

Cross-cultural ministry can be stressful for most people. First trips are challenging as it is a huge adjustment to experience developing countries initially. Each team member experiences life changes during the project, many of them enlightening and spiritually enlarging. However, travel is tiring, the food different, the sleeping arrangements possibly uncomfortable, the weather challenging, the language barrier frustrating, and the hard work exhausting. This combination produces stress. Turning adversity into teachable moments may mean that volunteers need to see challenges not as interruptions but as points where they have reached the end of personal resources. Then, everyone is in a position to learn new and exciting lessons about the power or sufficiency of Christ and other important personal lessons. Teachable moments occur when team members realize how much Americans are pampered and accustomed to having their way. Consider how the team's rights and comforts are insignificant compared to Christ and His sufferings here on earth. He was not concerned about His comfort, what He ate, or where He slept. *"We can adapt to some discomforts or differences for the cause of Christ. These are the experiences that can make the mission life-changing. We desire to direct ourselves toward dependence upon God, not being self-reliant or allowing unhealthy emotions to distract us from God's purposes."*

High-context cultures refer to places where people have much history together. People operate as if everyone is an insider and knows how to behave. Latin America, Asian, and Middle Eastern countries are difficult to visit as an outsider. People in low-context cultures (for example, America, Western Europe) have connections for shorter durations, therefore, less is assumed. Information is more straightforward and understandable for the western mindset than the assumed behaviors of the high-context people.

Independent individualism is often valued in the developed world, and decisions are based upon what the individual deems is best for his/her life. A westerner is likely to say, "I'll think, do, and go where I want, and be responsible to no one but myself." The "collective society" is much more important in many other countries, where people view themselves less autonomously and more as members of groups. They're concerned about the effects of actions upon the group as a whole, and decisions are made by consensus rather than individually. They are not always purely unselfish, but they're programmed to think about the goals and the needs of the group rather than to consider their own individual needs first.

Power distance refers to how "far apart" leaders and followers feel from each other. In many countries, titles and status are revered; superiors and subordinates are unlikely to socialize together; and leaders cannot be questioned by subservient people.

Physical proximity differs in high-contact and low-contact cultures. Proximity is measured by how close individuals stand when in casual contact with acquaintances. North Americans often prefer 20 inches between people, Latinos like 14-15 inches, and Middle Easterners are comfortable with 9-10 inches.

Time perception varies in cultures. North Americans are much more time-conscious and time-driven than those in many other cultures and think the clock is what determines when events start and end. Punctuality communicates respect, excellence, and conscientiousness. In contrast, less-industrialized cultures are far more interested in emphasizing the priority and the obligations of social relationships. Events begin and end when all participants feel the time is right, rather than artificially imposing clock time. A watch may not be needed on the mission field. Nothing runs on time—buses, trains, church services, meetings, and cultural events. The best advice is to relax, to kick back, and to leave the day planner at home. *"It is said of North Americans, 'they have the watches, but we have the time.'"*

* *"If we in North America say we'll meet at noon, it means that everyone is expected to be present about one minute before noon. In other cultures, it's different. If a meeting is planned for noon and the host is having a conversation with a friend, the conversation takes precedence over his/her timely arrival at the meeting. If s/he breaks off the conversation by looking at a watch and saying there is a meeting across town at noon, it could easily cause offense."*

* *"Our dental team attended church. We were told that church started at a certain time. We were there before the appointed time and then a few people arrived and fellowshipped. Then more arrived and started singing. The actual service started after thirty minutes. The pastor had noticed me looking at my watch and said, 'If the purpose of church is to worship God together, why would we start before everyone is here?'"*

* *"In many developing countries, the people don't just work toward finishing a task. They build friendships in the process. When shopping, they learn all about the shopkeeper—his children and his wife's recent operation. Relationships are built, and the shopper walks out with the shopping item and a new friend. That new friend just might come to church with him next Sunday!"*

* *"In some countries, such as parts of India, driving conditions can be so unpredictable that a distant meeting time can only be approximated. If you need to be at an appointment by a specific time—for example, with a high church leader—make sure you leave with enough time built into your schedule."*

Nonexistent privacy, in particular, can be unnerving to North Americans, where living is all about capitalizing on and demanding private space. In most other cultures, privacy is not a priority or a possibility. It may be normal to be jammed into public transportation and to be required to share bathrooms.

Cleanliness standards are a challenge in some places. In many cultures, people might not be in the habit of bathing daily. Notions of cleanliness do differ. In some places, a wet bathroom is considered a clean bathroom.

Oppressive poverty can affect team members. Some volunteers are grief-stricken by the need they see. Very few countries enjoy the standard of living to which the team is accustomed. *"It may help to remember that material wealth is not always synonymous with happiness. This does not excuse the vast economic disparity witnessed in travel. However, it is important to remember that we are not on the mission to share material wealth but to share the richness of knowing Christ."*

Social status, social stratifications, castes, or hierarchical pyramids occur in many cultures. It is good to be aware of these principles. *"In Mozambique we were thought of as a cross between Superman (due to our high-tech dental equipment) and Santa Claus (due to our generosity.)"*
* *"In the Dominican Republic, there is a social pyramid defined by skin color where whites hold higher status and black-skinned people—like Haitians—are at the bottom."*
* *"One missionary expressed offense and accused us of racism as we were sweating taking out a difficult tooth, commenting that Africans had harder bone, longer tooth roots, and stronger muscular-skeletal systems than many from other*

races. We had to explain how it was different to pull teeth on people from varying racial backgrounds due to the genetic makeup of their tooth and bone structures. He finally understood."

CDS' members work with an international team in Cambodia.

Educational levels of the national adults and children are helpful in understanding physical and spiritual well-being. Assessing their work environment, lifestyle, and everyday routines are clues to oral, medical, and mental health issues. Lack of oral hygiene, nutritional deficiencies, infectious disease, and other stressful conditions may be endemic and can affect how the team views and treats patients.

International holidays or religious celebrations are important to honor in the countries to be visited. This is especially important if plans take the team there during those times and may involve adjustments. *"One team worked on a local holiday ('because we came so far and didn't want to waste a day'), and ended up offending the local nationals."*

Shrine etiquette is important to know. Hindu and Buddhist temples, Muslim mosques, and even some Christian churches may require scarves on women's heads. Sometimes wraps are available to rent or to borrow. It's often considered inappropriate to wear shorts or above-the-knee clothing in many places of worship, and women should cover their shoulders. Many places of worship require the removal of shoes before entering. Pointing toes at any image of the Buddha is considered sacrilegious. Some temples and mosques are off-limits to travelers who don't practice the faith or to women. Respectful silence is necessary when visiting a house of worship. Cameras are often prohibited. *"In Moldova we visited an Orthodox Church, and they wouldn't sell us a cross from the gift shop because we weren't Orthodox. Since we felt we are Christians like they are, it did hurt our feelings."*

Culture Shock

Culture shock is the psychological disorientation that results from living or working in unfamiliar environments when experiencing different cultures.

Adjustment phases during culture shock are common, as noted by Dr. F. Serio, D.D.S.[61]

1) A "romantic/tourist" phase occurs initially when everything seems quaint, and the excitement and the euphoria of new experiences blur cultural differences. The new culture is fascinating and full of observations and new discoveries. There is an initial engagement with functioning in an unfamiliar environment.

2) A "lost-that-loving-feeling" phase follows. Curiosity gives way to frustration as feelings of irritation, anger, and helplessness often join with fatigue. These feelings may be pronounced if a volunteer is sick. Language barriers, obvious differences in public hygiene, traffic safety, food accessibility and quality may heighten the sense of disconnection from the surroundings. Homesickness, loneliness, and hostility at the situation and conditions may set in. There is an overwhelming urge to change everything so that conditions are the same as they are at home.

3) A "recovery" phase occurs when the new culture's ideas and practices do not seem as strange. Problem-solving skills in dealing with

the culture develop and acceptance begins. The culture begins to make sense and negative reactions are reduced. Self-confidence returns. There is a gradual adjustment in the development of a level of comfort with the culture and the situation.

4) Cross-cultural "acceptance" phase has been reached when differences are understood and expected. Humor and relaxation returns. Adaptation, or biculturalism, occurs when coming to an understanding of the situation on national terms, not the volunteer's terms.

Contributing factors often bring culture shock: unmet expectations, unrealistic goals, lack of results, familiar values questioned, and misunderstanding of cultural rules. Symptoms of culture shock may include homesickness, boredom, withdrawal from the group, irritability, excessive need for sleep, exaggerated cleanliness, family or team tension and conflict, stereotyping and hostility towards host nationals, inability to work effectively, and psychosomatic ailments. *"Culture shock is a real phenomenon, especially for those who have never left their own country. As much as you read, and as well as you are coached, you can never be fully prepared for the impact of the international environment on your senses and emotions. The language and food are often different; the activity is intense; and the smells are peculiar. You're always on your guard to avoid sickness. It is difficult to abandon all of the reflexes you've accumulated over your lifetime. Since the U.S. has only 4% of the world's population, there's no reason to believe that the rest of the world behaves the same as North Americans."*

Environmental changes can influence culture shock. Changes in one's mental status from jet lag, dehydration, and sleep arousal patterns due to unfamiliar noises contribute to discomfort. *"Have enough personal familiarity to know when something is genuinely important—like if you are going to faint or if you feel yourself in the presence of legitimate harassment. On the other hand, many overwhelming and apparently urgent feelings of discomfort can be managed by telling yourself that 'it's just a feeling' and thinking back to other times when you have encountered false, but overwhelming sensations. This may be just your mind playing tricks on you."*

Addressing issues when an individual is experiencing culture shock is important. Each person's adaptation will determine how effective s/he will be and the benefits s/he will receive. These are suggestions for adaption:

* Get ready to trust the Lord actively and deliberately. Believe God will provide and prepare to flex.

* Look for logical cultural beliefs behind everything in the host culture that seems strange, difficult, confusing, or threatening. Take every aspect of the experience and search for patterns and interrelationships. Try to trace actions, habits, or ideas that appear "odd" to their underlying values. The differences seen, while foreign and unexplainable to you, make perfect sense to the nationals. It can be fun to discover the reasons.

* Suspend judgment and avoid the temptation to generalize. (Example: "All Latin Americans are...") Embrace—not disparage—the host culture. Listen, observe, and try to understand.

* Ask the national hosts when confused about important cultural issues, do's and don'ts, how to greet nationals correctly, and male/female issues.

Cultural adaptation tips help people adjust. As Dr. L. Greene (missionary physician) says, "These experiences remind me of the mountain climber's explanation for why he does what he does: 'It's just like fun, only different.'"[62] Dr. Tim Dearborn gives the following advice.[63]

* Laugh. Find the humor in the situation and specialize in laughing at yourself (not others).

* Listen. St. Francis had it right. Seek first to understand, rather than to be understood.

* Learn. God hasn't sent you into the culture to be its judge.

* Love. It's the universal language.

* Live. Enter in, enjoy the differences and live as a servant.

Labeling Countries

Labeling terminology varies when describing countries. "Developed country" and "developing country" have been chosen for this manual, but there are many labels used to refer to countries. Most commonly, the criteria for evaluating the country's degree of economic development is all a subject of debate. The criteria include the gross domestic product (GDP), the per capita income, the level of industrialization, the amount of widespread infrastructure, and the general standard of living. Whatever term one uses is a generalized stereotype which may be occasionally useful but will be inaccurate much of the time. Some terms follow:

* Developed, industrialized, or a "more economically developed country" (MEDC) is a sovereign state that has a highly developed economy and advanced technological infrastructure. Developed countries are often described as having post-industrial economies—meaning that the service sector provides more wealth than the industrial sector.

* Developing countries have a lower Human Development Index (HDI) relative to more developed countries. The HDI is a composite statistic used to rank countries by levels of human development, including a measure of health, education, and income. Developing countries are in the process of industrialization.

* Undeveloped countries are pre-industrial and demonstrate an almost entirely agrarian development.

* The "Third World" term arose during the Cold War to define countries that remained non-aligned with either NATO (the North Atlantic Treaty Organization—the U.S. Western European nations and their Allies representing the First World), or the Communist Bloc (with the Soviet Union, China, Cuba, and their Allies representing the Second World). This description is often now considered negative. The Third World was normally seen to include many countries with colonial pasts in Africa, Latin America, and Asia.

* The "Majority World" term came about in the early nineties, when the Bangladeshi photographer, Shahidul Alam, began advocating for this new expression to represent what had been known formerly as the "Third World." The term highlights the fact that these countries are indeed the majority of humankind. It also brings to sharp attention the anomaly that less than ten countries—whose decisions affect the majority of the world's peoples—represent a tiny fraction of humankind. Thus, it is a descriptive term of where most of the world lives. Alam

argued that "Majority World" defines the community in terms of what it is, rather than what it lacks.

* The "Fourth World" term refers to sub-populations that are socially excluded from global society, such as hunter-gatherer, nomadic, pastoral, and some subsistence farming peoples living beyond the modern industrial norm. This sub-population may exist in a first world country, but with the living standards of those of a third world or developing country.

* Least Developed Countries (LDC) may be seen as having strong negative connotations that reinforce the stereotypes about poor communities and represent them as icons of poverty. By considering only the economic development, there is also the question of summing up a nation which may have great cultural heritage as less developed. According to the United Nations, an LDC exhibits the lowest indicators of socioeconomic development with the lowest Human Development Index (HDI) ratings of all countries in the world. A country is classified as LDC if it has poverty with a very low per capita income, a human resource weakness—based on indicators of nutrition, health, education, and adult literacy—and economic vulnerability—based on instability of agricultural production, instability of exports of goods and services, economic importance of non-traditional activities, merchandise export concentration, handicap of economic smallness, and the percentage of population displaced by natural disasters. Other terms and statistics may introduce the label of a "less economically developed country" (LEDC).

* "Two-thirds World Church" or "Majority World Church" show that, since the year 2000, more than two-thirds of the Christian church lived outside North America and Europe. This term was coined by church leaders gathered from these nations at the 2004 Lausanne Committee for World Evangelism in Pattaya, Thailand.

CAUTIOUS STEREOTYPES

Stereotypical labeling involves a preconceived idea that one group of people may have about another nationality, culture, sex, or race of people. A stereotype is held as a standard, a formula, a pattern, or a mold describing another group of people. Travelers must be cautious when making cultural or stereotypical assumptions about others or when thinking their perceptions are accurate.

Developed country residents often hold stereotypical ideas about international people from less-developed countries. Negative stereotypes may include these traits: innocence, laziness, inefficiency, slowness, indifference, poverty-stricken, uneducated, corrupt, requiring help, and much controlled by culture and customs. Positive stereotypes include the observances that developing people often live interdependently with intergenerational family members, live more in harmony with nature, and hold to spiritual, contented, and servant-oriented lives.

Developing country nationals often negatively think that people from developed countries are aggressive, harshly pragmatic, tense, discontented, corrupt, wealthy, materialistic, dominating, loud, obnoxious, overbearing competitive, selfish, self-centered, hold an attitude of national superiority, and are preoccupied with efficiency. Positive stereotypes of developed country people include their superior education, reliability, strong individualism, confidence, organization, efficiency, and tendency to have more secure and favored lives. *"Every country has citizens who drag it down, but we must guard against feeling culturally nearsighted or superior because of our resources, our education and skills, or our confidence. We only can thank God's grace for the advantages we've been given. Others may be remarkable in how they have overcome obstacles to live in trust and optimism."*

❖ *"We've discovered that often our American behaviors can be offensive and unattractive to people in other lands. With our warm, outgoing mannerisms, natural curiosity, and freedoms, Americans are not always understood by the citizens of other countries. Americans appear loud and boisterous."*

❖ *"In overcrowded lands, people who live in close proximity with thin-walled houses have learned to speak softly. We were warned to keep our voices down, as we didn't wish to be thought rude."*

❖ *"Americans value cleverness and joking, but that is often foreign to other cultures. They don't always understand the laughter and think the humor might be at their expense."*

* *"Face saving' is important in some 'shame or honor' cultures. It is the all-important issue in many Eastern cultures like China and Japan. A cross between pride and social status, 'face-saving' is all about appearances; yet, its cultural roots run deep. Shame someone publicly, and that friendship may be lost for life; making him/her look good will help the team go far. What makes people lose and gain face is complicated, but respect is the key issue. It is treating people with a sense of worth, since there is an emotional significance and self-worth that is attached to how others feel about themselves."*

BODY LANGUAGE

Body language may have significant meaning in other cultures. The bottom of the foot should be flat and facing down in many cultures (for example, Thailand and Bali). Blowing one's nose in public is considered rude in some places (for example, the Philippines). *"The head is considered sacred in SE Asia, so it is improper to touch a person's head."*

Anger expression is seen in many cultures as the greatest of sins. Crossing arms or putting hands on hips, as well as raised voices and confrontations, are considered bad form.

Hand symbols in cultures differ. The way hands are used in America may be obscene in other cultures. (For example, the "thumbs up" sign is not a positive gesture in some cultures.) The left hand is not used in some cultures. Another example is using both hands—or only the right hand—to give and to receive objects. Never use only the left hand. *"In Bali it's also impolite to point with the index finger. Gesture with the whole hand instead."*

Eye contact, in general, is acceptable among members of the same gender; but direct eye contact can be inappropriate between genders. However, when talking to an elder, many people tend to look down out of respect. This practice can also be true with women speaking to men. In some Muslim and Latino cultures, a woman who meets a man's eyes is considered brazen or inviting. It is best to avoid drawing attention. When possible team members should radiate confidence, while being discreet and unassuming. Guests should maintain a calm, mature approach in all situations. *"In Cambodia, a young girl was quite upset when an older American man knelt to talk to her when she was sitting in a chair, with his head below hers. The older, more respected person must have his head higher."*

    "In East Africa, raising both eyebrows at the same time means 'yes.'"

CAREFUL COMMUNICATION

Considerate communication with the nationals is well worth the effort. Language use helps one to become an insider, as everyone appreciates an attempt at using the local language. It's smart to follow these guidelines:

    Use signs and simple words, smiling often while acknowledging others.

    Ask questions, listen to people's stories, and find out how they live and what they believe.

    Make friends and discuss worldview issues—although questions should be considerate.

Offensive words can be unknowingly spoken to people from other countries, and it is wise to understand what may offend. Words such as "dirty," "squalid," or "filthy" may be truly descriptive but may be considered rude. However humble the "hut" or the "shack" may be, it is the best the people can afford and should be called a "home."

Cultural colloquialisms can be troublesome. Expressions are frequently not translatable in other languages in a way that will give the meaning they have in America. It is safer not to use them. (For example: to "make a pig of yourself" is a common expression in America. But in some lands, calling a person a pig, even in jest, is a serious insult.) It could take a long time to undo the damage caused by the careless use of phrases.

Critical complaining or sarcastic remarks are inappropriate within earshot of nationals or internationals. Many locals understand enough English to know what is being said.

Individual favoritism has no place in the field. Volunteers are cautioned to avoid lavishing praise on one national individual above the others. Be kind and friendly to all, but not to one person more than another.

Contact information generally should not be shared. It may be best not to give e-mail addresses, phone numbers, or Facebook contact information to nationals. One of the joys of a mission trip is meeting and interacting with foreign nationals. Logic and common sense are necessary if corresponding back to the field after returning home. Americans are often seen as very wealthy and generous people, and this perception could result in requests that can be awkward to handle and can create difficulty for the national missionaries or church. The local host leader can provide guidance when unsure about any request from a local person.

Appropriate greetings vary in cultures, so ask the host how these should be handled. Usually, a handshake and a smile are the standard greeting etiquette for both genders. Handshakes tend to be energetic and very often linger a bit. Sometimes close female friends may hug and kiss when they meet. *"A smile is a universal and primal thing, mighty beyond words. We use a smile whenever possible."*

    *   *"Every country seems to have its own way of greeting, so we check first, if possible. In Kenya, adults had a three-part handshake— clasped hands in "soul brother" style changing to a hand shake, and then back to the clasped hands. For children, we placed a hand on the child's upper forehead—almost to the hairline. I was patting their heads and was told to just place the hand on the forehead once briefly."*

    *   *"In some countries the women kiss on both cheeks, and in some countries they kiss on one cheek."*

    *   *"In India, we placed our hands under our chins, with 'palms together,' and bowed."*

Initial contact is quite formal in many places, and titles are often important. Politeness dictates use of the person's first and last name until invited to use his/her first name. International visitors should call their business counterparts by their title and last name unless requested to do otherwise (for example, "Reverend Smith"). After first meeting the eldest or most important person in the room, it is often customary to greet everyone in the room. This is done with a handshake and eye contact for everyone before talking to a particular person.

Multi-language conversations must include everyone present—using an interpreter if at all possible. *"One Moldovan spoke for a half hour with his friends in front of us and never summarized the topic, although we knew he spoke English. We felt very uncomfortable without even a brief translation of what they discussed. It was a good reminder to always include others in some way whenever conversing around those of other languages."*

Opposite gender discretion is a must. It is prudent to avoid being alone or talking alone with someone from the opposite sex. Even married couples should limit excessive shows of affection. In Muslim countries it's often considered improper for a male to kiss a female or even to offer his hand to a women until she has offered hers first. *"Cambodians find public affection so inappropriate that even newlyweds are forbidden to kiss at their wedding ceremony."*

Cultural misunderstanding and misinterpreted expectations will likely occur in some situations. *"In India, a hesitant or bland version of 'yes' probably meant something a little closer to 'no.' There was also a conflicting cultural stigma about 'yes' too quickly. To be polite one has to be asked to dinner at least three times and then it is acceptable to say yes."*

    ✦   *"Be careful in complimenting indigenous people's possessions, since their cultural tradition is then to give it to that person. We had several incidents where this happened, and we are now more careful. Our daughter was sharing the gospel in the home of a woman who was known for her chickens and commented on the nice chickens. At the end of the visit, the lady picked out her best chicken, wrung its neck, and handed the bleeding carcass to my daughter!"*

Technology use while on the mission field is controversial. Some say cell phones and social media is a distraction, and others think it is important to keep others aware at home of happenings on the mission field. *"We* *encourage team members to take a break from phone and social media contact, minimizing use, or detoxing from technology altogether, if possible."*

* *"Do not promise that team members can call home. They are there to serve and to focus on the mission. Give an emergency number to family members— usually the sponsoring leader's cell phone number or the ministry's number. Our policy is usually 'no news is good news.' Parents and families should not expect a call. They will hear in the event of a problem. We suggest that each team creates an e-mail or phone/prayer chain list so that word can be passed along at home."*

* *"We think that supporters expect to hear from us frequently, before, during, and after the mission trip. Don't disappoint them. Nothing sparks an interest in God's work around the world like being involved in events as they are happening."*

* *"Some groups ban iPods and cell phones by make the following appeal: 'We're using common transportation, so while on the road we also need to converse with fellow team members and listen to common music. This will keep us focused on one another and strengthen our fellowship. And this will open us to pay more attention to the people we're going to serve.'"*

Food Customs

Safe food questions are appropriately asked of the host country leader privately. Some meal items might cause stomach problems for visitors.

Gratitude expressed for the accommodations and food—whatever they may be—is greatly appreciated. The nationals are most likely giving the best they have to offer. *"Food is an idol for some team members, and it can become the focus of attention on mission trips. I like to think that I eat to live, not that I live to eat. But some mission experiences can teach us how much our gluttony controls us. In my month in Honduras, I had 83 meals of rice in a row, including breakfast. The rice left over at the end of the day was, with a little sugar, our breakfast cereal the next morning. We learned how the majority of the world eats every day, month, and year."*

Lunch meals are the main meals of the day in many countries. Dinner becomes a light snack or may be another full meal. Dining late at night is common in hot countries.

It is customary to share a plate of food in Senegal.

Different protocols for eating exist. All team members need to watch how the locals eat and may ask questions. Not all restaurant menu items listed are available. Since ordered food can come out separately and slowly, is it polite to eat before the others receive their meals? Patience is often required. *"In Malaysia it is considered bad manners if the food touches the hand too far up the finger, past the second knuckle."*

    ✦   *"When in India and many other countries, eat only using the right hand. The left is used for bodily hygiene and is considered unclean."*

    ✦   *"In Bangladesh, we were given our own fork and spoon at the beginning of the trip and were expected to bring it with us the entire two weeks. Many villagers ate with their fingers and did not have silverware."*

    ✦   *"A Muslim hostess may not join the meal, as they often eat separately from the men."*

    ✦   *"In Hong Kong the international guest can offer to pay, even though it will probably not be accepted. Do not offer to split the bill, as this will result in the loss of face for the host."*

* *"Placing chopsticks parallel on top of a bowl is considered bad luck and synonymous with a funeral ritual and death in some places."*

Local invitations from a national family should be accepted if possible, as it might be offensive to the hosts if the invitation is refused. Dining together is a great opportunity; however, the host national should be contacted for advice. It is a great chance to experience and to learn much about an international country. There is something spiritual about sharing a meal together. Meals can be a prolonged, adventurous social event. *"It isn't always crucial to know what exactly is being eaten."*

* *"It is often appropriate to bring some sweets or flowers for the host. If in doubt, ask national leaders what is expected."*

RESPECTFUL CLOTHING

Clothing strategies often are revealed after consulting the Internet or the international news to prepare for the expected weather for the destination. Altitude can greatly affect the temperature and the humidity within a country. Layering clothes maintains comfort in a range of hot or cold weather and involves having light undergarments that can be worn during the day while it is warm, and then adding a long-sleeved shirt or sweater in the evening. A long-sleeved shirt helps avoid insect bites and protects against sunburn irritation. Clothing should be versatile and professional unless construction jobsites are the goal. (See Personal Packing in Chapter 22.)

Appropriate dressing by team members shows honor to the culture. Women should dress modestly and have their shoulders covered. Women should not wear shorts or pants unless given permission by the host organization. Men should not wear shorts either, unless cleared by the nationals. It is usually acceptable for women to wear Capri pants, jeans, and shirts with sleeves. Tank tops, spaghetti straps, and uncovered midriffs are not allowed. It is impolite for men to remove shirts in public in some cultures. Clothes or accessories that advertise inappropriate topics, the military, and nationalities should be left at home. The mission team members are representing their faith, not the government. If swimming is anticipated, a modest bathing suit is appropriate. *"I wear a Canadian hat at times if I am concerned about a locality that may not favor Americans."*

Conservative Christians often live in rural areas of developing countries. Local women often do not wear pants, shorts, jewelry, or makeup. One dentist's wife said, *"I often face a 'wardrobe dilemma.' I only take one carry-on of clothes since our other luggage is all dental. It's usually gratifying to enjoy the life of minimalism as a refreshing change from American culture. Since most of our trips take place in extremely poor areas, I usually pack a few older, inconspicuous clothes from home, my hospital scrubs to work in, and leave at home my diamond wedding ring and other unnecessary accessories. It is not unusual to feel concerned that I've packed the wrong clothes, but I choose not to focus on that. I aim to be ordinary and modest."*

* *"When in doubt, I take a conservative outfit or plan to buy one locally."*

Shoe removal inside a house is expected in some places and reflects cleanliness and respect.

APPROPRIATE GIVING

Local tipping questions can be asked of the national hosts. Better yet, the national hosts can take care of tipping for the group. The Internet tipping resource is www.tipping.org. Tips are expected and assumed in some places. *"In Egypt everything is accomplished with extra cash incentives, and everyone assists for a price. Tips are expected to enter the doors of the airport, to send bags to the airline, to use the restroom, and to obtain water. Worse, there are no set fees. Service providers are usually supported by tips and not by their employers. We had compassion for the individuals once we understood the system. Even if we didn't like it, we accepted it as a cultural norm."*

* *"An American doctor and wife attached themselves to our team for an 'after-mission' short cruise. When the expected—and basically required—tips were given to the crew, they refused to contribute. We explained that it's the only income the workers get, and it would be rude to refuse; they still wouldn't give.*

We decided to pay their amount out of our team's fund, since we couldn't insult the workers in that way."

 ◆ *"In SE Asia, tipping is not a local custom; but it is expected of internationals, especially at larger hotels, restaurants, and for taxi use. If the service is poor, do not feel obliged to tip."*

Persistent begging is handled best by the trip and country host leaders. Locals will sometimes give an emotional plea for assistance for their struggling family. It is easy to meet nationals who seem especially deserving of help. They may have winsome personalities and fervent testimonies. Caution is necessary. While their need is valid and team members may have the ability to help, it is not appropriate for a plea to be made directly to team members. There's no pressure to meet these needs and commitments. *"Give all financial help through the missionary in charge, the field project coordinator, the local pastor, or wait and send it to the organization. Let the supplicant family know that the individual team members are giving all help through the local pastor or leaders. The responsible person there will know how to present the help in a way that will not hurt the ministry. Don't worry about not getting credit for the gift from the nationals. God knows of the gift, and it may be better if the nationals don't know."*

 ◆ *"There are many other nationals in that country who also need help just as much or more. It would be easy to create havoc in the church if offers to help include only a few individuals. The others may assume the missionary singled them out for help over the rest."*

 ◆ *"If a choice is made to personally give to beggars, it is best to carry small bills or coins. Another option is to give to Christian-based local ministries working with the poor, since money begged for is sometimes used for drugs or alcohol."*

Gracious kindness is appreciated by local waiters, hotel employees, clerks, and other nationals. Teams go with the goal to show the love of God. If not pleased with a service or a situation, it is advisable to be calm and constructive. It is not culturally appropriate to make demands or to show dissatisfaction. In most cases it is better to seek help from a leader or a guide before frustration sets in.

Flight attendants who give good service will greatly appreciate acknowledgement. They have a demanding job and are not allowed to accept tips. But, a smile and a "thank you" may make their day.

CONSIDERATE PHOTOGRAPHY

Respectful photography with cameras and video equipment should be followed. "Point and shoot" can insult the dignity of others. People in extreme poverty or difficult life circumstances should not be considered a spectacle. Being compassionate will be appreciated. If in doubt about photographing a scene or a person, the team leader should be consulted. Any objection by others to photography should be respected. It is unacceptable to sneak a shot and to make an enemy.

Photo opportunities may present as picturesque or amusing—such as people carrying baskets on their heads, riding small burros, or going about some other common custom of their country. It is polite to ask the missionary/project coordinator to get the photo subject's permission for the team to take photos. The national will know whether a small coin should be exchanged for the privilege.

Relationship focus is best when taking pictures. *"Before setting forth on a summer mission trip, youth from a North American church used disposable cameras to take pictures of 'home' to show their young mission partners in Mexico. The Mexican youth received cameras and the same instructions. When the youth compared their photos, the North Americans noticed that most of their pictures depicted possessions, while most Mexicans took pictures of people. The North Americans thought long and hard about why their worldview seemed more defined by stuff than by relationships. They pondered how to pay more attention to family and friends."*

Photographing children is usually a delight to all involved. Children crowd to see the digital camera screen after taking a photo. With the Internet, it is easy to email pictures to the national host—if approval to do so is obtained in advance. *"A Polaroid camera is a wonderful door opener in many instances.*

Offer to give children a picture of themselves if they will let the group take one to keep. We used this well in Guyana, but Polaroid film is very expensive and fogs in airport machines (so does some printer film). A local printer might help if the host national knows of one. Also, this takes much time, so is best handled by someone on the support team."

Prohibited photography include pictures of government officials, government sites, police or military personnel or installations, international airports, border crossings, bridges, or oil refineries. International governments fear subversive interests. Many houses of worship, historic sites, and tombs in Egypt are off limits, and the guards may confiscate memory cards from digital cameras. Pictures of people without clothing can be misconstrued or illegal in some cases.

Memory cards can be separated from cameras when not taking pictures. It's a simple method to ensure that any photographs taken will be safe even if the camera is stolen. *"I travel with two cameras: a digital SLR for the majority of the shots, and a small disposable camera to use when asking strangers to take pictures of me. As much as I tend to trust other people, I'm not ready to hand over my $1,000 camera to someone I don't know."*

Planning scripts to share upon the team's return ensures a focus for the pictures. The main aspects of the clinic or project can be illustrated as it develops. The people are the focus when shown in their best setting. The radiant spirit of transformed Christians communicates well in pictures and it is fair to show the scenes the team would want shown of them in their own country.

Camera knowledge will help. A telephoto lens without a flash and high-speed film might take less obtrusive pictures. Since award-winning pictures are most often close-ups, a telephoto lens will get closer while people are acting naturally. A camera with fill flash may yield better pictures of dark-complexioned people. A lens brush will help keep the camera clean. Cameras and film should not be left in hot vehicles.

A team member juggles for the delighted children in Swaziland.

CHILDREN INTERACTIONS

Children everywhere are similar in that they are almost always happy, have abundant energy, and simply want to play. Preparing props or games to use around children can ease many situations, helping to connect beyond the language barrier (for example, Frisbees, soccer balls, softballs). Stickers and small toys from thrift stores are great icebreakers that are easy to pack. *"Wherever you go in the world, kids seem to know 'the rock, paper, scissors' game."*
 • *"We had great fun teaching international children the 'Hokey-Pokey.'"*

Acknowledge children with love and caring around the clinic. It is important to be "safety conscious" and "soul conscious" with youth.

Children can "seem to be in the way;" but if a child is driven from the work area, it may cause a hurt that is difficult to heal. A team member or a national person could be assigned to provide ministry with some games or Sunday School-type activities the team has prepared ahead. Children need to feel appreciated and wanted. Dr. Wes Stafford (children's advocate and founder of Compassion International) says, "Every child you encounter is a divine appointment. You have the power and the opportunity to build the child up or to tear the child down. A life can be launched with as little as a single phrase, an uplifting word, or an act of kindness. The spirit of a little child is a lot like wet cement. When a child is young, it takes little effort to make an impression that can last a lifetime."[64]

Favoring children over other children can hurt feelings. *"We use a stuffed animal that patients can hold when in the dental chair. We gave it to our last patient, who we thought was the only child around. When another child came back to comment, we told her the child had been a good patient. 'I was, too!' she answered. We knew then we'd made an error and also said the wrong thing. We made several mistakes in that instance and learned a lesson!"*

Gift suggestions for children include these items:
- Toys: inflatable balls (pack deflated), matchbox cars, blocks, sticker books, puzzles, baseballs, magnet boards, hand puppets
- Games: educational DVDs in local language, chalk for hopscotch or drawing, jump ropes, deck of cards, and dominoes
- Craft or school supplies: notebooks, pencils, backpacks, calculators, construction paper, blunt scissors, clay, markers, crayons, beads and string, school glue or glue sticks
- *"We've enjoyed making chickens out of dental gloves. Blow it up like a balloon and tie it off. The fingers fan across like rooster headdresses, the thumb becomes a nose, and eyes and a smile with teeth can be drawn on with a marker. The children love them, and they are sturdier than regular balloons."*

Savvy Shopping

Local products can be interesting to purchase. Woodcarvings, glass, pottery, clothing, gems, furs, and rugs may be obtained at greatly reduced prices in many countries.

Polite bartering is a way of life in many places, and it's a great way to break the ice. Haggling adds to the shopping experience in markets. Bargaining will vary from country to country. *"We found in India, for example, the first counteroffer was 40% of the asking price and hopefully the negotiation can meet in the middle. In Turkey, it was usual to bargain only for a 10-15% reduction. Ask national host personnel what they consider the local bargaining rules to be."*

Bartering tips may help:

* Always be polite, but firm. Even if the item is not purchased after bargaining, it is important to leave on good terms.

* If the item cost seems affordable, it doesn't have to be an "amazing deal." It is not necessary to haggle over pennies or even dollars, if one considers the merchants' lifestyle. The extra income could make a big difference in their lives. If it seems reasonable, then it is fine to pay a little more.

* Most tourist shops will take foreign currency (especially dollars and euros) and give change in the local currency. Larger establishments often take major credit cards and will package and ship items (like a rug) to the buyer's home.

A happy child holds a glove "rooster balloon" in Nepal.

⁕ The negotiation, the purchase and the relationship made with the merchant is a process to enjoy and not to rush. Chat and have fun with it. It is best not to look at the price of the same item later in the market, as it may be upsetting. Satisfaction with the item and the experience is the goal.

⁕ Part of the shopping strategy is to look disinterested in the item desired. It is best not to ask the price right away or to touch the item. After asking the price, start to leave if the item seems too costly. The merchant will usually offer a better price. It may cause offense if the shopper makes an offer and then backs out.

* A larger discount may be part of the bargain if interested in buying more than one item.

* Souvenirs made from wildlife skins (including reptiles and shells) can't be exported.

* Shipping and payment arrangements should be communicated early in the negotiations. If paying by credit card, the price may be higher. If paying in cash, see what kind of discount this will add. If shipping an item, make sure that there is agreement upon shipping method and time frame.

* The shopper should not feel pressured into buying something not wanted. *"At the Great Wall in China, I was cornered by several hawkers and felt forced to buy an overpriced t-shirt to get them to leave me alone. When my husband noticed I was missing, he came back and found me crying and upset over their pushiness and intimidation tactics."*

CROSS-CULTURAL DEBATES

Smoking/drinking prohibitions on mission trips is a decision many Christian mission teams accept, even though some team members feel this is not specifically denounced by Scripture.

* Cultural sensitivity often dictates this policy. In most overseas projects, smoking and drinking are viewed by the nationals (especially those in rural churches) as inappropriate behavior for Christians. *"As guests in their country, we defer to their standards and norms, since we do not want to compromise our witness."*

* Due to rampant alcoholism, many developing countries have health issues, socio-economic problems, and family, church, and community upheaval. In many countries, drinking is considered inappropriate (for example, Muslim countries). *"We try to support those cultural beliefs and rise above any possible criticism as we attempt to display Christ-like examples."*

* In many mission locations, there are restrictions against smoking in certain areas. Smokers tend to withdraw from others when finding a location to smoke. This works against the goal of the unity that is nurtured on missions.

Dancing activities can also be objectionable in some national churches and welcomed in others. Checking with local hosts is advisable.

Dating habits may differ in other cultures. Singles should be sensitive culturally and careful with other singles on their team or among nationals. Many teams make it a policy that "dating" or coupling on mission trips is not allowed. The purpose of the short-term experience is to concentrate on each team member's personal relationship with God and to work together as a team. Dating hinders these objectives and will cause an individual to possibly forfeit a life-changing experience. *"An in-country dental assistant who was about the age of one of our single women flirted with her, but he spoke only his national language. The team member's friendliness was misinterpreted, and the situation was uncomfortable for her."*

Interaction policies established between youth and adults are helpful. Some missions involve minors either within a team or with nationals. The customary procedure is the "two adults" rule—where a minimum of two adults should be involved in the supervision of youth at any given point. Team members should avoid any situation where they are out of visual contact with others when talking to singles or those of the opposite gender. Displays of encouragement, such as a pat on the back or a hug, should be done only in the presence of the group.

CHAPTER 19

Financial Issues

————◆————

GENERAL INFORMATION

Before traveling, knowing how to access more money abroad in case of emergencies is prudent. Only cash is accepted in some countries because exchange rates are so volatile due to inflation. Local establishments may not be familiar with traveler's checks or credit cards. The local national host will help with these concerns.

Team money is best handled by the sponsoring organization and/or local national leaders. Whenever possible it helps if the local host pays all team expenses, as s/he can communicate best and know the normal costs and customs. From the time the nationals pick up the team at the airport, they take care of the fees, transportation, food, lodging, and tips, and ensure the money is well spent. *"We have found the best scenario is to pay directly into a tax-exempt sponsoring organization, who works out a budget with the host country leaders who will take care of all team finances."*

Spending money for individual incidentals and for shopping is basic. It is a team member's individual choice on how much to bring relative to the in-country expenses and expected souvenir costs. Depending on the country, $100-$300 in cash or traveler's checks is usually a good estimate.

Carrying cash in large amounts into a country to pay expenses is sometimes unavoidable. The cash may be distributed amongst team members. To insure accountability, it is important that each carrier accepts the responsibility, counts the money, and records the amount, so that any lost or stolen money can be tracked. *"One team member was careless with safeguarding the team money and some was taken. He blamed the team leader for giving him less than the others and wouldn't accept any fault. It was* *uncomfortable, so now we have all team members count and record the team money they received.*"

Team money funds ("a kitty") can be assembled where every team member puts in some amount to be used to pay for group expenses such as meals, entry fees, and rest room tips not covered by the host nationals. It saves calculating each person's share at every stop. At the end of the trip, the remaining amount can be split among the members.

Money theft or loss of valuables out of international hotel rooms can occur. A suitcase or a briefcase that locks is helpful. A cloth suitcase can be cut open, but a hard side with tab locks is a good deterrent to theft. There is usually a disclaimer for hotel safes in international countries. Most hotels will not be liable for any loss, even if it is their safe, because several people will have the combination. *"I put my valuables in a hard-sided suitcase or keep them always on my person. My money and passport stay on me at all times. There are money security belts, bracelet, collars, socks, and ankle bands to keep money safely on a person. Try not to let anyone see where an individual's money and passport are kept."*

 ❖   *"Rather than locking individual bags, I've used a cable lock through the handles of several bags. Not that this would prevent a determined thief, but the opportunist who wants to grab and run will be deterred from taking this bundle from a train cabin, rental-car trunk, or loosely attended baggage room."*

Locking valuables in an organization's safe is preferable to keeping passports and cash with the team members. However, there are places where passports are required at security check points when traveling around the country.

Hotel Internet and phone usage are often billed to individual rooms. Team members who used these services must be prepared to pay their own bills.

Monetary rules of import and export are important. It is possible to leave from or return to the U.S. with as much money (currency, coin, traveler's checks) as is desired. But if the value is more than $10,000, the individual must fill out a Currency Reporting Form, available from U.S. Customs. The penalties for failing to report are severe. Since the regulations involving importing and exporting money to/from other countries may vary, do the homework.

Dental charging for services provided in other countries is important to some missionaries who do not wish to create an entitlement mentality in their constituents. Dr. David Stevens (Christian Medical and Dental Associations' executive director) says, "I once asked national co-workers why they wanted to charge people who are so poor. They said, 'Our greatest natural resource is our people. If you give it to us free, you make us beggars. If they pay for the clinic services, however, their dignity remains intact.'"[65] *"One missionary in Belize said, 'I charge the patients a small fee for services, which they come expecting to pay. I charge $5 for root canals, cleanings, and fillings. Extractions go for $2.50. I want them to value the dentistry and contribute to our ministry.'"*

Tax deductions for businesses or for those who itemize deductions (use schedule A of Form 1040) are allowed for mission trips as long as the expenses are paid to a qualified tax-exempt organization that demonstrates recognizable charitable work. (See IRS Publication 526.) Volunteer time can't be deducted, but any reasonable expense incurred as part of the mission can be considered as a charitable deduction or a business donation. Retaining receipts for plane tickets, supplies, expenses, transportation, food, lodging, and all costs incurred for tax deductions is advised. If it is difficult to keep receipts on food and lodging expenses, it is possible to access international per diem rates (average day rate costs) by country, published by the U.S. Department of State under www.aoprals.state.gov/default.asp.

A 501(c) (3) tax-exempt organization has been set up by some volunteer dentists through which to funnel all expenses, but it is complex and not recommended unless mission/humanitarian work becomes almost a full-time endeavor.

CURRENCY ACQUISITIONS

Money values constantly change in all countries. Exchange rates are figured against hard currency such as the dollar or the euro. Smart travelers call a major bank or look online or in a major newspaper for the comparable value of currencies. Carrying a "cheat sheet" that includes exchange rates and metric conversions is helpful. Currency conversions are available at www.oanda.com.

Exchanging money in the host country is usually much easier and cheaper than at a U.S. bank. The national leaders are adept at this and know where the best exchange rate can be found. Local banks generally offer better rates of exchange than hotels, restaurants, or stores. Rates are often posted in windows. Sometimes private currency transactions carry the risk of travelers being swindled or stuck with counterfeit currency. A calculator can help figure the value of goods purchased and the amount of change.

Before exchanging international currency back to American dollars at the airport when leaving an international country, it is wise to find out if there's a departure tax. Some countries ask for a fee before continuing to the gate and have only expensive options for those without local currency, such as an exchange booth with notably poor rates. Usually, what is left over is a small amount, which can be given at the airport to the host leader for the ministry.

Mint condition bills are required in many countries where exchangers desire clean, fairly new, undamaged American dollars without any writing, graffiti, folds, or wear. Before leaving home, any money planned for exchange should look new—or ask the bank specifically for brand-new bills. Most places take American dollars and will give back change in the currency of the local country.

Closed banks upon arrival in an international city can be a problem. If it is not possible to use an ATM, only the money needed for the night may be converted. Some exchange booths offer a less favorable rate after banks close and then switch to competitive rates when banks reopen.

Small bills are useful for tips or small purchases.

ATM use abroad is not advised for everyone and is not always available. Some international ATMs don't allow access to savings accounts. Experienced travelers carry their bank's local phone number (complete with area code), as 800 numbers generally don't work overseas. *"One friend always travels with what he calls the "trusty four"—American dollars (lots of ones and fives divided up and hidden in several locations), traveler's checks, an ATM card, and a credit card. He says, 'Some people think that traveler's checks aren't necessary anymore, but they really can be useful in a variety of situations. My ATM card wouldn't work on Easter Island, where most restaurants did not accept credit cards and wanted to be paid in pesos. Luckily, our hotel cashed my traveler's checks and gave me the pesos I needed."*

Credit cards and traveler's checks can be used in most places internationally. Card and check numbers as well as the phone numbers to call if lost or stolen should be kept in a save place. Credit card companies charge a finance fee for ATM withdrawals. Notify credit-card companies involving cards that might be used on the trip before leaving home. Without this notification, the company might put a hold on the card due to "unusual" activity—like a charge for a restaurant in an international place.

Funding Missions

Individuals support their own mission trips primarily and are glad to do it as a form of giving back of their time, energies, talents, and finances. Most dental practitioners are able to finance their own travels and can budget for a working, mission-oriented, adventure of sharing and giving. (See Chapter 2: "Mission Benefits.")

Raising support plays an important role in mission trips for many others. Some sacrifice is rewarding for individuals going on the trip. Donating for someone's mission service is also a remarkable opportunity for others. Supporters can know and be grateful that their contributions will serve God's purposes.

Involving others in prayer and financial support blesses many people. Sending letters soliciting support is often beneficial, and examples are shown later in this chapter. It is a great example of service for family, friends, and community members who watch how missionaries live as Christians. This volunteerism has helped to build the practice of dental personnel when patients realize that their dental professionals are giving back in humanitarian ways.

* Supporters give because they believe their gift will change lives. They need to understand how their gift will impact the people of the trip/country.

* People often donate when they feel informed. Enlightening them is helped by answering these questions: Why am I going? How will the money be used? How can others be involved? How will it positively influence me? When givers feel as much a part of the trip as those who will travel, they may donate more money. Informative communication with givers before, during, and after the trip provides a sense of participation. They need to know that their support is being depended upon.

* Donors contribute when they see that volunteers are completely committed and enthusiastic about the mission. People are excited to see others with a passion and are then inspired to support them.

Fundraising challenges require much planning and work. Regrettably, fundraising may be met with animosity and apathy. Though God could chose to meet the financial needs miraculously through unusual circumstances, He often provides financial support as team members observe the Biblical mandates listed later in this chapter.

Team participants often break costs into units. One financing model shows how the larger body of Christ works using both those who send and those who travel.

* 1/4 contributed by the team member
* 1/4 raised by the team member through support letters
* 1/4 raised by the team member through fund-raising events
* 1/4 raised by the whole team and evenly divided by participants

These fundraising questions may be included:

* What will the church leadership allow in fundraising efforts?
* Are there worthwhile and successful ways to involve others in fundraising?
* How will records of funds received be kept?

Fundraising ideas are limited only by the imagination and energies of those participating:

* People may attend a pancake breakfast, spaghetti dinner, box lunch, or golf tournament. The hope is that attendees will also give above and beyond the cost.
* Garage or bake sales are great for both individual and group fundraisers. With the current gourmet cupcakes fad, it's sure to be a hit either before or after church. All customers can be told about the trip and where their money is going. This is an excellent way to build relationships.
* A silent auction uses donated items from businesses connected with the church. Others auction off "white elephants" for a congregation-wide junk swap.
* School fundraiser ideas can be borrowed: half-baked or build-your-own pizzas, cheese and sausage combos, or cookie dough.
* Car washes work well for groups. Church leaders or a local car wash business can be approached to see if they will host the event. Then the group can pitch in to buy soap and sponges. A fee can be charged per car or the event can be donation-based. It can be fun, build teamwork opportunities, and provide good income.

Rent a team member. Door-to-door offerings for lawn and garden services may be exchanged for donations. Most neighborhoods have residents who could use the help. This will give team members the chance to witness to neighbors, to earn some support, and to serve people in their local area.

Local businesses may sponsor individuals on mission trips for a charitable tax-deduction. The best way to approach this is to write a cover letter asking for them to sponsor a portion of the trip, such as a day's worth of expenses. Businesses that are advertised or connected with the church may be the easiest to approach.

Churches may donate towards mission trips and set aside a portion of their budget for this. Presentations can be given to church leaders or small groups, and a support letter can be written describing the trip. A church mission committee may vote to support the mission or to allow a congregational offering.

Change collections encourage friends to do something useful with all those coins that accumulate. It can be emphasized that dollar bills are also acceptable.

Biblical Mandates

Biblical scriptures endorse the communication of a team member's need and a request for prayer partners.

Paul asked for assistance in carrying out his vision to share the Gospel. "...to have you assist me on my journey there. . ." (Romans 15: 24). "I planned to visit you...and then to have you send me on my way. . ." (2 Corinthians 1:16).

The rejection of people should not be feared. "When I am afraid, I will trust in you. In God, whose word I praise, in God I trust; I will not be afraid. What can mortal man do to me" (Psalms 56: 3-4)?

It is important to remember that everything belongs to the Lord. ". . . for the world and all that is in it is mine" (Psalm 50:12).

When sowing, results can be expected. "And God is able to make all grace abound to you, so that in all things at all times, having all that you need, you will abound in every good work" (2 Corinthians 9:8). "Do not be anxious about anything, but in everything by prayer and petition, with thanksgiving, present your requests to God" (Philippians 4:6). "And we know that in all things God works for the good of those who love him, who have been called according to his purpose" (Romans 8:28).

    ✦   Honesty with God, without apology, is essential. The financial need is not the only goal. As a child of the King and a royal ambassador, prayer is encouraged. "...whatever you ask for in prayer, believe that you have received it, and it will be yours" Mark 11:24).

    ✦   God can give His boldness to His followers when it is requested. "For God did not give us a spirit of timidity, but a spirit of power, of love and of self-discipline" (2 Timothy 1:7).

    ✦   It is best not to compete or to compare the results of one with others who are also raising support. "The acts of the sinful nature are obvious...jealousy...selfish ambition...factions...those who live like this will not inherit the kingdom of God" (Galatians 5: 19-21).

SUPPORT LETTERS

Support letters often result in a group of people who will join with the individual or team to pray and/or to contribute funds. These tips help in composing a support letter.

1) Word process the letter, if possible, or write in black ink.
2) Be concise and keep the letter to one page.
3) Write something interesting to engage the reader.
4) Include this information:
    ✦   the goals and the sponsors of the mission
    ✦   the location of the mission
    ✦   the dates of departure and return
    ✦   how others can participate through prayer (list 3-5 specific prayer items)
    ✦   the specific amount of financial support needs

* how to give financially (for example, "make checks payable to this church")

* provide a self-addressed, stamped envelope as this increases the chances of return

* a "thank you" for their consideration of being part of a support team.

5) Proofread the support letter and ask someone trustworthy to give feedback. Pray that the letter will be effective in communicating individual and team mission goals and that God would touch the hearts of people who read it. Pray that supporters will be blessed.

6) Consider sending the letter to 20 to 40 people, including relatives, old friends, neighbors, patients, or clients.

7) After sending the letter, contact each person by phone or in person to ask his/her response and to answer their questions. Write a note of appreciation immediately to those who commit to supporting in prayer and/or finances.

8) Within three weeks after the trip, write a follow-up letter to all supporters. Do this while the experience is still fresh. Tell them how God worked for individual and team mission goals. Include some new insights that occurred. Realize that their support may be needed in the future and that a thorough follow-up letter will be remembered.

Support Letter Example #1:

(Your address) followed by two blank lines

(Date) followed by three *blank lines*

(The recipient's address) followed by two blank lines

Dear Dr. and Mrs. Jones, followed by one blank line

When I heard the dental team's report to the church upon their return from Africa last year, I felt compelled by the Lord to join the next trip. They have decided to go to Mexico this year, and I plan to be part of the team. We will be holding dental clinics in several locations to draw the surrounding neighbors to each church. Local pastors will witness to our patients, invite them to accept the Gospel, and welcome them to the church. These congregations all have ties to our church denomination. A local dentist from a nearby community will be serving with us, and we hope to encourage several American missionaries who are there.

I am asking you to join with me as I praise God for this opportunity to serve on the mission field. Please also pray that our team will be unified and will be able to work in good health. Pray that those in the church and community will have open hearts to the Lord through our dental treatment and evangelism.

The cost of the trip is $2,500, due August 1ˢᵗ, which includes the on-site expenses and airfare. I have been able to contribute towards some of this cost myself and have received funds from my family and the mission committee at church. I am looking for 15-20 additional people who will be part of my "sending team" and who will pray for me and will contribute $50-$100 each towards the dental supplies needed to treat patients. If you would like to be one of my "senders," please return the tear-off section below. Checks should be made payable to: Denver First Church and mailed to Denver First Church, 100 Main Street, Denver, CO 34567.

Thank you for considering being a part of my team! I will keep you informed of our progress.

Yours in Christ,
(sign name, leaving 3 spaces for the signature)
Mary Smith

I would like to assist (name)_____for the missions project to Mexico

_____praying for her weekly before and daily during the mission trip

_____contributing $_____towards her financial needs

Name_____

Phone: _____

Address/Zip_____

A diverse team brings a six-chair dental clinic into the Dominican Republic.

Support Letter Example #2:

(Date)

Dear Friends and Family,

(Begin with some personal remarks about your life in general...)

I am writing to tell you about a wonderful opportunity I have to go on a dental mission trip in the spring of 20__. Christian Dental Society is a nonprofit organization which desires to impact healthcare by following Biblical principles. This trip will provide dental personnel with opportunities for international service in underserved communities, as well as personal spiritual growth. CDS is sending a mission team to_____ from March ____ to _____.

The majority of our time in _____ will be spent in _____ community. During our time there we will be utilizing a portable dental clinic to treat a wide variety of dental problems including extractions, fillings, and cleanings. In addition, we will be visiting schools in the community to educate children on the importance of oral hygiene. We also will be offering eyeglasses and sunglasses in our eye clinic.

I am extremely excited about the opportunity to have an impact in the lives of people in _____. I am anxious to put my dental training to work in a place that greatly needs it. For me, this trip is the perfect opportunity to combine my passion for healthcare with my desire to help those in need.

In order for me to attend the trip, I am responsible for raising support. The total cost is (insert price) per person which covers travel, lodging, meals, and miscellaneous expenses. If you would like to be a part of my financial support for the mission trip, any help would be greatly appreciated and is tax deductible. Please fill out the information on the enclosed slip to indicate your donation is to help me. A return envelope is enclosed for your convenience.

Many heartfelt thanks and blessings to you,

(Signature)

Disturbing Objections

The overwhelming numbers of underserved patients needing dental care at home is often an argument used to discourage dental personnel who desire to take their skills to the developing world. Other concerns involve the realization that since there are so many dental problems in the developing world, the team cannot hope to make a difference—"so why try?" These criticisms are answered by explaining that the primary reason for CDS dental missions is for the positive, faith-building results that will affect the nationals and the team. The dentistry is often the door opener and encouragement for the local ministry and the dental personnel to share their Christian faith with the community and the patients they are treating. See Chapter 2 for a summary of the multitude of reasons for going on a dental mission and for the many benefits reaped while serving. *"Since the dental needs are endless, extracting or filling one more tooth— or cleaning one more mouth— should not be the overriding goal of a dental mission trip. It is more important to share God's love and to be a witness to God's kingdom as the team uses their gifts to help others."*

The expense of short-term trips is also often criticized. It is true that mission trips may be costly; but, if one sees the money as an investment in the growth and the discipleship of others, it really is not. Dr. L. Greene (missionary physician) says, "Since youth are often engaged in the short-term mission effort, let's not hesitate to spend $1,000-2,000 to alter indelibly the mindset of a young person, to establish a world view of missions, to help a teenager mature spiritually, to inspire fervent prayer for missionaries, to change lives, and perhaps to plant the seed of a future missionary. It is said that approximately $500 million is spent on short-term missions in one year. Compare that to these expenditures that same year: chewing gum - $2 billion, video games - $6 billion, CDs and tapes - $14 billion. The expenditure on a short-term mission, therefore, actually seems insufficient by comparison." [66] *"When compared to the thousands of dollars people often spend on vacations that have little lasting significance, short-term mission trips bring a huge return."*
  * *"A mission trip is tax-deductible (often up to 50 % of costs can be saved)."*

"Participating in a dental mission trip gives a wonderful significance and refreshing outlook to the professionals who use their gifts to impact a hurting world. Dental team members experience a different culture and people groups as they go in obedience to the Great Commission. It is an investment in the spiritual life of all involved, giving understanding of God's purposes." (See Chapter 2: Convincing Reasons.)

Stewardship responsibility may provoke some people to ask if money should be sent directly to the mission field. Can the local nationals do the work better and cheaper without the international team? This objection may be correct in limited cases, such as some basic construction projects or to provide services already available locally—if the only goal of missions is to get the job done. This is rarely the case in dental missions. One cannot send money to provide nonexistent dental services. *"Since quality dentistry is not available in most developing countries, it is essential that dental personnel go to help in the many areas of great need worldwide and it opens the areas to the Gospel."*

Spending money wisely is often discussed. Remember the woman who poured expensive perfume on Jesus before His crucifixion? Her display was unusual, but Jesus certainly did not condemn it. Some of those nearby rebuked her harshly, "Why this waste of perfume? It could have been sold for more than a year's wages and the money given to the poor." Jesus said, "Leave her alone. Why are you bothering her? She has done a beautiful thing to me. . . I tell you the truth, wherever the gospel is preached throughout the world, what she has done will also be told, in memory of her" (Mark 14:3-9). "Short-term missions have been criticized for their expense. Since many missionaries are barely able to make ends meet with their meager support checks, church members ask if we should just divert the short-term money to the full-time missionaries. I don't think we have to make a choice. Let's do both! The support of the full-time workers is important, but one way to accomplish this task is to educate members of the congregation about the missionaries' needs (Dr. L. Greene).[67]

"Anthropologists advocate that the world's remaining tribal groups should be left to themselves. These people do not realize how naïve their notion is!" says Don Richardson (author of *Peace Child* and missionary to New Guinea). "It is a foregone conclusion that even if missionaries do not go in to <u>give</u>, lumbermen, crocodile hunters, prospectors, or farmers will still go in to <u>take!</u> The issue is not then, should anyone go in, because obviously someone will! Rather, the issue is—will the most sympathetic person get there first? As the one who got there first to live among the Sawi, it was my aim to combine faithfulness to God and the Scriptures with respect for the Sawi and their culture."[68]

CHAPTER 20

Airplane Flights

———◆———

FLIGHT BOOKING

Patient humor is often important when transportation arrangements are made. *"Getting there is half the fun! My trip to Honduras took six airline flights, one bus trip, riding on a burra (a push-cart on a railroad track), a canoe ride, and a hike. The destination was not really as remote as it sounds, but getting there was a real adventure."*

* *"A team member hailed a taxi and found it had no floor boards for his feet. He overlooked that annoyance, but then found that the back of his pants became wet due to rain-soaked seats!"*

Flight booking is best done by the team leaders—after checking with the in-country host or others who have traveled to that destination to see what recommendations they might have concerning airport locations and time schedules. Some nationals may not suggest late night arrivals or departures for safety or transportation considerations. Sometimes the sponsoring organization will make travel arrangements, and the team leader can avoid this responsibility. The sponsoring organization, hosts, or Internet sites can advise on airport tax fees, local baggage fees, costs of connecting flights, and requirements for visas. Some visas can be obtained at the destination airport or a border crossing, and some visas must be purchased ahead of time. (See Visa requirements in Chapter 21.)

Tickets/passports must match exactly. The name (including the middle name or initial) and the date of birth on each ticket must be the same as the individual's passport in order for the ticket to be valid. *"We know several people who had to buy completely new tickets at the counter before a flight, since their name on the tickets did not exactly match their passports."*

Booking engines are often the easiest and least expensive way to make travel arrangements online (for example, Orbitz.com, Expedia.com, and Travelocity.com). These are high-volume, online travel agents and are valid places to research flights, costs, times of travel, and to allow actual booking of the trip.

Travel agents can be extremely helpful and can be easier to work with than booking engines. They are especially useful in obtaining volume discounts for groups of ten or more. There are a number of travel agents who specialize in helping charitable mission groups obtain discounts. *"After checking the booking engines, I often ask if the travel agents can come up with better, less-expensive flights, and sometimes they do. To avoid some of the hassle of doing it yourself, or when coordinating numerous people leaving at different times from different locations, a travel agent can decrease the stress."*

Better fares for flights departing and arriving often occur at larger, hub airports. Sometimes it pays to transport to major cities to catch a flight. Weekends, holidays, or busy travel seasons can increase costs, so shopping for the best dates may significantly alter fares. Booking on either side of peak travel seasons or holidays can possibly save hundreds of dollars. There may be good deals at the last minute. When planning a mission trip, however, there are often numerous travelers and a fairly rigid schedule to follow. Therefore, it is best to plan ahead.

Flight times and airport choice considerations enhance a trip. Flying early in the morning might help to avoid bottlenecks, but it depends on the day of the week and the route. Since the proliferation of small commuter shuttles often clogs runways, a 7 a.m. weekday flight in a busy business corridor (for example, New York to Boston) may get caught in congestion. Also, not all airports are created equal. That is where the traveler's web site of the National Air Traffic Controllers Association (www.avoiddelays. com) comes in handy. It can help find the best time to fly from a particular airport and the best airports for any connections. It is also a good source for flight-delay updates.

Early booking generally provides the least expensive flights with the most options especially with groups. Booking 4-8 months early is recommended for a group wanting to fly on a certain schedule. Booking with a charitable organization or using the Christian Dental Society Designated Fund are excellent ways to make sure credit is obtained for charitable tax deductions.

Suitable seat selections are better and easier with earlier booking. Window seats are coziest for would-be nappers and for views, but window seats over the wing eliminate a picture window. On long flights, it is most convenient to be on the aisle for restroom and stretch breaks. Seats near lavatories are congested and noisy. Back-row seats don't recline. If the configuration has two seats on the side, this is preferable for couples. Getting stuck in a middle seat of four or five across in the center of a plane is designated for those who are not able to plan ahead.

One hour is needed between connecting flights in the U.S. and at least two or three hours to clear customs after arriving back in the U.S. before a connecting flight to ensure connections are made.

Travel insurance for airline flights may be worth paying for, if a cancellation is possible. Many team members cannot foresee any risks that might cause the cancellation of their trip. Paying for trip/travel insurance becomes an individual choice. Once booked, most flights are non-refundable unless there is a major, documented, life-or-death reason. It still may be extremely difficult to obtain reimbursement. Many trip/travel insurance policies cover trip cancellation. (See Travel Insurance in Chapter 17.)

Checked baggage fees are a moving target, and it is usually the team leader's task to investigate the individual airlines' online information. Most domestic flights now charge for a second bag, and some charge for both bags plus the carry-on bag. At this time, most international airline flights allow two, 50-pound bags to be shipped free. With local flights or smaller airlines between countries, the allowance for weight and bag dimensions and the number of bags—with associated fees—can vary greatly. When calculating the cost of transportation, bag fees may be a significant cost factor.

Checked bag receipts are important to keep in case the bag does not show up at the end of the flights. The receipt, the bag description, and the general contents are needed to file the paperwork to find the bag or to make a claim. A cell phone photo may help.

Separating items such as needles, anesthesia, and instruments into different bags will lessen the chance of having dental care affected if one critical checked bag is lost in transit. Containers and bags should be packed as tightly as possible. Soft items such as gauze, gloves, and masks can be used to protect more fragile articles. Items can be packed into waterproof plastic garbage bags to protect them against moisture. Hazardous materials, including anything combustible—such as butane torch fuel or other items that are considered combustible—cannot be shipped by air under any circumstances. Checking with the airline carrier for exact restrictions on shipped items may remove problems. *"I have not had any problems packing a small bottle or container of lubricant or ortho resin, but avoid large liquid containers and spray cans of disinfectant. I use matches to heat an instrument during endodontic procedures."*

⁕ *"We once shipped a spray can of disinfectant and got an angry letter from the airlines. They now have fines."*

Digital scales that are light-weight and hand-held are useful to weigh bags as close to 50 pounds as possible.

Light-weight gloves help protect operator's hands from scrapes and cuts when handling heavy luggage bags at home, in the airport, and on the mission field.

Rewards programs for air miles may be beneficial. Frequent fliers should sign up for them. Most international airways are allied with major U.S. carriers for frequent flyer miles. It's smart to accumulate "miles" on the major airline plans when possible. Some travelers get a credit card with an airline rewards program. Other tips include checking the travel restrictions when using accrued miles, using rewards before they go to waste or expire, and ensuring that miles are credited, by checking as soon as possible after the return flight. For record keeping, team members should save ticket stubs for proof, as disputes concerning "miles" or tax deductions may surface. The original boarding pass or documentation can come in handy months after completing the travel.

Pre-Flight Considerations

Before leaving home, arrangements must be made to cover home life.

* Mail or newspaper deliveries must be put on hold.
* Bills may need to be paid in advance or friend/family members are asked to help.
* Emergency contact information should be left with relatives or friends. This could include field contact phone or fax numbers or stateside sponsoring organization information.
* Air conditioning is turned up in the summer; heating temperature is turned down in the winter; and the water heater temperature is lowered to save on electricity and/or gas.
* Water lines into the house should be shut in case a water line freezes, especially in the winter.
* Perishables in refrigerators or on shelves should be addressed.
* Garbage is removed from the house.
* Care for pets, lawns, and plants is arranged.
* Window/door locks and lights on timers are checked.
* Neighbors, family members, or friends may be asked to check on the home periodically.
* Airport transportation must be arranged.

Passports, tickets, visas, immunization certificate, money, traveler's checks, and personal medications are important to remember. A list to be checked off at the last minute may help. Before leaving, the team leader should remind team members by e-mail or by text to bring their passports.

Airline schedules can be downloaded to get the most up-to-date information from individual airline websites before leaving home. When encountering a delay or a cancellation at the airport, the information needed to find another flight quickly will be available. If having to wait in long lines to be booked on another flight, a call to the airlines (800) number may be answered faster.

Passenger rights are important to know. There are rules concerning liability for lost luggage, compensation for delays, airline security, and other issues. The Aviation Consumer Protection and Enforcement Office's website details such rules at www.airconsumer.ost.dot.gov.

Airport security regulations and restrictions vary. Some airlines allow fingernail clippers and water bottles but most do not. Duct tape and zip ties must be in checked luggage, or they can be confiscated as items which can be used to restrain airline staff. Since duct tape is great for travel emergencies, a suggestion is to wrap a few feet onto a pen to make a miniature roll to carry. Containers over three ounces (like a larger tube of toothpaste) must be in checked bags. *"I place a copy of my diploma in every bag of dental supplies/equipment so it is the first thing customs officials see when they open the bag. They may not read English, but bureaucrats around the world recognize 'official' documents."*

Marked luggage will prevent others from innocently taking the wrong bag. A distinguishing mark—a bright ribbon, an identifiable sticker, or colorful ID tags—sets pieces apart. This distinction will help not only at the baggage carousel but also anywhere luggage accumulates, such as in a crowded hotel lobby. Bags must be labeled clearly, inside and out. The address (business address may be preferred over private home address), phone number (including cell), and e-mail addresses should be filled out clearly on luggage tags. Placing tags or cards with contact information inside the luggage in case the external tags are lost helps ensure luggage reaches the destination. *"When we have a large group of twenty or more people (which is at least forty bags), each bag is numbered and pictures are taken so we know what a missing bag looks like."*

Important items that are easily left on planes (for example, readers, tablets, and computers) should be labeled with return address tags. Personal items may be placed in a backpack or a large purse/bag that fits under the seat ahead—rather than on the floor or in the seat-back pocket. A business card may be taped onto the cover of a laptop. *"One security officer said they had an average of six laptop computers left behind each day, and most of the laptops had passwords that kept the owners' contact information hidden."*

Anti-nausea pills, such as dimenhydrinate (brand name Dramamine), are the most common over-the-counter medications used by travelers, although side effects may include drowsiness and dry mouth. For effectiveness, these must be started a day before departure. With a long trip, some travelers obtain a prescription from the doctor for scopolamine—a thumbnail-sized skin patch that is worn behind the ear.

Pre-flight exercising before heading to the airport usually gets one tired enough so that relaxation and sleep come easier on the plane. If there is no time for a pre-travel workout, a brisk walk through the terminal before boarding or a quiet place in an empty gate to stretch is recommended.

Dietary restrictions (for example, vegetarianism, lactose intolerance, or food allergies) are valid concerns and should be brought up to the airline before the flight. Then they can accommodate passengers, if possible, with appropriate meals on long flights.

Airport Concerns

Experienced travelers recommend arriving at the airport at least two hours before the plane is due to leave for overseas flights—three hours if the airport is large, frequently congested, or with the possibility of long lines at the security area. If the team is not all present to check in early enough, some bags may not get to the plane; and it is even possible that the airlines might cancel a late-comer's ticket. If bags are not checked in at least an hour before the flight leaves, airlines will not guarantee that the bags will get loaded on the plane.

Security requirements at the Transportation Security Administration (TSA) check points change often and differ in many locations. Global entry or pre-check passes help streamline airport security checks. Applications, fees, and instructions can be found at www.cbp.gov/global-entry/how-to-apply. TSA allows each person to carry on personal care products in three-ounce or smaller containers in a clear, quart-sized, resealable bag. Larger containers may be placed in the checked bag, but they will not be accessible until the final destination is reached. If this rule is not followed, the liquids will be discarded at the security check. The toiletry bag must be ready to be pulled out of the carry-on (for example, in a side compartment) with arrival at the security checkpoint, as it will often need to be put in the plastic bins separately from the carry-on. Items which can be used as weapons (for example, dental elevators and sharp objects) are confiscated along with items which could be used to restrain (for example, zip ties and duct tape).

Water bottle liquids are not allowed. *"We empty our water bottles before the TSA checkpoint and then refill them on the other side. Don't fill containers to the top since changes in air-pressure during the flight can cause the contents to expand and leak."*

Using restrooms shortly before boarding the plane can be a wise move. Planes may be delayed in taking off, and passengers may be discouraged from moving about the cabin. *"In bad weather or for mechanical problems, I have sat for several hours waiting for the plane to take off and could not get up to use the lavatory."*

Carry-on space for luggage in overhead bins can be filled quickly by other passengers. Boarding as soon as possible avoids those problems. If there is a tight connection for the next plane, it is inconvenient and can cause delays if carry-on bags have been checked due to lack of space in the aircraft.

Necessary items for the plane may include reading materials, earplugs, eye shields, neck pillow, socks, a sweater, several nutritious snacks (apple, granola bar, dried fruit), a full water bottle (filled or purchased near the gate after the security check), lip balm, toothbrush and toothpaste, eye drops, extra glasses, contact lens kit, pens, note paper, and a calculator. Everything needed for the flight should be removed from the carry-on bag before stashing it overhead. It is convenient to place these necessities under the seat or in the front pocket. Carrying toilet tissue or tissues in international countries and airports is necessary as it is not always provided.

Luggage problems rarely happen. However, airlines can lose items; and for reimbursement, many airlines require an itemized list of the exact contents. For further verification, pictures of the items taken with a digital or a cell phone camera will provide an undisputable record. Luggage receipts should be saved until the luggage is all accounted for. Replacement items can be purchased if a luggage item doesn't arrive (for example, a change of clothes). The inconvenienced traveler must save the receipts. The airlines will sometimes reimburse for those items up to a set amount determined by the airlines. Luggage bags or the contents can be damaged during transport by the airline. A claim for reimbursement, repair, or replacement can be made. The responsible airline baggage section is usually located in the baggage claim areas to file lost or damaged luggage claims. *"On 50 mission trips our luggage has only been delayed once, but we have never lost anything yet. God answers prayer."*

Airplane Comfort

Temperatures vary while flying. To stay comfortable it is wise to dress in layers, to include a sweater, and to wear socks and loose-fitting clothes. Socks leaving marks on legs are too tight.

A pillow and a blanket should be found when boarding long flights. It can be difficult to obtain these items once the plane has taken off. So even if not anticipating needing them, it's a good idea to snag them before sitting down.

Deep-vein thrombosis (DVT) avoidance is imperative. On flights of four hours or more, the dry atmosphere, combined with immobility, can lead to the rare—yet serious—condition of DVT. When blood flow is restricted, clots can form in legs. These clots can then break free and travel to the lungs, where they block the flow of blood. To prevent this, travelers periodically massage calves and thighs in a circular motion, get up and move around every hour or so, and do in-seat stretches. They also keep legs slightly elevated when the plane reaches its maximum altitude by propping them on footrests or a backpack. Walking around the terminal while transferring also helps. Certain people are also at higher risks for DVT and physicians may recommend that travelers on long flights wear compression stockings to decrease chances of DVT; check out the website www.dvt.net for more information about the condition.

Drinking water often is recommended. It is best if airline passengers drink eight ounces of fluid (preferably water) each hour. This practice helps with hydration and also forces frequent use of the bathroom, encouraging movement and stretching of muscles to prevent DVT. Excessive sodium in drinks or snacks during a long trip can cause feet to swell. Alcohol is best avoided, as the rule of thumb is that one drink in the air is the same as two or three on the ground. Frequent travelers carry an empty water bottle through the security line. If there is not a water fountain near the gate, a flight attendant can be asked to fill the water bottle and passengers should keep it close by in the seat pocket.

Eye shields keep out the light and assist with sleeping. It is recommended that an eye shield be broken in by using it at least once at home prior to the trip. The shield should fit snuggly over eyes but not so tight that it causes perspiration or a headache. A shield is an effective way to quiet a chatty neighbor. A dark shirt also works.

Silicone earplugs are best. Frequent fliers should consider noise-cancellation headphones. They have a built-in device that "hears" low-frequency sound just before a person does and generates a sound wave that cancels it out. Several manufacturers make them, ranging in price from $40 to $300.

Comfortable headphones which plug into the airplane's sound system make watching movies or listening to music or audio books more enjoyable.

Air circulated through airplanes is extremely dry. It is helpful to apply lip balm, moisturizer, and eye drops often. A toothbrush and toothpaste for overnight flights might not be provided by the airlines.

Face masks are now seen more frequently when traveling and will reduce respiratory germs, especially when sitting next to someone who appears to have a cold.

Compressible pillows can be found in various sizes and shapes and come in handy.

Team members sleep on the airport floor between
flights to the Dominican Republic.

Customs Inspections

Customs inspections when entering international countries usually go
well but are often a stress point. *"We have had little problems in fifty trips.
One country had restrictions on used medical equipment as they did not want
to have contaminated equipment. Another country restricted new equipment as
they thought it might be sold for profit. Others may want a bribe and some are*

just curious, wanting us to open every container to be inspected. Most countries are happy that we are helping their people and let us through with no hassle. All the equipment, supplies, and instruments travel fine as checked bags, and, with prayer, we always manage to get our items through."

* *"The custom officials at one airport kept us waiting for an hour, and we suspected they wanted bribes. We waited them out, saying 'no comprehende,' and they finally let us through after I gave each of them a toothbrush."*

* *"Two women assistants were carrying dental supplies and were singled out for official baggage checks at the border of an international country. They were taken to another location where the bags were stored and could not communicate in the local language. They'd wished the team leader or another team member had been allowed to go with them, as it was unnerving to be separated from the team."*

* *"The local rules must be followed when shipping equipment and supplies into the country. Fees may be expected and may vary greatly. It is better to carry everything needed for dentistry with the team in checked bags if at all possible."*

* *"Some teams try to get a contract or an official letter for the customs officials so that the team can enter without problems. Often, a local national from the ministry or an organizational representative who speaks the local language may meet us at the port of entry to validate our equipment and mission to the custom officials."*

Loud humor or joking in or around international airports, the customs, and immigration area upon returning to the U.S. is inappropriate. The officials can be strict and serious. Most places disallow use of cell phones when going through customs and passport checks.

Register valuables like internationally made cameras or other foreign-made, serial-numbered personal items and possibly even dental equipment with customs before leaving home. This foresight helps prove prior possession to customs on the return home. *"Although this is recommended by U.S. Customs, we have never experienced any problems and have avoided this hassle for now."*

When leaving the airport arrival hall, there will often be a mob of eager taxi drivers, baggage handlers, and tour operators that assail the team.

Their offers can be politely and firmly declined. Taxi prices should be settled before stepping into a cab.

Jet Lag

Jet lag occurs when traveling rapidly by air across three or more time zones. When the body's clock has to readjust, it can bring drowsiness in the day and insomnia at night, hunger at inappropriate times, lack of appetite, as well as irritable or lethargic feelings. The more time zones crossed, the worse jet lag can become. Many feel flying westbound is more difficult. Recovery is thought to take a day for each hour of the time difference between the international destination and the traveler's home.

Jet lag effects can be lessened but not avoided. Some travelers minimize jet lag by changing their bedtimes at home for about a week before a long trip overseas. They go to bed an hour earlier/later (to start to match the destination's schedule), get up an hour earlier or later, then two hours, then three—and so forth. Natural remedies, supplements, and recommendations to reduce the effects of jet lag can be found with medical consultations, health food store sources, and Internet research.

After boarding the flight, it is best to eat dinner without using stimulants and to get some sleep. Travel is extremely tiring; and the more rest received on the plane, the more prepared travelers will be to deal with the stresses of jet lag. Avoiding overeating and caffeine intake for twelve hours before, as well as during the flight, is helpful. Although caffeine can help keep one awake longer, it makes individuals wake up more often once they do fall asleep and so reduces total sleep time. Drinking at least eight ounces of water for every hour in the air—even if not thirsty—can help.

Sleeping pills with a short cycle may be helpful on overnight flights. The dosage must be timed correctly, or it may cause grogginess when landing. A plane is not the place to try out a pill for the first time. Many travelers use a nonprescription sleeping aid such as Tylenol PM (or Ambien—a prescription medication) for three nights after arrival for adjustment to the new time zone and for three nights after the return home. A poor night's sleep often results when sleeping pills are discontinued.

On landing, it's best to drop off luggage and then to sightsee or to enjoy an activity if arriving during the day, without napping, as sleeping just delays one's body adjustments. Everyone needs to adapt as quickly as possible to the local time for all daily routines—go for a walk, get some sun, eat and go to bed at the normal time for the new location.

CHAPTER 21

Documentation Paperwork

GENERAL CONSIDERATIONS

Paperwork necessities and issues involved in doing dentistry often can be addressed by the missionaries or national contacts. Sometimes they have worked with teams before and know what is required by their country. Most developing countries' officials do not question a short-term dental mission clinic done in an outlying community. Some countries may require a host national dentist to validate the clinic, while some countries require a national dental person to work with the visiting team. It may be a casual "drop-by" for several hours, or the nationals may work with the team every day. Each country is different in its attitude and approach to outsiders. *"We are careful to remember that it is their country and they are in charge. We do not go into another country with a 'know-it-all' attitude, planning to 'do it our way.' We have a servant's attitude, work within the parameters offered, and stay flexible."*

Paperwork processes may take several months before a mission trip. With authorizations, it may be possible to clear customs easily. With the proper paperwork, the team may be afforded the courtesy of any other practitioners in that country. Setting up a permanent clinic definitely requires local governmental approval and attention to appropriate regulations.

Dental licenses, dental degree paperwork, and drug certificate copies should be taken, although they are often not requested. These document copies can be reduced and laminated. *"These documents go with me everywhere. On several occasions overseas, I have had to produce my credentials for government officials while working on location."*

Passport Information

Correct names on passports must exactly match airline tickets or the team members won't fly without purchasing new tickets—costly! If a team member's name has changed, a current, valid, amended passport is necessary.

Passport expiration dates must be valid for six months prior to expiration when departing the country, in case teams would be detained for some reason in a country. *"A team member couldn't go to Uganda from Amsterdam because she had only three months left before her passport expired."*

Blank pages with an inscribed "VISA" on a totally blank page (some visa stamps take the whole page) must be present. A Russian visa requires two adjacent blank pages. Blank pages at the back of the passport without the "VISA" inscription do not count. *"Before going to Africa, one team member was required to stay overnight in Atlanta to get more pages in her passport from an American embassy before she could fly overseas. This split the team and special arrangements had to be made."*

Old passports should be stored away at home so that they are not taken by mistake. It is easy to mix them up. *"We had a team member grab the wrong passport, discovering it at an airport an hour away. It was a hassle to have someone quickly get the correct one and drive it to the airport, barely getting there in time for the flight."*

Obtain passports at U.S. Post Offices, which requires an application form, a certified copy of the birth certificate (first-time applicants), a method to prove the applicant's identity (for example, valid driver's license or government I.D.), payment of fee, and two identical passport photographs (2 x 2) inches—obtained at commercial photo centers, Walgreens, mail centers, and post offices with a plain white or off-white background only).

U.S. passports are valuable—worth $3,000 in some countries—and they do get stolen. It is important to have a copy of the first two pages of each passport to keep in a place separate from the originals. Replacement is much faster with passport numbers or ticket copies. Normally, new tickets must be purchased if passports disappear. Sometimes there is a wait of two weeks for a new passport to be issued by the U.S. Embassy in an international country, and fees have to be paid—sometimes by cash only.

Visa Requirements

A visa is a stamp placed in a passport by an official of an international country which permits visitation for a particular purpose and a specified period of time. "International Entry Requirements" from the State Department are online detailing each country. Some visas can be obtained upon arrival at the international country; some must be applied for and purchased on the Internet; and some must be acquired in the form of a stamp in the traveler's passport prior to departure from the U.S. Often the sponsoring organization or nationals will know this information. One of these options detailed below is required.

- Sometimes visas are issued at the international country's airport upon arrival. When headed to a country that requires a visa, travelers should look online or should ask their own country-based consulate—that represents the destination country—whether visas are also issued at the destination. In many cases (for example, Egypt), they are. Obtaining the visa upon arrival is a much simpler procedure and usually a money saver. It is smart to verify that the consulate is correct in stating that the visa can be obtained easily upon arrival. *"In some instances, such as Mexico, the visa can be a separate document (tourist card) issued without a passport, with only proof of citizenship necessary."*
- Some visas are purchased on the Internet (for example, Turkey).
- Some countries require obtaining a visa ahead of arrival. This process requires sending the traveler's passport, a fee, a form, and two passport-like photographs to the international country's U.S. Embassy or to a third party. The embassy or the agent will return the passport with the stamp in advance of the trip. These international countries (for example, China and Nepal) will not allow entry into their country without their stamp. That process alone can take up to six weeks or more depending on how fast the

mail can deliver and can return the passport. The process can be expedited with increased fees or by hand-carrying the paperwork to the consulate. Passports are valuable and should be sent by registered mail. Then there is proof that the passport was received. Website information concerning visas include www.travisa.com and www.travel.state.gov/content/visas/english/general/americans-traveling-abroad.html. *"There are services that provide passport visa approval, but they are usually unnecessary and expensive."*

Visa restrictions are specific to some countries. The team leader will check with the host and research particulars. Some countries (for example, India) may restrict entry if leaving the country and then reentering, even if the visa is still valid. With an Israeli visa stamped in the passport, entry into other countries may be denied. Israel has a removable paper visa that can be substituted for a stamp to prevent this denial. Some countries (for example, Senegal) require shot records and a validated cholera immunization on an International Immunization Certificate to gain entry.

Local hosts advise on the necessity of carrying passports and visas on individuals continually while in the country or on the safety of locking these documents in a secure place.

Other Legalities

Airport taxes are required by some countries. Airport tax is an additional fee that is frequently required upon arrival in or departure from an international country. The country hosts will advise on the cost which is usually a nominal fee and a minor inconvenience.

Various forms including custom, immigration and declaration papers are passed out in airplanes. It is helpful to have handy the flight and the personal passport numbers. When checking the box concerning the reason for the international visit, "tourist" is the best choice for a short-term mission team member—unless the host advises otherwise. If visiting in a category other than tourist, there may be additional paperwork and fees. *"In some instances the host is developing relationships with* *the government and wants the team to come as a dental/medical practitioner to establish credibility.*"

Possession of restricted and prohibited items when facing customs could result in arrest. Most restricted and prohibited items are common-sense articles such as alcohol, tobacco, and firearms. Other items would be plants, animals, seeds, flowers, meats, pets, drugs, pornography, poisons, antiquities, or copyrighted articles. The U.S. Customs Service website is www.cbp.gov/. It also has telephone numbers for direct access to the agency that would be concerned about particular imported items.

Minors sometimes have legal requirements that must be considered in advance. "*Mexico requires a notarized letter of consent signed by both parents for minors traveling alone or with one parent or guardian. If the parents are divorced, a copy of the parental custody agreement is allowed instead. The airlines enforce this rule before passengers board.*"

Travel advisories to a particular country may occur. If the American consulate advises travelers to check in with the office, team members should do so. In the event of an emergency, officials would immediately know the team's location for evacuation. The consulate is there to help in case of accidents or problems while in the country. For an extended stay, the team needs to have the consulate's telephone numbers and locations.

Dental Malpractice

Dental malpractice lawsuits are rare in most developing countries, and the incidence is negligible; but there can be only speculation on whether lawsuits may increase in the future.

Malpractice coverage is not usually provided by sponsoring organizations. If a team member desires to purchase malpractice insurance, the terms of the policies should be closely examined, especially exclusion clauses, liability limits, and policy periods. Most of the policies will be claims-made policies and will require the purchase of a tail (extended coverage for possible latent reactions to treatment) if there is concern that a lawsuit may be filed beyond the policy period.

Liability coverage is usually not purchased for current missionary travel. Since lawsuits are exceedingly rare, it becomes an individual risk/benefit/cost decision on whether to purchase insurance. Gallagher Charitable International Insurance Services specializes in overseas medical/dental malpractice insurance at gallaghercharitable.ajg.com, and a policy can be purchased for about $7 per day at www.internationalhelpers.co.gg. Gallagher Services can also cover the sponsoring organization in case there is an unfavorable result of a team member's actions, and they also protect against trailing claims.

Free clinic leaders may consider applying for the Congress-enacted Federal Tort Claims Act (FTCA) medical malpractice protection for volunteer free clinic health-care professionals through Section 194 of HIPAA (Public Law 104-191). If a volunteer health care professional meets all the requirements of the program, the related free clinic can sponsor him/her to be a "deemed" Public Health Service (PHS) employee for the purpose of FTCA medical malpractice coverage. FTCA deemed status provides the volunteer licensed or certified health care professionals with immunity from medical malpractice lawsuits resulting from their subsequent performance of medical, surgical, dental or related functions within the scope of their work at the free clinic. Claimants alleging acts of medical malpractice by the deemed volunteer health care professional must file their claims against the United States according to FTCA requirements.

GOVERNMENT POLICIES

Working cooperatively through a local government agency, with their sanctions or approval, is by far the best way to operate. They can provide the necessary freedom as a mutual trust is developed. Since a team has come to help them, most generally they will be receptive.

Some universities in international countries have reciprocity with universities in the U.S. There is an exchange of instructors at given times for each to work in the reciprocal countries. A wide variety of purposes including mobile clinics, and statistical research can be served with these programs. The length of stay may be several days up to a year's sabbatical. These programs are helpful, but many times funds are limited or nil.

Church denominations have missionaries in most countries of the world. Local missionaries can inform the visiting dental team of local restrictions and laws. Usually, it is permissible to deliver health services in conjunction with the local church, but most health services should be confined to church buildings or approved clinic sites. There are legal ramifications in some countries so that health care cannot be performed outside the respective church property or licensed clinic. To avoid causing the local group trouble, the team must use wisdom and must respect the laws, the customs, and the values of the local missionaries.

Governmental disapproval can occur in some countries. It may be risky business if the government is of another religion and uses harassment or oppressive tactics. Missionary work in some countries is illegal. Yet, there are hundreds of missionaries working freely in those countries and probably thousands of churches have been built. Dental and medical groups who travel in and out of these countries to work with missionaries enter as tourists. When crossing the border they carefully pack medical supplies and equipment to evade detection at the border. They can be turned back and not allowed to enter. Groups who obtain federal permission to enter will have a letter of invitation for the border guards to scrutinize. Some groups have obtained letters of permission from the state government where they will be working. All travelers must be aware of the laws of the country before traveling.

Prescription drugs transported across the border without authority to do so is unwise. Generally, it is best not to take narcotics and only a limited amount of antibiotics. The drugs must not be expired.

Local officials of communities will usually do their best to help health teams after the team's arrival. These officials live with the needy people and would be in trouble with the village if free health services were not permitted to set up. It is usually a political feather in the local officials' caps if they persuade a dental team ~~to visi~~it the village.

U.S. constitutional rights are a debatable issue when visiting another country. If one of the international country's laws is broken, the offender must pay the price just as any national citizen would. The U.S. State Department is very limited in what it can do if a U. S. citizen breaks the law in another country. Some countries still have the death penalty for drug trafficking. *"Even a simple auto accident can cause imprisonment. When driving, carry insurance for that country, since U.S. insurance is not valid in international countries. Normally auto insurance is only good a few miles over the border in Mexico. If renting an automobile, be sure to get local insurance with the contract."*

CHAPTER 22
Personal Packing

———

Airline policies, for most airlines, currently allow two, fifty-pound checked bags per person for overseas flights. A backpack, a purse, or a bag which fits under the seat can be taken along with a carry-on suitcase. Most people find that a backpack is the most utilitarian for the amount it holds and its usefulness throughout the trip. A flat purse can be packed if it might be helpful. Weighing checked bags with a small, digital, luggage scale to meet the fifty-pound limit is prudent. If there is extra room or weight, the developing countries always need clothes, shoes, and various items they may request. Use bags that can be carried easily through an airport or up several flights of stairs if needed. When possible, pack in hard-side suitcases that lock rather than cardboard boxes, as custom authorities will want to investigate boxes for import items. *"On our teams, each couple is allowed one, fifty-pound bag and a carry-on bag for personal luggage. The other three bags are filled with dental items. When we go as a couple, we carry a complete clinic in four checked bags and place personal items in our two, carry-on bags. It is best if all the containers have wheels."*

Small valuables are best kept in a pouch to be worn on the front of the body underneath clothing. Wallets can be placed in front pockets, and purse handles should cross the body where an arm can protect them from being snatched off a shoulder. A water-proof pouch can come in handy to keep sweat from molding money and a passport and may be needed if planning to shower or to swim in an insecure place. The pouch will keep important items dry if trekking.

Laundry options are often available on the mission field, so several changes of clothes usually suffice. Clothes that are easy to wash and dry easily are best.

* Laundry facilities or laundry personnel are available in most places, but they may be difficult to use if moving frequently.

* The laundry stomping method works well using a solid base in the shower stall. The day's dirty outfit is worn to the evening shower. (Usually with hot, steamy weather most people rinse off after a day's work.) Bar soap or shampoo is used to soap up the outfit under the arms while wearing it. Then one slips out of the outfit to "agitate" the clothes with the feet while showering. It is easy to rinse, squeeze out, and hang clothing items on plastic hangers. To construct a clothesline, the use of clothes pins, a small rope, some wire, or even dental floss works well.

* Ziplock washing machines also work. The dirty clothes and a squirt of soap (or shampoo) and water is placed in a large, re-sealable plastic bag. Shake the bag, dump the soapy water, add clean water, shake again to rinse the clothes (may repeat a couple of times) and then the items are squeezed out and hung to dry.

Packing hints follow with packing list suggestions provided in Appendix A.

* A master list is helpful that includes everything that might be needed on any given trip—from a normal vacation to a mission trip. Save the list on a personal computer and before packing, cross out anything not needed for the particular trip. When in doubt, leave it out.

* Pack early—even start a week or so before leaving. Packing can be stressful, so put aside enough time and set the desired mood (with music to enjoy). Some people set up an ironing board next to the suitcase, since ironed clothes lie flatter and arrive neater.

* Refining packing helps when the trip approaches. Some travelers recommend halving the packing list at the last minute; but if the list is done well, it may only need some light editing. A copy of the revised list can be kept for reference on the next trip. It may also be needed as a record in case luggage is lost or stolen.

* Luggage should be packed as lightly and efficiently as possible. Staying within weight or size limits is important. Prohibited liquid supplies are not included (for example, alcohol, H2O2, compressed air containers, or Cidex).

* Smaller planes often don't have room to store all the carry-on bags, and they must be checked at the gate. Important items to be used on the plane should be stored in the plastic bag which will go under the seat. If told to check the carry-on at the gate, the smaller bag will contain what is needed while on the plane.

* Folding techniques for clothes differ, and each theory has its advocates. Rolling clothing works well with duffels and soft-sided bags and will meet the needs of a casual traveler. "Interlocking" (wrapping slacks, say, around a bulkier clothing item) and the "dressmaker's dummy" approach (layering garments progressively over one another) are other good ways to minimize wrinkles.

* Plastic helps reduce wrinkles since plastic decreases friction. Individual items can be placed inside dry-cleaner bags, and they'll arrive in a reasonably preserved state. Resealable, plastic bags are good for stowing miscellaneous items. Compression bags protect clothes while adding space in the luggage. *I put plastic coverings on items that may not survive water damage. Water has saturated my luggage several times on trips.*

* Fabric softener sheets placed in the suitcase when packing will absorb odors and dampness and will keep clothing smelling fresh. This is most beneficial in warm, humid climates and while at sea. Humidity and moisture can adversely affect comfort, clothing, and electronic equipment on a trip into a jungle. Some supplies or equipment may need to be packed in plastic with moisture-absorbing packets to protect them.

* When packing, the suitcase is laid flat, and folded clothes are piled down the center. The heaviest items are placed where the bottom of the bag is when it's standing, so they won't crush other items. Rolled clothes fit into the spaces around the stacked clothes. Shoes are stuffed with socks, underwear, or small items which can be wrapped in plastic bags and wedged into unused crannies. Socks and underwear fill in remaining holes.

* Items can be "doubled up" by looking for ways to make the daily routine more travel friendly. Why pack hand, body, and face creams when one all-purpose moisturizer will do? Why pack laundry soap when shampoo will do? Shampoo can be left behind when using a soap that's everything in one. Liquids in the carry-on bag must be in three-ounce containers placed in a clear, quart-sized, plastic bag.

◆ Clothes amounts needed for trips of 4-5 days include one shirt per day, one layering jacket or sweater, one bottom per every two days (but never less than two pairs of pants), underwear for every day, and seasonal additions, like a bathing suit. If traveling for more than 4-5 days, follow the same numbers as above and plan on washing clothes instead of taking more.

◆ Clothing suggestions include the use of light-weight, wrinkle resistant, compact, and washable clothes. Dark clothes don't show spots or dirt and work for most situations. Pants that zip off to shorts provide options. T-shirts or polo shirts can be washed easily, are cool and modest, can double as pajamas or cover ups for swimming, are comfortable to wear after work, and can be given away at the end of the trip. The imprinted message can be a good conversation starter as long as the message is not suggestive or culturally questionable. If ordering "team shirts," consider designing one with a pocket on the upper chest for men. *"One team member duct-taped a pocket on his t-shirt because he missed having one so much!"*

◆ Long skirts with elastic waists for women are acceptable attire and are comfortable in all types of weather. In heat, they allow air to circulate up the legs. They are also convenient when encountering a squat toilet or when eliminating in the bushes. A cotton sarong (a loose-fitting skirt-like garment formed by wrapping a large strip of cloth around the lower part of the body) is lightweight, washable, and multifunctional—as a swimsuit cover-up, a picnic blanket, a temporary skirt to throw over capris in a temple, as an extra pillow, as an airplane blanket, emergency towel, or tablecloth.

◆ Two shoe pairs are usually all that's needed (one to wear and one to pack). Closed-toed shoes with good tread and some protection are a smart idea. Flip flops or sandals can be a second or a third pair as they pack easily. They keep feet cooler in hot, humid climates and can be used in hotel showers or for relaxing in the hotel. The long plastic bags from home-delivered newspapers can be used to slip shoes into for packing.

◆ Old clothes that are still wearable but that are not wanted anymore are best to take—those that may be ready for a thrift store. Along the way or at the end they may be discarded or given away when not needed. It will make room for souvenirs. Some travelers refer to this practice as "shedding."

* Essential items may be best taken in doubles—contact lenses, prescription sunglasses, or lip balm. It is wise to take copies of passports, driver's licenses, trip itinerary, doctor information, or credit cards. One copy is given to an emergency contact and two copies are carried on the trip, stowed in separate places.

* USB flash drives store medical and insurance contacts, confirmation codes, credit card numbers, photos from home, Power-Point presentation, addresses, and phone numbers. An inexpensive, thumb-sized drive fits in a secure zip pocket in a travel pouch. Without a laptop, one can insert the flash drive in most hotel or Internet café computers. Some USB flash drives password-protect data.

* Luggage organization is accomplished with extra resealable, plastic bags in different sizes. They keep freshly washed but not-quite-dry underwear separated from dry clothes, pills and vitamins separate from snacks, are good for packing shoes and wet swimsuits, can be used as trash bags in the van, make it easy to find everything from toiletries to flashlights, and keep papers dry and protected.

* Prescription medications must not be forgotten. A list of medications or a copy of the prescription will help if additional medication is needed. The pills are best in original bottles, so that customs won't ask questions about unidentified pills. The prescribing doctor should use the generic name and should note potency/dosage information on any prescription refill slips needed. *"My blood pressure pills fell out of my bag on the first day of the trip. Since I didn't have the bottle or a doctor's prescription, the local pharmacist called my pharmacy in America and was able to get me the correct medication."*

* Personal medicines that might be required during the day when away from the hotel room should be carried along with each team member. With significant or life-threatening allergies, a medical bracelet should be worn during the trip. The team leader and others should be advised of any medical conditions that might become a problem. Insulin users should check with their doctor for how to dose with dietary and time changes. It is smart to bring double what is needed and to pack half in the carry-on bag and half in checked luggage.

* Easily replaced items should be used and won't be sorely missed if they are lost, broken, or stolen. Valuable, sentimental, or fragile items should be packed in a carry-on bag. All expensive jewelry or electronics should be left home. This is not only for safety but also because of the message it sends to those the team is serving. For most non-Americans, jewelry is a symbol of extreme wealth and status. The display of expensive jewelry or costly electronics could invite a rush to judgment that the team did not intend to create and can be a theft magnet and a target for unwanted attention. Showing evidences of affluence, such as pictures of beautiful, expensive homes, cars, and even churches, may unknowingly hurt international people. Proximity and exposure to wealth can provoke a sense of poverty. International cell phones, iPads, fancy clothes, fat wallets, staying at plush hotels, and eating at extravagant restaurants can create more comparative poverty than most volunteers can imagine. *"No Christ follower should have too much while others have too little."*

* *"To avoid being a target, it is important to avoid the appearance of affluence. Carry a minimum amount of valuables and plan to have secure places to conceal them."*

* Extra clothes and basic toiletries should be packed in carry-on bags in case checked bags are lost. *"I always carry my loupes and headlight in my backpack as they are one of my most expensive and necessary items I need to do dentistry.*

* Hair appliances should be minimal with plans for simple hair care to suit the environment. Many places have humidity and heat that will wreck hair styles, regardless of how much effort is expended.

* Travel irons that are small and dual-voltage for wrinkled clothes are nice in some settings. A thin spray bottle may suffice to dampen wrinkled clothes for straightening (or it can be used as a mister to keep cool).

CHAPTER 23

Post-Trip Considerations

POST-TRIP EMOTIONS

Returning volunteers cannot expect that others will appreciate or understand their experiences or relate to their newfound points of view. Most people will listen politely for a few minutes and then want to talk about topics related to them. It is best to have a quick, three-minute synopsis of the highlights of the trip and have several pictures that capture the experience. That is often the only attention and time many people will give. *"I have team members prepare a one-minute, three-minute and a five-minute answer to the question 'How was your trip?' Think about what was the most meaningful thing that happened—that should be in the one-minute answer. Some folks who don't know the Lord will only give you that one minute—make it count!"*

"Overseas backlash syndrome" is one surprising experience faced by some returning team members. This sentiment occurs when well-intentioned people may question why a volunteer has provided services in another country when there is so much need in the home country. *"We tell them that we are following the Great Commission in Matthew 28:19-20 that instructs us to go to all nations. Even Jesus took His ministry to other regions."*

  • *"We remind them that there are many safety nets for people in the developed world, but few (especially for dentistry) in the developing world."*
  • *"I often engage them in a thoughtful, polite discussion about their own volunteer commitments to needy people."*

Life reentry brings common experiences and emotions that affect many people who have had meaningful cross-cultural encounters. It is as valuable a part of the experience as the trip itself. There are often stages of adjustment to reentry as follows (adapted from Lisa Chinn in *Reentry Guide for Short-Term Mission Leaders*).[69]

1) Fun. *"I can't wait for a hot shower...Oh, the delights of sleeping in my own bed...I really missed my family."* Initially, it is great to be home and to look at pictures from the trip. An individual's life and relationship with God feels changed, along with a new vision of the world. It feels like it's time to do things differently.

2) Flee. *"No one seems interested in my experience. Everyone here is so busy and life seems so fast. I really miss my team and new friends."* It is discouraging to see how materialistic, impersonal, less spiritual, and busy life at home seems to be. It feels lonely, and the community experienced with the team and the nationals is missed. People at home seem preoccupied with petty concerns and easily depressed by unimportant issues—especially when compared to the faith, the joy, and the community that was so evident on the trip. People at home may seem narrow without any world view, and many are ignorant of the plight of the rest of the world. Initially, team members may think that life felt more real, more solid, and more significant on the mission trip than it does at home. Because return isn't possible, one often relives memories, looks at pictures, and makes contact with team members. Even that is difficult because life sweeps returnees up with its pressures and busyness. *"Expect to be confused by emotions—even the macho people may sense disillusionment and stronger emotions than usual."*

3) Fight. It takes time to meld the past with the new experiences and the changes of the mission trip. Some depression can set in. *"People seem to take their faith so much more seriously over there...My church service seems so passionless. People are more interested in expanding their savings account than in saving the lost. We live as such isolated individuals. God calls us to intimate community. People at home seem indifferent to the real issues in life. Even the church fosters a self-indulgent, self-preoccupied spirituality. I feel like I'm being critical and feeling spiritually superior."*

4) Fit. *"I can't live here like people do there. I tried to live differently, but it's impossible. The cost of living is so much higher here. I have to accept it. I have to return to my normal responsibilities. I can't just drop everything. I've got so much that I have to do. I'm losing my friends because they see me as a 'mission fanatic.'"*

Each team member must try to acknowledge these issues, talk with those closest about the feelings, and consciously plan to be involved in life back home again. Understand that readjustment takes time. Integrate the experiences and the feelings with a plan for the future. Now it becomes important to fit in. The press of responsibilities has taken hold, and it's simply too hard to keep focused on the experiences from the trip. The memories are beginning to fade, and it has been hard to live differently. Even if promises were made to communicate with the people involved with the trip, it hasn't seemed to happen. Many people end the reentry process here. Their trip becomes a distant memory. There is a nagging guilt over not being able to live differently in light of what they learned. But other than giving money to mission projects, praying occasionally for the people they met, and looking forward to another short-term trip, they don't know what else they can do.

5) Fruitfulness. God wants to lead those from their trip experiences into life-transforming, creative fruitfulness. A new journey has begun. In fact, the second journey may be one of the primary reasons why God called the team member to the trip. Being led by the Spirit of God down the path of fruitfulness will take effort and time. Thus, the journey from mission tourism to global citizenship continues long after the return home. Patience and persistence helps. Keeping a journal chronicles the pilgrimage. God is the author of this quest, and of the faith, so God must be kept as a participant in the process.

COMPASSION FATIGUE

"Compassion fatigue" is a common emotional/mental state of weariness that can afflict anyone who has a tender heart for those who are needy and hurting in the world. Most Christians truly want to be caring and giving people, but the challenge is in learning how to sustain that compassionate state when faced with the overwhelming needs experienced in charitable work. *"Making compassion a foundation of daily spiritual exercise and religious habits is often the goal of Christians. Compassion can be cultivated. It takes practice; it is complex; and resistance will be a part of the process. Compassion fatigue is often emotional fatigue, and compassion is an attitude and not an emotion."*

Compassion fatigue can be combatted by following suggestions from David Best (president and cofounder of the "Towel and Basin" ministry that helps people discover their God-given visions).[70]

* Know the individual life-mission and call on your life. All people—not just those ordained as pastor or deacons—have calls to service. God has placed you on this earth for a particular purpose. Know your life's mission; then live within it.

* Make time for yourself. If you don't make time for yourself, no one else will. Jesus is our example. In places of solitude and silence, Jesus reaffirmed the Father's mission for His life. The crowds continued to cry out for his attention; yet, Jesus made time for himself. You must too.

* Discipline your life. Create some regular ritual and schedules. The traditional disciplines of the Spirit (for example, prayer, Bible study, church involvement) are a good place to begin. This frees you. For example, you don't have to think every morning, "Should I brush my teeth today?" In what areas of your life could you create disciplines and good habits?

* "The need is not the call." Recite this daily. There are so many needs around us, but God has created a vision just for you. God has formed the Body of Christ with many different members, each with different gifts. Some of the needs you see are for fellow members of the Body to fulfill. As you increasingly understand your life mission, make time for yourself and discipline your life. You will know at what time and to what needs you are to respond.

* Stay close to Jesus. He is the source of energy through prayer, Bible study, meditation, worship, solitude, and fasting.

Mission "Next Steps"

Learn about missions, unreached people groups, and investigate in-depth mission Bible studies suggested on these websites:

* Joshua Project www.joshuaproject.net
* Operation World and Mission Frontiers www.operationworld.org
* Traveling Team www.travelingteam.org
* 10/40 Window www.win1040.org
* The Kairos Course www.kairoscourse.org

Pray for unreached peoples, countries, and the persecuted church. *"I pray for those workers who made the clothes I'm wearing today—the country is on the clothes tag."*

- Global Prayer Digest www.globalprayerdigest.org
- Ethne to Ethne Prayer Initiative www.ethne.net
- Prayer Guard www.prayerguard.net
- Voice of the Martyr's website www.persecution.com/
- National Day of Prayer www.nationaldayofprayer.com

Get Involved with Finishing the Task.

- Take the *Perspectives on the World Christian* Movement course www.perspectives.org.
- Serve on the church mission committee.
- Correspond with and support a missionary.
- Reach out to local international students www.isionline.org.
- Attend a local or a national mission conference like Urbana www.urbana.org or the Global Missions Health Conference www.medicalmissions.com or the Christian Medical and Dental Association Conferences www.cmda.org.
- Search online evangelism and discipleship www.globalmediaoutreach.com.
- Learn how to evangelize by checking out e3resources www.e3resources.org.

Investigate Short-Term Trips.

- Christian Dental Society www.christiandental.org
- Website by Dr. William Griffin www.dentalmissiontrips.org
- American Dental Association Mission website www.internationalvolunteer.ada.org
- Mission Finder www.missionfinder.org
- Short-term Missions www.shorttermmissions.com
- National Short-term Mission Conference www.nstmc.org
- Christian Medical and Dental Associations with Global Health Outreach www.cmda.org

Commitment can bring full-time service.

* Attend Christian Medical and Dental Associations' Dental Residency program www.dentalresidency.org.

* Attend a one-year mission program. Examples include Cru www.cru.org, Youth With A Mission www.YWAM.org, Operation Mobilization www.om.org, Wycliffe Bible Translators www.wycliffe.org.

* Enroll in Bible College as preparation for ministry among the unreached.

* Go to an unreached people as a "tentmaker" www.globalopps.org/links.htm.

CHAPTER 24

Inspirational Thoughts

———◆———

Christian Dental Society members say that dental mission trips are intoxicating, habit-forming, and provide invaluable experiences, and they open doors to adventures in serving God by giving to others. The acquired understanding and growth have shifted world views to a new perspective. Those who serve time and again agree that the efforts are totally worth the sacrifices.

    *   *"We always seem to be blessed beyond what we have possibly given to others. Going on a dental mission truly is a precious and amazing experience, giving satisfaction like nothing else."*

    *   *"The urge to continue sharing our dental skills with the rest of the world has become irresistible. Each visit to a different land is a unique experience."*

    *   *"Our lives will never be the same. Dental missions transformed our kids from consumers into servers. We can't wait to take our grandkids."*

    *   *"Always dreaming of places where we'd like to serve, we return home to America feeling truly blessed with new friendships all over the world."*

    *   *"It's the hardest job I've ever loved. Even though I am sometimes exhausted after a few days of demanding dentistry on an international mission field, the warmth and the fulfillment of serving so many people in the Lord's name has become a pearl above price to me."*

    *   *"When people ask what country we've loved the most, we say, 'we just love the ones we're with!' We wonder if we should hang a sign: Will Work for Hugs!"*

    *   *"Relish the moment"* is a good motto, especially when coupled with the Bible's reminder that 'This is the day the Lord has made; let us rejoice and be glad in it' (Psalm 118:24). *It is the regrets over yesterday and the fears of tomorrow that cause much angst in our lives. Regret and fear are twin thieves that rob us of today. If we follow the will of Christ to serve others, however, we can rejoice in His leading and peaceful satisfaction every day of our lives."*

    *   *"It is courageous and self-sacrificing for a dentist to commit to a dental mission trip.*

The dollar cost of the mission trip is not the major factor. It is very difficult for dentists, especially solo practitioners, to leave their work. The loss of income and the office overhead costs continue in their absence. Often dentists must provide for staff members who usually rely on the weekly income. Dentists also feel a responsibility to their patients. Spouses and families must also support the dentist's use of vacation time for dentistry. Dentists don't exactly experience a vacation when they are doing the hard dental work required in an austere setting. BUT, it is totally worth these sacrifices, and many dentists have been blessed beyond measure!"

* *"Patients may actually have a more favorable view of the practice and will still be there upon the dentist's return. If volunteering becomes a part of the dentist's regular schedule, patients are likely to ask about the success of the last trip or about plans for the next one."*

* *"I feel that the risks people take reveal what they value. As a short-term dental missionary, I challenge believers to become 'risk takers for God.' We met a German missionary who was headed for Sudan. When asked if that was dangerous, he smiled and said, 'Well…life is also very hazardous in Germany, as people are dying daily in their beds, never having really lived for God!'"*

* *"I received this thank-you letter from nationals:* 'We cannot pay you with money for what you have done for us, but at least we can say thank you and pray to God and ask Him to bless you now and forever…Our smiles will always be our most valuable treasure, and only you have made it possible.' *With gratitude such as this, the rewards can far outweigh any volunteer's effort."*

* *"It is only when we attempt the impossible that we see God at work. A good friend once told me. 'Don't try to do something that you can accomplish by yourself. That's you working. Try the impossible. Then if it comes to pass you know that you've seen God working.'"*

I looked, and behold, a great multitude which no one could count, from every nation and all tribes and people and tongues, standing before the throne and before the Lamb" (Revelation 7:9).

…let your light shine before men, that they may see your good deeds and praise your Father in heaven" (Matthew 5:16).

"...whatever you did for one of the least of these brothers of mine, you did for me" (Matthew 25:40).

"...always giving thanks to God the Father for everything. . ." (Ephesians 5:20).

END NOTES

———

1   New International Version of the Bible. (Wheaton: Tyndale House Publishers, 1991).

2   Dr. H. Leon Greene. *A Guide to Short-Term Missions: A Comprehensive Manual for Planning an Effective Mission Trip.* (Downers Grove: InterVarsity Press, 2012), Kindle Location 59.

3   Dr. Burton Conrad, Dr. Roby Beaglehole, Dr. Habib Benzian, Jon Crail, Dr. Judith Mackay. *The Oral Health Atlas: Mapping a Neglected Global Health Issue.* (Brighton: FDI World Dental Federation, 2009), Dr. Burton Conrod, President, FDI World Dental Federation, 7.

4   Dr. Diarmuid Shanley, Beaglehole, et al., 74.

5   Dr. Poul Erik Petersen, Dr. Denis Bourgeois, Dr. Hiroshi Ogawa, Dr. Saskia Estupinan-Day, and Dr. Charlotte Ndiaye. "The Global Burden of Oral Diseases and Risks to Oral Health." *Bulletin of the World Health Organization*, September 2005, 662.

6   Beaglehole, et al., 61.

7   George Bernard Shaw, Irish playwright, critic, political activist (1856-1950).

8   Miguel de Cervantes, Spanish author (1547-1616), quote from *Don Quixote.*

9   Beaglehole, et al., 96-103.

10 Dr. Diarmuid Shanley, former dean, Trinity College Dental School, Ireland, 2008. Beaglehole, et al., 74.

11 Dr. Zaka, Madagascar physician, interviewed by Dr. Robert Meyer, November 2004.

12 Beaglehole, et al., 66.

13 Dr. Milad Hanna, Egyptian physician trained in the U.S., interviewed by Dr. Robert Meyer, November 2011.

14 Beaglehole, et al., 70.

15 Dr. Caswell A. Evans, College of Dentistry, University of Illinois at Chicago, 2006. Beaglehole, et al., 20.

16 Dr. Margaret Chan, World Health Organization Director-General, 2009. Beaglehole, et al., 49.

17 Dr. Ole Fejerskov, Dr. Edwina Kidd. *Dental caries: the disease and its clinical management.* Oxford: Blackwell Munksgaard, 2008.

18 Dr. Sarah Hodges, Pediatric Anesthesiologist, Uganda, 2009. Beaglehole, et al., 34.

19 Beaglehole, et al., 81.

20 Department of Health and Human Services. *Oral Health in America. A Report of the Surgeon General.* Rockville, MD: U.S. Department of Health and Human Services, National Institute of Dental and Craniofacial Research, National Institutes of Health, 2000.

21 Beaglehole, et al., 39.

22 Dr. Aubrey Sheiham. "Oral Health, General Health, and Quality of Life." *Bulletin of the World Health Organization*, September 2005, 644.

23 Jonathan Kozol, U.S. writer and educator, 1991. Beaglehole, et al., 38.

24 Dr. Richard Carmona, U.S. Surgeon General, 2002. Beaglehole, et al., 60.

25 Beaglehole, et al., 58.

26 Dr. David A. Livermore. *Serving with Eyes Wide Open: Doing Short-Term Missions with Cultural Intelligence.* (Grand Rapids: Baker Books, 2006), 20-24.

27 Sheiham, 644.

28 Dr. Li Xiaojing, Dr. Kristin M. Kollveit, Dr. Leif Tronstad, and Dr. Ingar Olsen. "Systemic Diseases Caused by Oral Infections." *Clinical Microbiology Reviews*, October 2000.

29 Pastor Don C.Richter. *Mission Trips That Matter: Embodied Faith for the Sake of the World.* (Nashville: Upper Room Books, 2008), 19.

30 Joanne Shetler with Patricia Purvis. *And the Word Came With Power: How God Met and Changed A People Forever.* (Portland: Multnomah Press, 1992), 119.

31 Pastor Max Lucado. *Outlive Your Life: you were made to make a difference.* (Nashville: Thomas Nelson, 2010), 9.

32 Helen Keller, author, political activist, lecturer, first deaf and blind person to earn a B.A. (1880-1968).

33 Dr. Os Guinness. *The Call: Finding and Fulfilling the Central Purpose of Your Life.* (Nashville: W Publishing Group, a Division of Thomas Nelson, Inc., 2003), x.

34 Pastor Rick Warren. *The Purpose Driven Life: What on Earth am I Here For?* (Grand Rapids: Zondervan, 2002), 15.

35 Bob Buford. *Half Time: Changing Your Game Plan from Success to Significance.* (Grand Rapids: Zondervan Publishing House, 1994), 18.

36 Bob Buford. *Finishing Well: What People Who REALLY Live Do Differently!* (Brentwood: Integrity Publishers, 2004), 140.

37 Dr. Richard G. Forbes and Dr. William C. Topazian, D.D.S., editors. *Spiritual Issues & Choices in Dentistry.* (Bristol: The Christian Medical and Dental Associations, 2000), 73.

38 St. Augustine, Christian Theologian and philosopher (354-430).

39 Francis Bacon, Renaissance philosopher (1561-1626).

40 Dr. David Stevens. *Beyond Medicine: What Else You Need to Know to Be a Healthcare Missionary.* (Bristol: Christian Medical & Dental Associations, 2012), 85.

41 Forbes and Topazian, 78-80.

42 Dr. Roger J. Smales. "The Atraumatic Restorative Treatment (ART) Approach for Primary Teeth: Review of Literature." *American Academy of Pediatric Dentistry* 22:4, 2000.

43 Mother Theresa, Roman Catholic Religious Sister and missionary (1910-1997).

44 Helen Keller, author, political activist, lecturer, first deaf and blind person to earn a B.A. (1880-1968).

45 Loren Eiseley, American anthropologist, educator, philosopher, and natural science writer (1907-1997).

46 Lynelle DeRoo, BSDH. *Brush for Life.* Interviewed by Dr. Robert Meyer, DMD, May 7, 2015.

47 St. Francis of Assissi, Catholic saint, religious deacon, confessor, and founder (1181-1226).

48 Bruce Tuckman. "Developmental Sequence in Small Groups." *Psychological Bulletin*, 1965: Reprinted in Group Facilitation, Spring 2001: 384-99.

49 Livermore, 31-33.

50 Richter, 24.

51 Pastor Kevin Johnson. *Mission Trip Prep: A Student Journal for Capturing the Experience*. (Grand Rapids: Zondervan Publishing House, 2003), 133-175.

52 Pastor Lynne Ellis with Pastor Doug Fields. *Mission Trips from Start to Finish: How to Organize and Lead Impactful Mission Trips*. (Simply Youth Ministry, 2008), 103-104, 107-108.

53 Dr. Tim Dearborn. *Short-term Missions Work Book: From Mission Tourists to Global Citizens*. (Downers Grove: InterVarsity Press, 2003), 84-85.

54 Dr. Donald G. Bloesch. *The Struggle of Prayer*. (Colorado Springs: Helmers and Howard, 1988), *vii-viii*.

55 Pastor Bill Hybels with LaVonne Neff. *Too Busy NOT to Pray: Slowing Down to be with God*. (Downers Grove: InterVarsity Press, 1998), 9-11.

56 Pastor Dutch Sheets. *The Beginner's Guide to Intercession: How to Pray Effectively*. (Ventura: Gospel Light Regal, 2001), 9.

57 Dearborn, 73-79.

58 Mission to the World, Presbyterian Church in America Mission Board. *Mission to the World: Short-Term Missions Individual Manual*. (Lawrenceville: Mission to the World, 2004), GEN 3-7.

59 The material was adapted from an article by Pastor Paul Borthwick, Minister of Missions, Grace Chapel, Lexington, MA. Mission to the World, GEN 2-3.

60 Dearborn, 88.

61 American Dental Association Division of Global Affairs and Dr. Francis G. Serio, editor. *International Dental Volunteer Guide*. (Chicago: Division of Global Affairs, American Dental Association, 2009), 42.

62 Greene, Kindle location 1716.

63 Dearborn, 46.

64 Dr. Wess Stafford with Dean Merrill. *Too Small to Ignore: Why the Least of These Matters Most*. (Colorado Springs: WaterBrook Press, 2007), 9.

65 Dr. David Stevens and Dr. Gene Rudd. Short-Term Missions: Answers to Your Questions—and to the Questions You Need to Be Asking! *Mission Survival Kit: Practical Tips for Successful Short Term Mission Service. Bristol:* Christian Medical and Dental Associations, 2014.

66 Greene, Kindle Location 169.

67 Ibid., 159.

68 Pastor Don Richardson. *Peace Child: An Unforgettable Story of Primitive Jungle Treachery in the 20th Century.* Ventura: Regal Books, A Division of GL Publications, 1976), 118-119.

69 Dearborn, 94-95. (Adapted from Lisa Espineli Chinn, *Reentry Guide for Short-Term Mission Leaders.* (Orlando: Deeper Roots, 1998), 14.

70 David M. Best. "How You Can Combat Compassion Fatigue." *Nazarene Compassionate Ministries (ncm.org),* 18-19.

Additional Resources

Bond, Marybeth. *Gutsy Women: More Travel Tips and Wisdom for the Road.* San Francisco: Travelers' Tales, 2001.

Christie, Dr. William B. *Gloria's Smile: My Dental Teaching Mission in Peru: A Story of God's Amazing Faithfulness.* www.booksurge.com, 2009.

Corbett, Steve, Brian Fikkert. *When Helping Hurts: How to Alleviate Poverty without Hurting the Poor...and Yourself.* Chicago: Moody Publishers, 2012.

Dickson, Murray. *Where There is No Dentist.* Berkeley: The Hesperian Foundation, 1983.

Hobdell, Martin, Poul Erik Petersen, John Clarkson, Newell Johnson. "Global Goals for Oral Health 2020." *International Dental Journal,* 2003: 285-288.

Johnstone, Patrick. *The Future of the Global Church: History, Trends and Possibilities.* Downers Grove: InterVarsity Press, 2011.

Judge, Cindy. *Before You Pack Your Bag: Prepare Your Heart.* Wheaton: Campfire Resources, Inc., 2000.

Kidder, Laura, Stephanie Butler, Kelly Kealy eds. *Fodor's 1,001 Smart Travel Tips.* New York: Fodor's Travel, a division of Random House, Inc., 2011.

Lamb, Dr. Ron. *Portable Mission Dentistry.* Broken Arrow: World Dental Relief, 2002.

Meyer, Dr. Bob and Diane. *Truth, Teeth, and Travel: Heartwarming, adventurous journeys into fascinating, exotic cultures; Volume 1 and Volume 2.* Wheaton: OakTara Publishers, 2013.

Miley, George. *Loving the Church...Blessing the Nations: Pursuing the Role of Local Churches in Global Mission.* Waynesboro: Gabriel Publishing, 2003.

Newell, Marvin J. *Commissioned: What Jesus Wants You to Know as You Go.* ChurchSmart Resources, 2010.

Obrecht, Dr. Dawn V. *Mission Possible: A Missionary Doctor's Journey of Healing.* Steamboat Springs : Dr. Dawn Obrecht, 2008.

Ohlerking, Dave. *Walk With Me: Through Some Hard Places of the World.* Baton Rouge, Louisiana: Ready Writer, 2008.

Paulose, Moses. *Missionary Challenge: A History of Body of Christ Ministries, Rameswaram, TN., India.* Rameswaram: Body of Christ Ministries, 2009.

Piper, John. *Don't Waste Your Life.* Wheaton: Crossway Books, 2003.

—. *Let the Nations Be Glad.* Grand Rapids: Baker Academic, 2005.

Saint, Steve. *The Great Omission: Fulfilling Christ's Commission Completely.* Seattle: YWAM Publishing, 2001.

Stearns, Bill and Amy. *2020 Vision: Practical Ways Individuals and Churches Can Be Involved.* Bloomington: Bethany House Publishers, 2005.

Stevens, Dr. David with Gregg Lewis. *Jesus, M.D.: A Doctor Examines the Great Physician.* Grand Rapids: Zondervan, 2001.

Stiles, J. Mack and Leeann. *Mack and Leeann's Guide to Short-Term Missions.* Downers Grove: InterVarsity Press, 2000.

U.S. Department of Health & Human Services: Food and Drug Administration, Center for Devices and Radiological Health: Office of Device Evaluation . "Guidance Documents (Medical Devices and Radiation-Emitting Products)." *Updated 510(k) Sterility Review Guidance K90-1.* August 30, 2002. http://www.fda.gov/MedicalDevices/ DeviceRegulationand Guidance/Guidance/GuidanceDocuments/... (accessed September 26, 2014).

"Using ART in Mission Dentistry." *Dentistryinfo*, August 10, 2010.

Warren, Rick. *The Purpose Driven Life: What on Earth am I Here For?* Grand Rapids: Zondervan, 2002.

Woodbridge John D., ed. *Ambassadors for Christ: Distinguished Representatives of the Message Throughout the World.* Chicago: Moody Press, 1994.

Yohannan, K. P. *Revolution in World Missions.* Carrollton: gfa Books (a division of Gospel for Asia), 2004.

Yun, Brother with Paul Hattaway. *The Heavenly Man: The Remarkable True Story of Chinese Christian Brother Yun.* Grand Rapids: Monarch Books, 2002.

Appendix A

Packing List

* Paperwork
  - [ ] Current passport with photocopy, airplane tickets, travel insurance documents, emergency numbers, agenda, driver's license if needed
  - [ ] Health certificate (shot record), medical insurance documents, physician's name, clinic phone numbers and addresses, blood group, allergies, current medication list, prescriptions
  - [ ] Copy of dental license, diploma, letter from sponsoring organization
  - [ ] Emergency contact family information
  - [ ] List of packed dental items, pressure pot sterilizer validation letter
* Personal items
  - [ ] Bible, notebook, pen or pencils for journaling and documenting
  - [ ] Toiletries: toothbrush, toothpaste, dental floss, soap, shampoo, shower cap, deodorant, razors, shaving cream (prepare for no electricity), feminine hygiene items, hand lotion, lip balm, other necessities
  - [ ] Cell phone, e-readers, music players, laptop with chargers, reading books
  - [ ] Sunglasses, contacts, eye glasses (if applicable), eye shield for sleeping on plane
  - [ ] Battery-operated alarm clock, if cell phone can't be used
  - [ ] Translator aids such as dictionary, phrase book, electronic translator, map of country
  - [ ] Favorite headphones for airplane or for listening to music
  - [ ] Earplugs for the plane, external noise, or snorers
  - [ ] Sewing kit (pocket size)
  - [ ] Photos of family and friends, but nothing showing affluent lifestyle
  - [ ] Name tags or cards for team members and local helpers
  - [ ] Electric adaptor plugs for country visiting
* Health and safety items
  - [ ] Personal medications, vitamin supplements (if applicable)

- □ Personal first-aid kit (Team leader should have kit in Appendix I)
- □ Insect repellent with DEET at least 15%, mosquito netting, if needed
- □ Sunscreen, lip balm
- □ Small travel packs of tissue (Toilet paper is not always available.)
- □ Hand sanitizer or packets of wipes
- □ Flashlights, headlights, or flashlight application on phone
- □ Zip ties to secure luggage
- Valuable items
  - □ Travel wallet or pouch to carry valuables inside clothes, extra suitcase key in pouch
  - □ Small calculator for local currency transactions or use phone
  - □ Cash for tourism and incidentals (some $20, $5, and $1 bills to equal $100-$300)
  - □ Credit card, traveler's checks (card and check numbers, phone contacts in case of loss or theft)
  - □ Camera supplies, charger, extra batteries, data disc
- Clothing and accessories
  - □ Casual clothes, belt (See Chapter 22)
  - □ Two or three scrub sets for clinic work
  - □ One nice outfit for church (women: skirt; men: collared shirt, nicer pants)
  - □ Light-weight rain jacket
  - □ Hat or head covering for intense sun
  - □ Sweatshirt or sweater, if cold weather is a possibility
  - □ 1-2 pairs of comfortable, close-toed shoes, sandals for warm areas
  - □ For construction projects: work gloves, hat, bandanna, lightweight long pants, sturdy shoes/work boots
  - □ Flip-flops for dirty shower/bathing areas
  - □ Swimsuit
  - □ Light robe for common bathrooms
  - □ Light-weight gloves to protect hands during baggage handling
  - □ Plastic bags to store items, to store dirty or wet clothes, and to protect clothes from dampness
- Food/beverages

- ☐ Snacks: nuts, power bars, dried or fresh fruit, dried or packaged meat, pouched tuna, peanut butter, crackers
- ☐ Water bottle that is durable and portable
- ☐ Water purification tablets or water purifiers if unsure of a good source of pure water
- ☐ Flavored, healthy drink mixes to add to water to make hydration more pleasurable

* Comfort items to consider taking
  - ☐ Small sleeping pillow with pillowcase for comfort
  - ☐ Bed sheet, as sometimes not provided
  - ☐ Sleeping bag or blankets if host says these are needed
  - ☐ Several plastic hangers to hang and to dry clothes
  - ☐ Washcloth, bandana, or small towel, as many hotels do not provide them
  - ☐ Travel iron with dual voltage
  - ☐ Hair dryer, curling wand with dual voltage

Appendix B

Surgical Checklist (See Chapter 7-9.)

- Dental equipment:
  - ☐ Dental chair
  - ☐ Operator stool with backrest
  - ☐ Patient head rest attached to back of chair, if standing for extractions
  - ☐ Dental operating unit (DOU) and accessories
    - ☐ Handpieces with correct attachments
    - ☐ Suction tips
    - ☐ Air/water syringe tips
    - ☐ Surgical burs
    - ☐ Burs to adjust acrylic, to smooth sharpness
    - ☐ Handpiece lubricant
    - ☐ Extension cord and surge protector
    - ☐ Extra fuses
  - ☐ Battery-operated handpiece, if no DOU:
    - ☐ Suction apparatus
    - ☐ Irrigating syringe and needle; cups for expectorants
    - ☐ Surgical burs
    - ☐ Burs to adjust acrylic, to smooth sharpness
    - ☐ Handpiece lubricant
  - ☐ X-ray unit, intraoral sensor, viewing screen
  - ☐ Air-abrasion and/or hydro-abrasion unit, abrasive powder
  - ☐ Dental loupes or protective eyewear
  - ☐ Headlight (LED), charger or batteries
- Anesthetic supplies:
  - ☐ Anesthetic syringes
  - ☐ Intraligamentary syringe, needles
  - ☐ Anesthetic carpules
  - ☐ Anesthetic carpules, a few without epi
  - ☐ Needles, assorted per practitioner
  - ☐ Topical anesthesia

- □ Cotton tip applicators
- □ Needle recapping guard
* Examination items:
  - □ Trays to hold instruments
  - □ Mouth mirrors
  - □ Explorers
  - □ Periodontal probes
* Forceps, assorted:
  - □ Upper universals for pedo and adult
  - □ Lower universals for pedo and adult
  - □ Cowhorn # 23 for lower molars
  - □ Operator specific forceps
* Instruments:
  - □ Elevators, assorted
  - □ Luxators, assorted
  - □ Periosteal tissue elevators, assorted
  - □ Curettes, assorted
  - □ Scalers, assorted
  - □ Curved hemostats
  - □ Root tip picks
  - □ Cheek retractors
  - □ Mouth props, assorted
  - □ Bard Parker holders and scalpel
  - □ Bone file
  - □ Rongeurs
  - □ Tissue scissors
  - □ Mono-bevel chisel and hammer
* Suturing supplies:
  - □ Suture holders
  - □ Sutures
  - □ Suture scissors
  - □ Tissue tweezers
* Disposables:
  - □ Gloves for dentists and assistants
  - □ Masks for dentists and assistants

- Gauze (2 x 2)
- Bibs or drapes for patients and instrument trays
- Bib clips to hold patient drapes
- Disposable cups or baggies for extra gauze and medications
- Disposable cups for expectorants
- Trash bags and waste baskets
- Toothbrushes and floss for patients
- Tissue hemostatic agents
- Gel foam and dry socket paste
- Fuji IX power liquid to patch holes
- Medical items:
  - Blood pressure cuff and stethoscope
  - Epi-pens or epinephrine with injector for anaphylaxis reaction
  - Albuterol Sulfate inhaler
  - Analgesics (Motrin 200 mg tabs and Tylenol 325 mg tabs)
  - Antibiotics (Pen V K 500 mg tabs and Clindamycin 250 mg tabs)
- Miscellaneous items:
  - Protective eyewear for assistants and patients
  - Mirror for patient instruction
  - Containers to organize, store, transport items
  - Sterilization equipment and supplies (See Appendix E.)
  - Surgical scrubs or smocks
  - Plug adaptors for specific country
  - Converters (proper size) for electrical equip

Appendix C

———◆———

Restorative Checklist (See Chapter 5-9.)

❈ Dental equipment:
- ☐ Dental chair
- ☐ Operator stool with a backrest
- ☐ Dental operating unit (DOU) and accessories
  - ☐ High- and slow-speed handpieces with correct attachments
  - ☐ Suction tips
  - ☐ Air/water syringe tips
  - ☐ Surgical burs
  - ☐ High-speed burs
  - ☐ Latch slow-speed burs
  - ☐ Acrylic and polishing burs/discs
  - ☐ Bur blocks
  - ☐ Handpiece lubricant
  - ☐ Surge protector and extension cord
  - ☐ Extra fuses
- ☐ X-ray unit, intraoral sensor, viewing screen
- ☐ Dental loupes or protective eyewear
- ☐ Headlight (LED) with charger or spare batteries
- ☐ Curing light, cordless and charger and accessories:
  - ☐ Composite gun to insert composite
  - ☐ Composite materials, assorted colors
  - ☐ Flowable composite and tips
  - ☐ Composite bonding agents, dentist specific
  - ☐ Etching gel and tips
  - ☐ Sealant material and tips
  - ☐ Bard Parker handles and # 12 blades
  - ☐ Interproximal instruments
  - ☐ Composite finishing and polishing burs
- ☐ Amalgamator and 220V converter, if necessary, and accessories:
- ☐ Amalgam

- □ Amalgam carriers
- □ Amalgam wells
- □ Packing instruments, assorted
- □ Carving instruments, assorted
- □ Excavators, assorted for caries removal
- □ Chisels, assorted
- Anesthetic supplies:
  - □ Anesthetic syringes
  - □ Intra-ligament syringes and needles
  - □ Anesthetic carpules
  - □ Anesthetic carpules, a few without epi
  - □ Needles, assorted per provider
  - □ Topical anesthesia
  - □ Cotton tip applicators
  - □ Needle recapping guard
- Examination items:
  - □ Trays to hold instruments
  - □ Mouth mirrors
  - □ Explorers
  - □ Periodontal probes
  - □ Tooth sleuth
- Rubber dam set up:
  - □ Rubber dam material
  - □ Rubber dam punch
  - □ Rubber dam forceps
  - □ Rubber dam frames, assorted
  - □ Rubber dam anterior, premolar, and molars clamps
- Interproximal items:
  - □ Tofflemire holders
  - □ Tofflemire pedo, regular, and wide bands
  - □ Clear matrix bands
  - □ Curved, special matrixes
  - □ Wedges, assorted
  - □ Spreaders, holders for matrix
  - □ Tissue forceps or tweezers

- ☐ Sandpaper polishing strips
- ☐ Floss
- ✴ Additional instruments or items:
  - ☐ Scalers and curettes, assorted
  - ☐ Sharpening stone
  - ☐ Articulating forceps
  - ☐ Mixing pad and spatula to mix
  - ☐ Bib clips to hold patient drapes
  - ☐ Protective eyewear for assistant and patient
  - ☐ Mirror for patient instruction
  - ☐ Containers to organize, store, transport items
  - ☐ Sterilization equipment and supplies (See Appendix E.)
  - ☐ Surgical scrubs or smocks
  - ☐ Plug adaptors for specific country
  - ☐ Converters (proper size) for electrical equip if needed
- ✴ Disposable items:
  - ☐ Gloves for dentists and assistants
  - ☐ Masks for dentists and assistants
  - ☐ Bibs or drapes for patients and instruments trays
  - ☐ Trash bags and waste baskets
  - ☐ Gauze (2 x 2)
  - ☐ Cotton rolls and dry angles
  - ☐ Disposable cups to give pain medications and for patient expectorants
  - ☐ Toothbrushes and floss for patients
  - ☐ Glass-ionomer/resins, light-cured
  - ☐ Articulating marking tape
  - ☐ Base or liner material
  - ☐ Glass-ionomer Fuji IX material
  - ☐ Tissue hemostatic agents
  - ☐ Retraction cord
- ✴ Medical items:
  - ☐ Blood pressure cuff and stethoscope
  - ☐ Epi-pens or epinephrine with injector for anaphylaxis reaction
  - ☐ Albuterol Sulfate inhaler

- □ Analgesics (Motrin 200 mg tabs and Tylenol 325 mg tabs)
- □ Antibiotics (Pen V K 500 mg tabs and Clindamycin 150 mg tabs)
- • Miscellaneous items:
  - □ TMS pin and post kit
  - □ Stainless steel crown (SSC) kit, cement, pliers, and scissors
  - □ Pulpotomy supplies
  - □ Crown cement
  - □ Endodontic kit
  - □ Prosthetic kit

Appendix D

Hygiene Checklist (See Chapter 7-9.)
* Dental equipment:
    □ Dental chair
    □ Operator stool with a backrest
    □ Dental operating unit (DOU) with hook up for ultrasonic scaler
        □ Slow-speed handpieces with correct attachments
        □ Air/water syringe tips
        □ Polishing cups
        □ Prophy paste
        □ Handpiece lubricant
        □ Surge protector and extension cord
        □ Extra fuses
    □ Ultrasonic scaler with tips and 220-volt converter, if needed
    □ Air-abrasion and/or hydro-abrasion unit and abrasive powder
    □ Loupes or protective eyewear for the hygienist
    □ Headlight (LED) with charger or spare batteries
    □ Curing light with charger, if doing sealants
* Examination:
    □ Trays to hold instruments
    □ Mouth mirrors
    □ Periodontal probes
    □ Explorers
* Anesthetic supplies:
    □ Anesthetic syringes
    □ Anesthetic carpules
    □ Anesthetic carpules, a few without epi
    □ Needles, assorted per provider
    □ Topical anesthetic
    □ Cotton tip applicators
    □ Needle recapping guard
* Instruments and miscellaneous:

- Hand scalers, assorted
- Curettes, assorted
- Sharpening stone
- Tooth model and brush to teach oral hygiene
- Mirrors for patient instruction
- Protective eyewear for assistant and patient
- Bib clips

- Disposable supplies:
  - Gloves for hygienist and assistant
  - Masks for dentist and assistant
  - Bibs or drapes for patients and instrument trays
  - Trash bags and waste baskets
  - Gauze (2 x 2)
  - Cotton rolls and dry angles
  - Toothbrushes and floss for patients
  - Disclosing tablets or solution
  - Disposable cups
  - Sealant syringes with tips
  - Etching gel

- Medical Items:
  - Blood pressure cuff and stethoscope
  - Epi-pens or epinephrine with injector for anaphylaxis reaction
  - Albuterol Sulfate inhaler
  - Analgesics (Motrin 200 mg tabs and Tylenol 325 mg tabs)
  - Antibiotics (Pen V K 500 mg tabs and Clindamycin 250 mg tabs)

- Miscellaneous items:
  - Containers to organize, store, and transport items
  - Sterilization equipment and supplies (See Appendix E.)
  - Surgical scrubs or smocks
  - Plug adaptors for specific country
  - Converters (proper size) for electrical equip

Appendix E

—◆—

Sterilization Checklist (See Chapter 9.)

- ☐ Disinfectant wipes
- ☐ 4-quart Presto stainless steel pressure pot
- ☐ Extra ring seal for pressure pot
- ☐ Weight added to top of pressure pot for 24 psi (Order from CDS.)
- ☐ Electrical heating element (1,000-1,500 watts in 120-or 220-volts)
- ☐ Extension cord with in-country adaptor for heating element
- ☐ Two tubs (about 6" X 10") to wash instruments (soapy tub and rinse tub)
- ☐ Cup (small patient cup) and pitcher to put water in pressure pot
- ☐ Liquid dishwashing soap in small container (Add several drops to soapy tub.)
- ☐ Small scrub brushes to clean instruments
- ☐ Pipe cleaners or tiny brush to clean suction tips
- ☐ Wire brush to clean burs
- ☐ Three kitchen mitts
- ☐ Loud timer for 10-minute sterilization time
- ☐ Heavy-duty gloves to clean instruments
- ☐ Tea strainer to hold burs and rubber dam clamps
- ☐ Tray to hold hot, sterilized instruments
- ☐ Patient bibs to place on tray to absorb moisture (may cut in half)
- ☐ Tongs to remove hot, sterilized instruments
- ☐ Trash bags
- ☐ Duct tape to attach garbage bags in a convenient place
- ☐ Sterilization instructions from CDS website
- ☐ Sterilization validation letter from CDS website

Appendix F

—◆—

Dental Phrases for Interpreters (See Chapter 8.)

* We are here to help and to show God's love.
* Please sit down in the chair and lie down.
* What is your chief concern or problem area? How can we help?
* What type of pain? What makes it hurt? How long has it been hurting?
* Does it hurt to tap on the tooth or to wiggle the tooth?
* We can save, repair, or fix the tooth.
* We cannot fix the tooth, and it needs to be extracted or removed.
* Do not be nervous. We will not hurt you.
* Do you have any of these medical concerns: pregnancy, heart condition, diabetes, infectious diseases, bleeding problems, jaw or joint problems?
* The dentists will give a dental shot or anesthesia.
* The dentist will apply topical anesthesia so you will not feel the shot very much.
* When the dentist gives the shot, wiggle your toes and think about something nice to distract yourself, and you will not feel the shot very much. It is like a mosquito bite.
* The anesthesia will make your lip, tongue, or cheek numb for several hours. Do not eat afterwards until the numbing goes away, as you may bite your tongue or lip.
* These are other common terms: open your mouth, close your mouth, bite, swallow, spit, blood, bleeding, infection, swelling, pressure, dental suture, gums, jaw bone, drill the tooth, and tooth roots.
* Move up in the chair, please.
* Get up from the chair, please.
* Please put your chin up or chin down.
* Wear these glasses to protect your eyes.
* This patient drape will help protect your clothes.
* Here is a toy animal for you to hold which will help you relax.
* We sterilize all instruments.

- Do you brush/floss and have a toothbrush/toothpaste?
- Your gums bleed because they are inflamed.
- You have dental calculus/tarter.
- During extractions, you will feel pressure, but not pain.
- This is a tooth pillow to help hold your mouth open.
- This is a dental drill, suction, air/water syringe, needle.
- Dental amalgam is silver, and dental composite is a white filling for front teeth.
- The curing blue light hardens the white fillings. It is not hot.
- A root canal removes the tissue within the tooth which contains the nerve.
- Common dental terms include: dental crown, dental bridge, removable partial, denture, implant, orthodontics.
- A "rubber dam" is like a rain coat and will isolate the tooth for a filling.
- A tooth ring will hold the rubber dam in place.
- Bite on the marking tape to check that the filling is the right level.
- Instructions after extractions: Bite on the gauze so that the bleeding will stop. Do not talk or spit, but swallow.
- Pain pills can be taken every 4-6 hours, as needed.

Appendix G

———————

Health History Form
Health History

Name: _____ Age:____ Date: _____

Are you in good health? Yes □ No □ Are you pregnant? Yes □ No □
List any serious illnesses, operations, or hospitalizations in the last five years:

_____

_____

List any drugs or medications you are taking:

_____

_____

Describe any heart problems you have:

_____

Do you bleed easily, or are you on a blood thinner? Yes □ No □
Have you had a bad reaction or are you allergic to anything? Yes □ No □
Do you suffer from any other sickness not listed that we should know about?

_____

_____

Patient's signature:

_____

Appendix H

Tooth Extraction Instructions

* Tooth extraction wounds usually heal quickly without complications.
* Dental numbing often leaves the lips, teeth, and tongue numb after an extraction. Avoid chewing and do not drink hot liquids until numbness wears off in several hours.
* Control of bleeding: Keep the pressure gauze sponge in for 30-60 minutes with constant, firm, biting pressure (no chewing or talking). Replace the gauze for another 30-60 minutes if fresh blood is present. There is often slight oozing of blood mixed with saliva, which may last for a day. This is normal, so don't be alarmed. *"I always tell the post-extraction patient, 'This could easily bleed until you go to bed tonight.' It is never a problem if the bleeding stops sooner than they expected. But it is always a problem if it bleeds longer than expected."*
* Oral rinses: On the day the tooth is extracted, it is important to help the blood clot stabilize. Do not rinse the mouth and avoid spitting, smoking, eating hot food, drinking carbonated beverages, drinking through a straw, or sucking on the wound. Gentle rinsing with water should begin on the day following a tooth extraction. Continue to brush teeth, gently brushing around the extraction site for two days after the extraction.
* Facial swelling: Some swelling may occur and is expected. To minimize swelling, avoid vigorous physical activity immediately following the extraction. Swelling usually goes away in a few days.
* Pain control: If medication was given for pain, take 1-2 pills every six hours with water, if needed.
* Nutrition: It is important to drink fluids and to eat soft, nutritious foods. Clear liquids, juice, soup, and soft food are advised for the first two days.
* Rest: After the first day, activity levels can be increased.

Appendix I

Basic First-Aid Kit

Someone should take a first-aid kit in a carry-on bag and should keep it with the team at all times. Carry a multi-purpose knife/scissors and nail clipper in a checked bag and add to the kit while in country. Be sure to take these items back out when flying home to get by security officials. Listed medications are popular recommendations and similar drugs can be substituted in each category.

- ☐ Pain medications: Motrin 200 mg tabs and Tylenol 325-500 mg tabs
- ☐ Antibiotics for infections: Z Pak, Amoxicillin 500 mg, Clindamycin 150 mg
- ☐ Thermometer
- ☐ Traveler's diarrhea: Ciprofloxacin 500 mg tabs
- ☐ Antacids: Pepto Bismol tabs
- ☐ Antiemetic: Compazine 5 mg tabs for nausea and vertigo
- ☐ Malaria prophylaxis: Doxycycline 100 mg tabs or Mefloquine 250 mg tabs
- ☐ Anti-allergy medication: Benadryl 25 mg tabs
- ☐ Anti-itch hydrocortisone cream
- ☐ Antibiotic ointment
- ☐ Antifungal cream: Tinactin
- ☐ Female vaginitis products: Monistat for those prone to yeast infections
- ☐ Cold medication: NyQuil, DayQuil, Afrin Nasal Spray
- ☐ Cough lozenges, sugar-free
- ☐ Decongestant: Sudafed 30 mg tabs
- ☐ Eye drops: Visine
- ☐ Antiseptic: Betadine to clean wound
- ☐ Small bandages, assorted sizes and moleskin
- ☐ Gauze pads, rolls of adhesive tape
- ☐ Ace bandage for sprains
- ☐ Small tweezers, needle to remove slivers
- ☐ Sunburn ointment: Aloe Vera
- ☐ Vaseline and lip balm

Appendix J

———◆———

Lead a Seeker to Faith in Jesus Christ

❖ In acknowledging God as the Creator of everything, we accept our humble position in God's creation. "You are worthy, our Lord and God, to receive glory and honor and power, for you created all things, and by your will they were created and have their being" (Revelation 4:11).

❖ We must realize that we are sinners; and, therefore, we are condemned to death. "For all have sinned and fall short of the glory of God" (Romans 3:23). "For the wages of sin is death" (Romans 6:23).

❖ God loved each of us so much that He gave His only begotten Son, Jesus, to bear our sin and die in our place. "God demonstrates His own love toward us, in this: While we were still sinners, Christ died for us" (Romans 5:8). Although we cannot understand how, God said our sins were laid upon Jesus and He died in our place. Jesus became our substitute. In the Bible, a jailer asked his prisoners, Paul and Silas, how he could be saved. They replied, "Believe in the Lord Jesus, and you will be saved" (Acts 16:30-31). We believe in Jesus as the one who bore our sins, died in our place, was buried, and whom God resurrected. It is Christ's blood and resurrection that assures us of everlasting life when we call on Him as our Lord and Savior. "Everyone who calls on the name of the Lord shall be saved" (Romans 13). Jesus says, "I am the way and the truth and the life. No one comes to the Father except through me" (John 14:6).

❖ It is God's grace that allows us to come to Him and is not a result of our efforts or work. "For it is by grace you have been saved, through faith-and this is not from yourselves, it is a gift of God-not by works, so that no one can boast" (Ephesians 2:8-9).

"He saved us, not because of righteous things we had done, but because of His mercy" (Titus 3:5).

* All that we need to do is to accept the gift that Jesus is holding out for us right now. "That if you confess with your mouth, 'Jesus is Lord,' and believe in your heart that God raised him from the dead, you will be saved. For it is with your heart that you believe and are justified, and it is with your mouth that you confess and are saved" (Romans 10:8-9). God says that if we believe in His son, Jesus, we can live forever with Him in glory.

"For God so loved the world that he gave his one and only Son, that whoever believes in Him shall not perish but have eternal life" (John 3:16).

* We pray to accept the gift of eternal life that Jesus is offering right now. We review with the seeker what this commitment involves and have him/her repeat these statements.

I acknowledge I am a sinner in need of a Savior.
I repent and turn away from sin.
I believe that God raised Jesus from the dead.
I trust that Jesus paid the full penalty for my sins.
I confess Jesus as my Lord and my God.
I surrender control of my life to Jesus.
I receive Jesus as my Savior forever and accept that God has done for and in me what He promised.

* We help the seeker pray a prayer similar to this: "Father, I know that I have broken your laws, and my sins have separated me from you. I am truly sorry, and now I want to turn away from my past sinful life toward you. I believe that your son, Jesus Christ, died for my sins, was resurrected from the dead, is alive, and hears my prayer. I invite Jesus to become the Lord of my life, to rule and to reign in my heart from this day forward. I am now placing my trust in You alone for my salvation, and I accept your free gift of eternal life. In Jesus' name I pray. Amen."

✦ Everyone receives the Holy Spirit the moment they receive Jesus Christ as their Savior. "Having believed, you were marked in Him with a seal, the promised Holy Spirit, who is a deposit guaranteeing our inheritance until the redemption of those who are God's possession- to the praise of His glory" (Ephesians 1:13-14). A possession of the Spirit is an identifying factor of the possession of salvation.
"You, however, are controlled not by the sinful but by the Spirit, if the Spirit of God lives in you. And if anyone does not have the Spirit of Christ he does not belong to Christ" (Romans 8:9).

✦ We welcome new Christians to God's family and encourage them in ways that will help them grow closer to Jesus. The Bible tells us to follow our commitment in these areas:

✦ Loving God and people becomes a priority. "'Teacher, which is the greatest commandment in the Law?' Jesus replied: 'Love the Lord your God with all your heart, and with all your soul, and with all your mind. This is the first and greatest commandment. And the second is like it: Love your neighbor as yourself. All the law and the Prophets hang on these two commandments'" (Matthew 22:36-40).

✦ Time is spent with God each day. It does not have to be a long period of time, but it is helpful to develop the daily habit of praying to Him and reading His Word. We ask God to increase our faith and our understanding of the Bible. "Do not be anxious about anything, but in everything, by prayer and petition, with thanksgiving, present your requests to God. And the peace of God, which transcends all understanding, will guard your hearts and your minds in Christ Jesus" (Philippians 4:6-7). "Jesus replied, 'If anyone loves me, he will obey my teaching'" (John 14:23).

✦ We follow God's commands that Christians meet regularly for worship, prayer, Bible study, and assistance to each other, "Let us not give up meeting together, as some are in the habit of doing, but let us encourage one another" (Hebrews 10:25).

* Telling others the good news about Jesus is important. "Jesus said to them, 'Go into all the world and preach the good news to all creation. Whoever believes and is baptized will be saved, but whoever does not believe will be condemned'" (Mark 15:16).

* Baptism in obedience to the commands of Jesus is a public testimony of our salvation. "You are all sons of God through faith in Christ Jesus, for all of you who were baptized into Christ have clothed yourselves with Christ" (Galatians 3: 26-7).

Index

Decay, **1**, **4**, 43, 48, 59, 61, 66, **80**, 111. *See* Caries

Deep Vein Thrombosis (DVT), 227

Dental. *See* Chair, Diagnose, Equipment, Hygiene, Instruments, Materials, Opportunity, Patients, Portable, Restorative, Students, Supplies, Surgery, Treatment

    capabilities, 25, 29, 72, 74-75, 130, **136-138**

    clinic, dental, xiv, 25, 70, **72-73**, 86, 88, **94- 95**, 99, 109, 118, 121, 130, **136**, 138, 145, 155, 164, 196, 204, 212, 214, 233, 238-239

    experiences, 18, 29, 32, 54, 72, **75-78**, 85, 102, 105, 116, 120, 149, 172, 241

    needs, xiv, **1-7**, 28, 50, 64, 77, 80, 83, 86, 91, 122, 130, 136, 214, 215, 249

    operating unit, 37-39, **40-41**, 43, 55, 56, 61, 65, 72, 76, 104, 110, 137, 267, 270, 274

    organizations, xvi, **22-23**, **41**, **72-73**, 212, 220

    phrases, **89**, 158, 180, **287-288**

    resources for, xii, xvi, 22-23, **41**, 44, 54, **72-73**

    set-up, xi, xii, 11, 16, **38**, 52-54, 61, **74-79**, 84, **134**, 135, 140

Designated funds account, *See* Christian Dental Society

Developed country, **x**, 1-2, 4, 18, 34, 50, 57, 71, 92, 94, 148, 169, 175, **182-184**, 247. *See* Church

Developing country, **x**, **1-5**, 48, 62-63, 71-72, 97, 100, **102**, 156-157, 174, 192, 215-216, 233, 237. *See* Church

    characteristics, **10**, **37-38**, 43, 51, **64**, 94, **159**, 162-164, 168-170, **182-185**, 200, 241

    experiences, **50**, **72**, 92, 105-106, 128, 176, **184**, 247

Devotions, 28, 33, 36, 125, **139-142**, **147**. *See* Bible

Diagnose, dental, **5**, 39, **56**, **61**, 83, 87

Disclosing solution, 66, **111**, 275. *See* Brushing teeth, Clean teeth, Hygiene, Prevention

Diseases, 6, **9-10**, 28, 32, 161. *See* Caries, Decay, Gingivitis, Periodontitis

    infectious, **92-95**, 102, 106, 136, **159**, 162, 178, 277

    connections between dental and medical, 6-7

    oral, xii, 1, **3**, 5, 8, 18, 22, 65, 66, 113

Disinfection, 92, **100-102**. *See* Sterilization

Documentation, records, **105-106**, 202, 208, **233-240**. *See* Legalities

Donations, x, xvi, 21, 72, **146**, 204, 208-209, 214

Pregnancy, 6, 106, 277

Pressure pot, 45, 55, 82, 93, **98-100**, 264, 276

Prevention, 5, 51, 65-66, **108-113**, 136, 159-160. *See* Hygiene

Privacy, 78, 130, 154, **177**

Prosthodontics, 40, 43, 50, 51, **68-69**, 86, 273

Prophylaxis medication, **60**, 64, 95, 160, 281. *See* Antibiotic, Post-exposure prophylaxis

Pulpotomy, **64**, 273

Relationships, 13, 32, 34, 115-119, **123-124**, 143, **152**, 174, 176, 181, 194, 208, 236, 248. *See* Friendship, Mentorship

Resources, general, **3**, 5, 15, 29, 32, 48, **65**, 77, 105-106, 134, 157, 174, 184, 191, 199, **211**, 259. *See* Christian Dental Society, Dental, Organizations

Restorative, xvi, **38**, 59, 65-66, 106. *See* Clinic, Dental, Organize, Portable, Supplies

appendix checklist, 270-273

equipment, instruments, **xv**, **39-44**, 50-56, **60-64**, 72-73

materials, **47-48**, 60, **70-73**

portable trip instructions, 50-56, **74-91**

Rubber dam, **42**, 51, 54, 55, **63**, 94, 99, 271, 276, 278. *See* Restorative

Safety, xii, **23-24**, 33-35, 78, 82, 87, 95, 115, 130, 132, 135, 145, **155-171**, 179, 186, 189-190, 196, 202, 218, 236, 246, 255, 264. *See* Accidents

dangers, 5, 25, 28, 44, 93, **95**, 147, **155-156**, 159, **162**, **164**, 172-173, 254

fears, 10, 48, 68, 87-88, **91**, 150, 154, 195, 209, **253**

risks, 6, 16, 19, 23, 25, **27-28**, 94-95, 97, **157**, 159-162, 168, 205, 220, 227, 238, 239, **254**

safety nets, 3, **247**

security, 79, 100, 150, 203, **223-227**, 281

Scales, weigh bags, **221**, 241-242

Scrubs, 54, 75, **94**, 192, 265, 269, 272, 275

Sealants, 22, **47**, 55, 63, **65-66**, 83, 270, 274-275

Sexual issues, 36, 147, 183, **188**

Serve, serving, xiv, 17, 21, 31, 33-34, 97, 114, **127-128**, 131-132, 145, 181, 184, 209. *See* Mission, Opportunities, Volunteer

God, 8, **9**, 11, **16**, 22, 115, **126-128**, 130, **134**, 140, 144, **250-253** on missions, xvii, 13-15, **23-24**, **27-29**, 72, 84, 120, 122, 123, **125-126**, 132, 143, 189, 204, 212, 215, 233, 246

Sharing, xi, xvi, **18-19**, 29, 73, 114, 119, 122, 126, 128, 136, 144, 187, 190, 195, 203. See Mentoring, Teaching, Testimony

beliefs, xiv, 8, 12-14, 77, 111, 117, 139, 142, 145-153, 209

Sharps container, **57**, 62, 82, **94-95**, 99, 100

Shopping, 118, 132, 137, 155, 174, 176, 179, **198-200**, 202, 219

Sightseeing, 128, 129, **132**, 137. *See* Holidays, Vacation

Significance, purposeful, x, **16-17**, 20, 34, **50**, 114, 117, 119, 120, 126, 129, **134**, **137**, 143, 144, 150, 153, 175, 201, 207, 210, 215-216, 250

Social status, 3, 23, 85, 147, 172-176, **177**, 183, 185. *See* Cross-cultural

Spiritual, xvi, **8-10**, 12-14, 17, 21, 23, 28, 29, 32, 33, 50, 76, 114, 117, 129, 134, 135, **139-145**, 152, 153,174, 178, 184, 191, 214, 215, 216, 248, 249. *See* Bible, Christian, Evangelism, Outreach, Prayer, Testimony

gifts, x, 15-17, 51, 116, 215, **250**, 282-283

Sponsor, national hosts, (too numerous to list as they advise, plan, and take responsibility for the team). *See* Gate keeper, Leadership, Missionary, Organizations, Organize, Planning, Serve, Volunteers

Spouse, 13, 28, 34, 36, 120, **127**, 154. *See* Volunteers

Stainless steel crowns, 48, **64**, 273

Statement of faith, xiii. *See* Christian Dental Society

Sterilization, xvi, 4, 13, 18, 38, **43**, 44, 45, 51, 52, 54, 55-56, 60, 61, 62, 66,72, 75, **76**, 82, 84, **92-93**, 95, **97-100**, 101, 102, 110, 120, 127, 136-137, 159, 264, 272, 275, 277

appendix checklist, 276

techniques, 97-100

Stool, dental, **40**, 56, 61, 65, 267, 270, 274. *See* Equipment

Stress, xi, **xii**, 13, 20, 32, 40, 78, 105, 114, **117**, 119, 152, 174, 178, 219, 229, 231, 242

Students, dental, xvii, 11, **18**, 34, 68, 116-117, **121-128**, 251

Success, xii, 16, 17, 86, 88, **114-117**, 121, 123, 126, 127, 134, 140, 151, 208, 254

Suction, dental, **40**, **42**, 45, 56, 61, 65, **66**, 82-84, 103-104, 110, 267, 270, 276, 278

Tourism, 13, **20**, 22, 132, 136, 162, 259, 265. *See* Sightseeing, Tourist, Vacation

Tourist, **156**, 164, 167-168, 173, **174**, 179, **198**, 235-236, **239**

Transportation, transport, xiv, 23, 25, 29, 41, 45, 53-54, 60, 64, 66, 74, 93, 100, 114, 125, 129, 155, **163-164**, **177**, 189, 202, 204, 218, 219, 221, 222, 226, 239, 269, 272, 275. *See* Airplane

Traveler's diarrhea, **161-162**, 281

Treatment, dental, 2, 3, 5, 18, 43, 47-49, 50-70, **79-84**, 90-91, 92, 99, 109, 114, 122, 130, 212. *See* Atraumatic Restorative Treatment, Hygiene, Restorative, Surgery

capabilities, limitations, 50, **74-75**, **77-78**, 80, 85-86, 105-106, **136-138**

Trust, **xiii**, **10**, 12, 17, 28, 76, 77, 90, 104, 119, 124, 144, **155-156**, 181, 184, 195, 206, 209, 211, 238, 283. *See* Healing touch

distrust, **12**, **87**, 88

Ultrasonic scaler, **43**, 55, 65, 83, 274. *See* Hygiene

Universal precautions, **93-94**, 95, 106, 159. *See* Infection control

United States State Department, **24**, 157, 235, 240

Vacation, 13, **20**, 118, 124, 128, 215, 242, 254. *See* Holidays, Sightseeing, Tourism

Valuables, xii, 1, 9, 104, **131**, 203, 230, 234, 236, **241**, 246, 265. *See* Safety

Visas, 129, 218, 222, 234, **235-236**

Volunteers, 11, 21, 32, 73, 75, 77, 94, 96, 104, 118, 119, 129, **134-135**, 156, 158, 168, 169, 172, 174, 177, 179-180, 187, 204, 207, 246, 247. *See* Organizations, Spouse, Teamwork

dental, xiv, 84, 122, 123, 128, 207, **238**, 254

non-dental, xii, 48, 88, **120**, **127**

qualifications, 24, **27-29**, 32, **117**

Waste, infectious, **102-104**. *See* Infection control

Water, drinking, **5**, 15, 20, 35, 55, 75, 104, 111, 129, 131, 137, 159, **161**, 163, 169, 192, 223, **225-227**, 231, 266, 280. *See* Traveler's diarrhea

hydration, 35, **168**, 180, 227, 266

purification, **165-168**, 169

Weather, **25-26**, 157, 163, 174, 191, 225, 242, 244, 265

World Dental Relief, 72

World Health Organization, 1, 3, **24**, 48

X-ray, **43-44**, 56, 61, 267, 270, *See* Equipment

Made in the USA
San Bernardino, CA
01 March 2016